THE UNIVE... ... O
WIN...

The Politics of American Actor Training

Routledge Advances in Theatre and Performance Studies

The Politics of American Actor Training

Edited by Ellen Margolis and Lissa Tyler Renaud

Routledge
Taylor & Francis Group
New York London

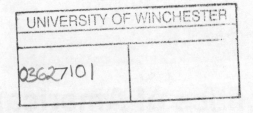
First published 2010
by Routledge
711 Third Avenue, New York, NY 10017

Simultaneously published in the UK
by Routledge
2 Park Square, Milton Park, Abingdon, Oxon, OX14 4RN

Routledge is an imprint of the Taylor & Francis Group, an informa business

First issued in paperback 2011

© 2010 Taylor & Francis

Typeset in Sabon by IBT Global.

Library of Congress Cataloging in Publication Data

The politics of American actor training / edited by Ellen Margolis and Lissa Tyler Renaud.
   p. cm.—(Routledge advances in theatre and performance studies ; 11)
   Includes bibliographical references and index.
  1. Acting—Study and teaching—United States.   2. Drama in education—United States.   I. Margolis, Ellen, 1959–   II. Renaud, Lissa Tyler.
   PN2075.P65 2009
   792.02'807073—dc22
   2009016040

ISBN10: 0-415-80121-4 (hbk)
ISBN10: 0-415-89653-3 (pbk)
ISBN10: 0-203-86777-7 (ebk)

ISBN13: 978-0-415-80121-8 (hbk)
ISBN13: 978-0-415-89653-5 (pbk)
ISBN13: 978-0-203-86777-8 (ebk)

Contents

Acknowledgments

The editors would like to thank those who supported our work on this book:

Julia Alderson, Kiril Bolotnikov, Norma Bowles, Harry Elam, Rinda Frye, Laura Gattoni, Robert Goldsby, Breanna Grove, Les Hasbargen, Elizabeth Levine, Alfonso Lopez-Vasquez, Terry O'Day, the Pacific University College of Arts & Sciences, Ryan Reed, Harriet Renaud, Roxane Rix, Bill Smith, Karima Wilner, Leigh Woods, our many anonymous readers, and our families.

Special thanks to Talia Rodgers of Routledge, London; to our production coordinator, Terence James Johnson; and to our editor, Erica Wetter.

Introduction

Ellen Margolis and Lissa Tyler Renaud

In place of politics of serious public issues, one that engages the public broadly, we have politics defined broadly by entertainment and television values—image, artificial bids for attention span, spin and the rest—and narrowly by what are called "wedge issues," representations of ideological hysteria. All these developments have consequences for artistic content.

Michael Janeway, *American Theatre*, 2000[1]

Put these two train wrecks together: first, the explosion of the Entertainment Industry, defining so much of our culture and our economy, filling so much of the vacuum in our political culture. Second, the "culture wars"—the shift into escapism, identity politics, consumer gadgetry, cults of markets and money. Add those all up, and it's hardly surprising that there is so little today of what theatre is historically about: a theatre of ideas and of the soul.

Ibid.[2]

It is surprising that there isn't already a book addressing how these developments are reflected in actor training. We have heard these matters debated in the proverbial hallway conversation for many years, expressed informally in half-formed anxieties and experiential knowledge about power relationships. When the editors of this book brought forth these issues in a panel session at the 2004 Association for Theatre in Higher Education (ATHE) Conference in Toronto, there was consensus from an exciting mix of academic and professional theatre people that the topic of actor training and its politics—the powerful undercurrents of their professions—needed to be formalized in fully-articulated, published, and disseminated work. We have been galvanized by enthusiastic remarks, in subsequent private discussions and public presentations, that such a project is "long overdue." Although there are certainly well-known books on specific approaches to acting, anthologies of essays from theoretical and historical perspectives on acting, and individual articles that explore some of the challenges of actor education, questions about the politics of acting pedagogy in the U.S. have not heretofore been treated in a single volume.

As co-editors, we have gathered an impressive group of theatre scholars, professionals, and teachers to write on "the politics of American actor training." Here, thirteen prominent academics and artists view actor training through a political, cultural, or ethical lens. We invited our writers to tackle fraught topics about power as it plays out in American acting curricula and classrooms, asking them to address their pieces to people at the top of the profession, to those who are unfamiliar with important, prevalent questions about our nation's acting training as it now stands, and to anyone in a position to make concrete changes. Consequently, the book not only identifies complex issues and assesses them, but also proposes new and practicable ideas to serve administrators, department chairs, conservatory heads, teachers, critics, as well as students and actors. Our collective aim has been to assess current and past training policies and practices, and to propose new ideas that will inform twenty-first-century actor training in America.

* * *

The title of the book communicates one of our highest priorities: to challenge professional American actor training in the full range of its settings—universities, conservatories, institutes, private studios large and small, and inside and outside the U.S.—that is, wherever professional American actor training may be found. Other choices followed from this fundamental decision to be inclusive in this sense. For example, we chose not to divide scholars and practitioners, but instead to encourage chapters from both sides of the figurative aisle. We were struck by the writers' interest in being part of a book that set aside conventional divisions, and were deeply impressed that so many of them have the expertise to combine both theoretical and practical perspectives in their chapters. In addition to their academic degrees, the authors all work in positions of responsibility in the world of acting training, and all add compelling views from their particular trenches. Therefore, the resulting book features chapters from a wide range of disparate voices—from theorists, directors, and teachers, to administrators, actors, and historians. In support of this range, we chose not to strive for consistency of tone, but to encourage widely differing writing styles, from the experiential to the theoretical, and from the meditative to the statistical.

Yet another outgrowth of our choice to look beyond the usual categories of practice and theory was our decision to highlight actor training across the country, because the editors represent the many who disagree with the premise that the best of the training happens at a handful of elite East Coast schools. The methods of schools such as Julliard, NYU, Carnegie Mellon, Yale School of Drama, Neighborhood Playhouse, Stella Adler Conservatory, and the Actors Studio dominate the popular image of and mainstream discourse on actor training. The realities of actor training across the nation, however, encompass a wide spectrum of complex factors, and our goal has been to focus on many of these widely unacknowledged complexities, to give a truer, more inclusive picture of American actor training.

It comes as no surprise that acting teachers accustomed to thinking of themselves as defining American training, can feel challenged by questions that persist nationwide about the assumptions that were inherent in their own training and in the training they offer. This book intends to give a fair hearing to persistent, questioning voices, thereby contributing to the national dialogue the diverse perspectives and proposals needed to keep American actor training dynamic and germane, both within the U.S. and abroad.

* * *

Scrutiny of the teacher–student relationship has a long history, and many have written on the transmission, use, and maintenance of power in the academy. In our time, Paulo Freire's seminal work on the colonialism inherent in Western education brought new energy to this inquiry. Freire's work intertwined several branches of thought pertaining to educational practice, oppression, and liberation. In response, educators committed to Marxism, feminism, civil rights, and identity politics picked up the challenge, exposing unspoken forces at play in classrooms and laboratories. This scrutiny, though, has not been applied with equal thoroughness to the acting studio. What questions are particular to—or particularly charged in—the training of actors?

This book, *The Politics of American Actor Training*, has gone through many stages of development, and the authors in it have brought to it the force of their own motives and divergent ideas. But it should be noted that Paulo Freire's influential work, *Pedagogy of the Oppressed*, underlies all formal discussion of power in education. Contemporary educators in all disciplines have been inspired and challenged by Freire's rejection of the teacher–student dichotomy and his model of a symbiotic, reciprocal relationship between students and teachers. In the field of acting, one might find special resonance in the multiple connotations of the verb "to act," or respond to Freire's notions of the student as a social Subject, acting upon his or her environment. Freire asserted a "culture of silence" within which colonized people—and in the "colonized" Freire includes, by extension, students—are granted limited vocabularies and expressive channels, and are thus cut off from access to centers of power or means to mobilize. One doesn't have to stretch these notions very far to suggest similar limitations and oppressions in the looming presence of the theatre profession, with its scant opportunities, devaluing of rigorous training, and unpredictable points of entry. At the outset, then, Freire's ideas served as both specific models and metaphors for the theatre.

At the same time, the last few years have seen the inevitable changes in performance/cultural theory and in related fields.[3] With the publishing cycle for theatre journals much faster than for books, and the online culture blogs changing our thinking faster than either journals or books, there is a lag time between when ideas become current, when they are advanced in the print media, and when they are implemented in an acting program or rehearsal. The editors' intention for this book is neither to be leading-edge in theoretical terms, nor to forge new theory. Where appropriate, the book points existing theory at the acting studio; in other cases, the chapters use other means to bring additional weight to existing conversations.

We have been fortunate in having a rigorous, silent army of anonymous readers at critical junctures, and have been delighted to see our book spark in them such varied theoretical associations and suggestions for further development of our topic. Readers made their own insightful connections with work ranging from Carl Jung's on archetypes and the collective unconscious to Lev Vygotsky's on social learning. Others saw obvious links to cognitive psychology, or urged histories of university systems, degrees, and capitalism. Like the writers in this book, our early readers have brought their own orientations to this political look at current actor training. Although direct treatment of those areas lies outside the purview of this book, readers will find some of the ideas suggested in one or more of the chapters, and we will watch with interest for further work from others on these promising subjects. As it stands, this book aims to add to the robustness and sophistication of American actor training inside and outside America.

* * *

The fourteen chapters fall roughly into two groups. Part I deals with the larger contexts that determine today's U.S. actor training: historical, social, colonial, and administrative. Part II addresses matters of identity as they emerge in classrooms and rehearsal halls: identity politics, access, and marginalization.

The two sections overlap, but they are also linked in their essential concern: the relationship between the distinctive American acting culture and its political subtext. One might argue for almost any chapter to be in the other section, and this is rather deliberate; the two sections are two approaches to the same topic, and are of the same "stuff." We have wanted to come at the politics of U.S. actor education from two directions as a strategy for best surrounding and capturing our subject. Nevertheless, there is enough difference in focus that we are putting the chapters into two sections for the reader's convenience. This is not meant to divide the entries, but only to propose an organization for them.

INTRODUCTION TO PART I

In the West, some of those who gained recognition and fame came into contact with official culture . . . which enthusiastically accepted them and swallowed them up, as it accepts and swallows up new cars, new fashions, or anything else. In Bohemia the situation is essentially different, and far better than in the West, because we live in an atmosphere of complete agreement: the first [official] culture doesn't want us, and we don't want anything to do with the first culture. This eliminates the temptation that for everyone, even the strongest artist, is the seed of destruction: the desire for recognition, success, winning prizes and titles, and last but not least, the material security which follows.

Ivan Jirous, *A Report on the Third Czech Musical Revival*, 1975[4]

Culture is politics.

Tom Stoppard, Introduction to *Rock 'N Roll*, 2006[5]

In America, we do not describe the relationship between authorities and artists in terms of first and second, or official and unofficial cultures, but we know we have these separate cultures, that they are in contact, and that the goal of their contact is material security. Instead of those words, we speak in terms of government subsidies and university support, grants, and endowment awards—language that attempts to communicate its own kind of "atmosphere of complete agreement." Nevertheless, it barely masks some disquieting truths: that the cultural system that forces the interdependence of authorities and artists often hobbles both, that cultural activity has no organic function in our society so that organizations funding the arts do so from self-interest, that the support from above shifts the artist's focus from community to money, that funding inequities seriously divide artists among themselves, and that our artists are sometimes forced to strike some devilish bargains with those with power to make the leap from surviving to thriving.

In Part I, our concern is how these larger dynamics surface in actor training. The following questions served as points of departure: What are the economic realities at work where training programs use their financial status to substantiate their excellence? How has actor education adapted to the business model where the student–teacher relationship changes to an employer–employee one? Does a pedagogical vision of inspiring responsible, resistant thinkers extend to the acting class? Do teachers in a conservatory setting have an obligation to indoctrinate students into the traditional power relationship in the professional theatre? Are instructors obliged to interact with the marketplace, or to ignore it? Does the unlikelihood of earning a living as an actor cause us to preach a conformist mindset out of fear for our students' futures? What are the limits of responsibility when preparing students for life in a profession that barely sustains itself economically?

Further: How do actor training programs regard non-traditional casting practices, such as colorblind casting? Should teachers acknowledge race when choosing material for scene study, and if so, are minority students then underserved if they do not train in the classic plays of the European

theatre? Even as training nationally becomes less centered on the Stanislavsky legacy of psychological realism, how can we extend our new forms of
training to embody true plurality?

INTRODUCTION TO PART II

> I feel that even the current token adherence to "multiculturalism" is
> often little more than a patronizing capitalist designation for "The
> Other." But we also witness serious inquiry in which the dogmas of
> the past are rethought and debated. Indeed, the periphery is affect-
> ing the center in many ways, and previously marginalized cultures
> are not only influenced by but also act upon the mainstream culture.
> New paradigms are called for, and new artists will find them, and
> new critics will have something to write about.
>
> Peter Selz, *Beyond the Mainstream*[6]

In some segments of the country, current discourse is energetically highlighting the politics of representation in the theatre, from perspectives
including black studies, feminist studies, queer studies, and disability studies. In other parts of the country, such conversation about "cultural identity" is still in the future. In segments of the nation in which those identity
issues have been at the forefront for some years, there is already, as scholar
Michael Millner writes, "a sense of exhaustion around the whole project of
identity."[7] Still other people fear that this exhaustion will lead to dismissal
of the concerns expressed in the argument around identities, long before
they have been meaningfully addressed.[8] Ultimately, with identity politics
variously yesterday's, today's, or tomorrow's news, we can only say that
some of this thinking has made its way into the professional theatre—at
least into the non-profit theatre—in a lasting way. As for actor training
across the nation, it remains largely unchanged in this regard.

It was felicitous for the editors that one of our astute, unnamed readers
expressed a position that will strike a familiar note for many:

> Special pleading by one or another excluded group—the multicultural
> agenda of the 1980s—is no longer enough. (It never was!) It's not just
> a matter of "access" or "casting policies" within programs. MFA pro-
> grams would turn their backs on their mandate if they began accepting
> lots of disabled actors and completely ignored dominant cultural values
> in their casting policies; that's the hard reality. This is about institu-
> tional power in the academy and its links to global capital.

Although these comments are limited to university programs, they can
be made about all actor training programs, since all necessarily contend
with defining their relationships to the dominant culture. Not contend-
ing with it aligns a program with conventional forces by default. As the

demographics of the United States change at record speed, this not-contending becomes increasingly less tenable, both ethically and practically. Therefore it remains an urgent project for those of us in the acting field to gather useful language and concepts to articulate the changes around us, to keep our actors training in ways that connect them to the world both as it was, and as it is.

With that project in mind, we looked for questions and answers that might move us forward. These questions provided the impetus for Part II: How are gender, class, and race expressed and perpetuated in acting studios and training programs? What physical and/or vocal gestures of race, class, gender and sexuality do teachers reinforce or even require their students to perform? Are teachers obligated to train young men and women to fit the world of images (physical types, gender roles) likely to be recognized and readily consumed in the professional theatre or the entertainment industry? What cultural assumptions do teachers pass along to students regarding what an actor looks and sounds like? What codes are at work in their communication? How do choices about dramatic literature used in training affect a student's ideas about his or her own potential?

INTRODUCTION TO THE CHAPTERS

Any inquiry into American actor training is likely to touch on our theatre's consumption of Konstantin Stanislavsky's work, around and against which much American training has defined itself. In her chapter "Stanislavsky and Politics: Active Analysis and the American Legacy of Soviet Oppression," Sharon Marie Carnicke notes that "mistaken assumptions still hold," assumptions that can be traced in part to politics as the term is ordinarily construed. Presenting research that will break new ground for many readers, Carnicke traces in historical terms the political dynamics that defined and limited Western reception of Stanislavsky. Looking at Soviet propaganda as a force behind the mis-transmission of Stanislavsky, Carnicke notes that governmental policies allowed the Moscow Art Theatre to bring only Realist productions (as opposed to more controversial works in its repertoire) to the United States in the 1920s. Additionally, she describes a conflict between two of Stanislavsky's assistants whose differing views of the master teacher's work and inter-personal conflicts ultimately determined how the Method of Physical Actions prevailed, in its dissemination throughout Europe and the U.S., over the method of Active Analysis.

The nature of cultural exchange emerges as a theme in other chapters as well. Chandradasan, one of India's leading directors and theatre scholars, offers his forceful perspective on "The Influences of American Theatre Training on Indian Theatre," delineating how Western funding agencies in India have served to de-politicize and deracinate theatrical forms that had previously been both politically grounded and deeply connected to

community and place. Citing American granting practices and global economic factors, Chandradasan describes the impact of American capitalism
on the Indian theatre of the last half-century. Chandradasan also offers a
window onto the appropriation of South Asian dance forms by the American avant-garde in the 1960s, and the problematic effects of introducing to
formal theatre education in India a "professionalism" modeled on Broadway norms far afield from the realities and values of Indian theatre.

Beyond our nation's borders, globalization gives us ever-increasing
opportunities to interact with diverse theatre traditions, while at the same
time extending the reach of American marketing and popular culture. Having spent several years as a visiting professor in Asia in the middle of a long
career running a studio in California, Lissa Tyler Renaud is particularly
qualified to comment on the subtexts of intercultural educator exchanges.
In "The Wild, Wild East: Report on the Politics of American Actor Training Overseas," Renaud takes a candid look at how American training
fares when it is exported for consumption by students whose views of U.S.
culture have been determined by translations of uncertain reliability, and
whose understanding of theatre education is formed by constantly changing political relations throughout their region and the world. Like Chandradasan, Renaud notes the sometimes corrupting influences of competitive
grant opportunities; together, their chapters are an incisive commentary on
the ironies of cultural colonialism as it plays out in the studio.

Several of the educators here describe the learning that continues to
shape their teaching, much of it at the hands of their own students. With
"Actor Training Meets Historical Thinking," Jonathan Chambers draws
on a pivotal teaching moment in his classroom that enhanced his own education and teaching. In a model of engaged pedagogy, Chambers reflects
on what he learned from allowing beginning acting students to work on
Sarah Kane's *Crave* despite its uneasy fit with the objective/obstacle model
in which they were training. Examining the unspoken hegemony of Realism in the acting classroom, Chambers goes on to unravel assumptions that
"the System" is culturally neutral, and documents the experiences that have
led him to bring awareness of Realism's particular and material history
into his acting classes. In a poignant counterpoint, Derek S. Mudd, now a
doctoral student in performance studies, reflects on the rigidity of approach
that marked his experiences as a student in two MFA acting programs a
decade apart. Having been failed by instructors who embraced their roles
as unassailable experts and refused even to acknowledge their student's
investment in and understanding of the roles he prepared for, Mudd now
challenges himself to become a responsive and engaged theatre educator.

This field may be especially anxious because of the economic realities
that bear on the American artist and actor. In a challenging chapter, Leigh
Woods reflects on the history of formal training programs within the academy over the past three decades and the ways in which such programs
address—or fail to address—the realities of students' potential careers. To

move past current limitations, Woods suggests community-oriented projects through which acting students might be guided to wider ambitions and their talents directed to serve a sense of community that includes but is not confined to art and the academy. In this way, writes Woods, "Acting can be reconceived as a kind of common language spoken . . . by many."

Also arguing for inclusivity half a world away from the theatres where Chandradasan notes that Western "professionalism" is a mixed blessing, Ellen Margolis considers both the politics of professionalism in the theatre and the assumptions of the academy, two dovetailing sets of beliefs that marginalize adults with family or other personal obligations and systematically drive individuals with full personal lives out of her profession. In "Arrested or Paralyzed? Reflections on the Erotic Life of an Acting Teacher," Margolis connects the special imperatives of theatre education to her experiences of being transformed by the insistent presence of her students.

From her perspective of over thirty years of professional and academic theatre work in the U.S. and abroad, Lissa Tyler Renaud shines a harsh light on the confusing and corrosive effects of the marketplace on aspiring actors. In her "Training Artists or Consumers? Commentary on American Actor Training," Renaud looks at changes in a profession overcome by commercialization, and at training that needs to adapt to technology and to a generation of acting students who are unconvinced that they need a real education in theatre, the arts, or the humanities. Challenging us to dignify the field of actor training with antidotes to the anti-intellectualism and cheap over-specialization that prevail, Renaud argues for the importance of a multi-disciplinary, historically-informed actor training in every sort of studio.

With "Beyond Race and Gender: Reframing Diversity in Actor Training Programs," David Eulus Wiles asserts that the academy has deeply internalized the rules of the commercial marketplace and the stereotypes prevalent in the larger society when it comes to actor training, especially at the graduate level. Arguing for the most progressive possibilities of higher education, Wiles notes that theatre educators in the academy have the opportunity to challenge and perhaps change notions of what constitutes appropriate appearance onstage. Similarly, in her chapter "'Typed' for What?" Mary Cutler laments that unreconstructed gender roles are unconsciously reinforced in training programs through teachers' selection of material, and that instructors' anxieties for their students' futures are especially manifest in the narrow range of material selected for the American College Theatre Festival's national scholarship program. Inspired by Rhonda Blair's feminist critiques of actor training, Cutler takes up the challenge of helping to liberate her students from limiting stereotypes.

Wiles' and Cutler's contributions resonate with "Changing Demographics: Where is Diversity in Theatre Programs in Higher Education?" in which Donna B. Aronson describes her efforts and successes at encouraging greater diversity in theatre at her former home institution in Texas, prompted by concerns that her department did not reflect the largely Hispanic makeup of its campus or the local community. Aronson's desire for an inclusive model has led her to consider how theatre programs might go beyond desegregating; here she suggests how theatre might be used to encourage diversity and enhance communication throughout a campus community. A past president of the Association for Theatre in Higher Education, Aronson also reflects on the worthy journey that lies ahead for the profession at large.

Several of our contributors describe the real impediments confronted by actors from traditionally under-represented groups and offer visions for pertinent cultural change. In a chapter at the crossroads of the practical and political, Victoria Ann Lewis chronicles the achievements of a number of disabled actors-in-training, and of the instructors who came to appreciate that their vocabularies were enhanced and assumptions challenged by working with these students. As a documentarian and activist for this population within the theatre community, Lewis goes on to present a manifesto for access. Similarly, in a chapter aimed at helping professional and academic training programs to enhance the quality of preparation offered to their Latino students, Micha Espinosa and Antonio Ocampo-Guzman examine how programs in the United States currently train actors of Latino heritage. Here, the authors identify three signal challenges: the complexities of bilingualism, complicated and conflicting messages Latino actors are likely to have internalized about their own physicality, and the particular difficulties of preparing Latino students to work in an industry that tends to relegate these actors to stereotypic roles.

Venus Opal Reese's "Keeping It Real Without Selling Out: Toward Confronting and Triumphing Over Racially-Specific Barriers in American Acting Training" proposes a training approach designed to serve racially- and historically-conscious African American playwriting. Drawing on Ron Eyerman's theorizing of collective trauma as cultural memory, Reese deliberately works against an idea of traditional European/American acting that she associates with "emptying out," instead inviting students—through improvisation, writing exercises, and class discussion—to bring their full and authentic voices to any role.

CONCLUSION

It has not been our purpose to exhaust this enormous topic in this one book, but to provide those in actor education with a rich and engaging way into a larger, inevitable conversation. Even a book such as this one, with an inclusive philosophy, does not attempt to cover each minority population, or each disability, or each of any underrepresented group. The effects of American training are observable in many more cultures globally than have been discussed here. Sometimes there have been complex obstacles to securing input from members of groups not used to being approached. In any case, we found that the chapters included work together well to offer an adventurous survey of trends in thinking on the subject. We hope our selection of chapters will heighten awareness of many other voices, while engaging everyone interested in how American theatre training expresses our national identity, in the globalization of arts education policy, and in the politics of curriculum decisions wherever our actor training is keeping American actors relevant.

NOTES

1. Michael Janeway, "Who's Teaming Up in the Tug-of-War Among the Two Theatre Sectors, Pop Culture and the Press." *American Theatre* (New York: Theatre Communications Group, December 2000), 86.
2. Ibid., 87.
3. On this point, two books deserve special mention for their ambitious scope and rigorous application of theory: Ellen Donkin and Susan Clement's *Upstaging Big Daddy: Directing Theatre as if Gender and Race Matter*, and more recently, Ann Elizabeth Armstrong and Kathleen Juhl's *Radical Acts: Theatre and Feminist Pedagogies of Change*.
4. Ivan Martin Jirous, "A Report on the Third Czech Musical Revival." *Primary Documents: A Sourcebook for Eastern and Central European Art since the 1950s*. Laura Hoptman and Tomas Pospiszyl, eds. (Cambridge, MA, and London, England: The Museum of Modern Art, New York, and MIT Press, 2002), 56–65. Quoted in Tom Stoppard's introduction to his *Rock 'n' Roll*, revised edition (London, England: Faber and Faber, 2006) xx.
5. Stoppard, *Rock 'n' Roll*, ibid., xix.
6. From Peter Selz's introduction to his *Beyond the Mainstream: Essays on Modern and Contemporary Art* (Cambridge, England: Cambridge University Press, 1997), 10.
7. The full passage from Michael Millner's "Post Post-Identity" reads: "If the 1990s were characterized by a rich and sophisticated reconceptualization of identity—as performative, mobile, strategically essential, intersectional, incomplete, in-process, provisional, hybrid, partial, fragmentary, fluid, transitional, transnational, cosmopolitan, counterpublic, and, above all, cultural—the new millennium has been frequently marked by a sense of exhaustion around the whole project of identity. The fatigue is palpable even among some of those left cultural critics most responsible for identity's ascendancy. Terry Eagleton's recent *After Theory* (2003) closes with a call to move on: cultural theory 'cannot afford simply to keep recounting the same narratives of class, race and gender, indispensable as these topics are. It needs to chance its arm, break out of a rather stifling orthodoxy and explore new topics.'" *American Quarterly* Volume 57, Number 2 (Baltimore, MD: John Hopkins University Press, June 2005), 541.
8. Writing on his blog about "Gay Male Poetry Post Identity Politics," poet Reginald Shepherd posted: "When I told a friend about this [Association of Writers and Writing Programs] panel, he said, 'No one sent me the memo that racism, heterosexism, and class struggle had ended and thus we can now put that silly business [of] the politics of identity behind us.' I told him he should check his mail more regularly, as lots of people have sent out that particular memo." At http://reginaldshepherd.blogspot.com/2008/02/gay-male-poetry-post-identity-writer politics.html.

Part I

1 Stanislavsky and Politics

Active Analysis and the American Legacy of Soviet Oppression[1]

Sharon Marie Carnicke

A CULTURE OF DISINFORMATION

In classes and rehearsals, U.S. acting teachers and directors invoke Stanislavsky's name as if they knew him well. In books and articles about theatre and performance, U.S. scholars refer to the "Stanislavskian actor" as if the phrase represents a clear and transparent concept. Yet, assumptions behind these references are not necessarily derived from clear-sighted visions of the Russian's work. Americans tend to think of Stanislavsky as a tyrannical director and teacher, exclusively committed to realism as an aesthetic style and personal emotion as the primary wellspring of great acting. In fact, he viewed the actor as an autonomous artist, saw realism as only one in a myriad of equally profound theatrical styles, and developed a compendium of acting techniques, with "emotional memory" as the most capricious and least effective.

In the twenty-first century, the mistaken assumptions still hold. As recently as March 2007 on the pages of *American Theatre*, director Charles Marowitz refers without irony to Stanislavsky as the "Father of psychological realism"; Marowitz's title "Getting Stanislavsky Wrong" is inadvertently self-referential, striking a truly ironic note.[2] Because of this persistent image of Stanislavsky, director Anne Bogart turns instead toward postmodern dance and the Japanese teachings of Tadashi Suzuki for her inspiration, accurately observing that, "The Americanization and miniaturization of the Stanislavsky System has become the air we breathe and, like the air we breathe, we are rarely aware of its omnipresence."[3] As a Russian scholar and theatre practitioner, my mission has been to bring that awareness and to clear the air. I have elsewhere examined the complex cultural, linguistic, and commercial forces that have shaped our myths about Stanislavsky,[4] and this article zooms in on one pernicious source behind his "Americanization and miniaturization": Soviet propaganda.

When Stanislavsky first stepped on U.S. soil in 1923, Soviet political forces had already begun to shape what we know of him. He had brought on tour his theatre's oldest and most realistic productions, because his new government was already promoting realism as the most desirable artistic style. With the Moscow newspapers full of insinuations that his trip to a country which had refused to recognize the U.S.S.R. constituted a betrayal of the Revolution, Stanislavsky could ill afford to showcase other work (such as his symbolist productions, for example) that was artistically and politically controversial at home.

Ten years after Stanislavsky's return to Russian soil, the Soviet propaganda machine had become even more aggressive in its manipulation of him. In 1934, he found himself confined to his home with virtually no access to the outside world. He was indeed very ill, but his quarantine was more than a medical prescription; it was political as well. In the atheistic communist regime, the uses he made of Yogi Ramacharaka's spiritual teachings alone were enough to make him politically traitorous. But when, in 1934, Stalin declared Socialist Realism to be the only sanctioned style for Soviet art, Stanislavsky became all the more dangerous for his experimentation with nonrealism and his stubborn support of his former protégé, Vsevolod Meyerhold (deemed, at that time, an enemy of the people for his theatrical productions). Stanislavsky's image as a theatrical hero on the front lines of "The Battle for Realism"[5] could best be maintained by keeping the actual man out of the public eye. He lived his last four years (1934–1938) in what was, for all intents and purposes, an internal exile, imposed by the state.

During this time, he turned his home into rehearsal space where carefully selected actors and teachers labored from early morning to late at night. Despite serious illness, he always appeared among them clean-shaven, in a suit and tie with a fresh shirt.[6] As his assistant, Maria Knebel, recalls:

> He had never before held back, but in those years at the studio his generosity in sharing his creative ideas took on a particular character. It struck me as courageous, tragic, and sublimely peaceful. It was as if he knew that death was close, and it engendered in him one desire—to give away everything while time still remained. I never heard him indulge in the grumbling of old age. He was deeply and joyously focused on the possibilities that our discoveries could offer to theatrical art.[7]

While Stanislavsky privately developed his System for actors using Yoga and theatricalist insights, his public image was carefully constructed in the press by selecting from his work only what would support communist directives. During those years, Stanislavsky's fictionalized *persona* as the patriarchal director committed exclusively to dramatic realism took center stage, while the artist's trial and error approach to acting was hidden away in his home studio.

After the 1923 and 1924 tours of the Moscow Art Theatre (MAT) to the United States, a group of young Americans were inspired by the Russian actors who had seemed so vitally alive onstage, so fully in control of their art. These young artists greedily drank in what they could learn of Stanislavsky's acting System, largely ignorant of how politics were spinning what they were gleaning of it. Thus, Americans became unwittingly and ironically complicit in developing his Soviet image. When Lee Strasberg, Harold

Clurman, and Cheryl Crawford founded the Group Theatre in 1931, they adopted the Soviet emphasis on realism and added an American spin by emphasizing Stanislavsky's early notion of emotional memory. By the end of the 1950s, Strasberg's teachings at the Actors Studio in New York had successfully promoted not only the Method, but also the now pervasive myth of Stanislavsky as a staunch advocate of psychological realism in drama and emotional authenticity in acting. As Strasberg quipped in 1965, "Many people in America think that Stanislavsky must be an American. Otherwise, how could he have possibly influenced the American theater to the extent that he has?"[8]

Stanislavsky's books on acting, alas, further contribute to the culture of disinformation that informed acting practice in the U.S. He published them in the late 1930s during the most repressive period of Soviet history, when Stalin purged the country of unwanted people, including artists who circumvented his policies on the arts, either through confinement (as in the case of Stanislavsky), or incarceration and execution (as in the case of Meyerhold). Stalin also purged unwanted ideas through the censorship and banning of books. While Stalinist politicians and critics worked hard to make sure that Russian actors and audiences interpreted Stanislavsky's influential teachings through a Marxist lens, Soviet editors and governmental censors who prepared his writings for publication did the same.

Stanislavsky first tried to save his System by arranging for its publication in the U.S. In 1931, he gave American translator Elizabeth Reynolds Hapgood rights to all his books, unaware that commerce would oblige her to abridge them severely.[9] To ensure publication in his native language, he used devices available to all Soviet writers to circumvent censorship. He wrote through indirection: hints, unidentified quotations from banned books (such as those by Yogi Ramacharaka), and suggestive analogies that create a rich subtext of radical thought. Without understanding the specifics of his political context, however, one can easily misread his surface apologies for socialist realism as genuine.[10]

Soviet politics has created such a widespread culture of disinformation about Stanislavsky and his work that the thinking of most theatre professionals and scholars still travels along these rails of thought. He does still seem to be the larger-than-life paragon of theatrical history that Soviet propaganda had made of him in the early twentieth century. No wonder he can strike an outdated note in the twenty-first! Russian director Adolf Shapiro echoes the sentiments of many today when he wrote that this paragon's "psychological" methods initially struck him as "insufficiently vivid and expressive, even boring."[11]

But this stodgy, old-fashioned *persona* had stolen the identity of a much more forward-looking man of the theatre, who sought the elusive and multivalent art of acting. The actual Stanislavsky had played with many ideas that Soviet philosophy would not allow and Americans were not in a position to find. Among these are his adaptations from Yoga, his use of modern dance techniques for the actor, his revisions of Diderot's concept of the actor's dual consciousness, and his innovative rehearsal technique, Active Analysis.[12]

In this chapter, I tell one specific story of how the Soviet political machine constructed the Stanislavsky myth by suppressing Active Analysis and replacing it with a politically correct version known as The Method of Physical Actions.

ACTIVE ANALYSIS IN PRACTICE[13]

During his confinement at his home, Stanislavsky worked with a select group of actors to develop a rehearsal technique in which actors examine the dynamics of human interaction through purposeful improvisations. He used this new technique for rehearsing traditionally scripted plays (including those by Molière and Shakespeare), for dramatizing prose works (like the short stories of Anton Chekhov), and for devising performances entirely from the actors' improvisations.

Before improvising, actors map the interaction they wish to explore by asking three basic questions:

1. What is the main "event" that should occur? This question interrogates the narrative level of acting. For a scripted play, the event must jibe with the text. A concise answer to this question provides a target to guide actors as they improvise.
2. What is the dynamic function of each actor in the interaction? Some play "impelling actions" which move purposefully toward the event; others play "counteractions" which resist, delay, or seek to prevent the targeted event. In this stage of work, actors consider the force and direction of their actions and anticipate the collisions that are likely to occur between them as they improvise the scene. This step assumes the structural importance of conflict to drama.
3. Actors now identify strong, active, and playable verbs that will embody the actions and counteractions they have identified and that might naturally produce the target event. Those who impel the scene choose verbs that will take them toward the event; those with counteractions choose verbs that resist the forward movement of the scene. During improvisations, actors are expected to stick to their chosen verbs (*what* they are doing), even when they find that they must shift tactics (*how* they do it) from moment to moment as the interaction unfolds.

The actors now improvise the scene, keeping in mind the event and their chosen verbs. During improvisations they may use whatever text they remember, paraphrase the dialogue, or work silently. In this way, they test their understanding of the scene's structural dynamics. Two examples of such mappings for the improvisational, hence "active," analysis of a scene might be:

Sample Event 1: The Breakup of Two Lovers
Impelling Action: To call it quits (Tactics that might arise: To let him down easy, to state the case, to berate, to suggest alternatives, to walk out, etc.)
Counteraction: To seduce (Tactics that might arise: To flatter, to tease, to wheedle, to allure, to prod, to give myself, etc.)

Sample Event 2: A Politician Wins a Vote
Impelling Action: To inspire (Tactics that might arise: To lay out the plan, to envision a better future, to warn of impending dangers, to assure, to show confidence, etc.)
Counteraction: To judge (Tactics that might arise: To take the person in, to listen, to look, to argue, to assess, to evaluate, etc.)

After completing an improvisation, the actors evaluate their work. Did the event occur? Did the dynamic structure of actions and counteractions make sense? Did the improvisation elicit and express information about character, emotional content, self-image, power relationships, etc., that makes sense? Depending upon their answers, the actors now revise their map of the scene and repeat the improvisation. This process of analysis, improvisation, and evaluation is repeated until the group has achieved what they wish. When working with a script, the group often notices that memorization seems to occur of itself, or comes with extraordinary ease following a series of such improvisations.

While "action," expressed by an active verb, is generally familiar through Hapgood's awkward translation "objective," the notion of "counteraction" is not. While improvisations are often conducted in rehearsals, they rarely track the scene so closely. In Active Analysis, improvisation does not imagine the characters' back stories, but drafts the cast's eventual performance.

THE POLITICAL SUPPRESSION OF ACTIVE ANALYSIS[14]

Created in his hidden home studio, Stanislavsky wrote virtually nothing about Active Analysis. Only eyewitnesses, who worked with him on it, could carry it forward into the future. But accounts of what had actually happened behind closed doors vary in direct relationship to the witness's politics. The real-life drama between two of Stanislavsky's assistants, Maria Osipovna Knebel (1898–1985) and Mikhail Nikolaevich Kedrov (1893–1972), best exemplifies how Soviet policies on the arts continued to suppress unwanted aspects of Stanislavsky's work in the Cold War period.

By 1949, Knebel had risen high in the ranks of the MAT. She had joined the company as an actor in 1924, specializing in character roles like that of Charlotta in Anton Chekhov's *The Cherry Orchard*. In 1936, Stanislavsky selected her to assist him with the experimental work he was conducting at his home. In 1942, she began directing for the MAT, and in 1943 she added the teaching of acting to her profile at MAT's newly created Studio-School.

From 1936 to 1938, Knebel simultaneously explored Active Analysis with Stanislavsky and on her own at a small alternative theatre, the Ermolova Studio, where she had been directing since 1935. While rehearsing two of Gorky's plays there, she consulted Stanislavsky regularly about her use of his new approach in production. Two years after his death, she codirected Shakespeare's *As You Like It* using Active Analysis for the first time from conception through performance. For this production, she worked as *rezhisser*, the director who assists actors in the creation of their characters. Her codirector, the production's *postanovshchik*, with responsibility for staging the play was at first skeptical about her process of rehearsing the actors, but when she showed him the results, he was completely won over to the new method.[15] From this time forward, she made it her mission to use, teach, and promote Active Analysis:

> There are a great number of paths in art. For me, the path was a rehearsal process, the method of Active Analysis. By that time, through my many experiences and in my work on Shakespeare and Gorky, I understood that this method strengthens the improvisatory nature of the actor, helps uncover the actor's individuality, and cleans the dust of time off literary works with wonderful images and characters in them.[16]

In 1949, despite her success at MAT and her commitment to Stanislavsky's work, Knebel was abruptly fired by Kedrov, who had been appointed the company's new Artistic Director. He had claimed the role of Stanislavsky's true heir when he staged for public production one of the last house projects, Molière's *Tartuffe*. But Knebel's continuing presence in the theatre clearly challenged his claim. She, like he, had assisted Stanislavsky in his last years; she, like he, had applied Stanislavsky's last experiments to the directing of classic plays. She, as easily as he, could have called herself Stanislavsky's heir.

If Kedrov's organizational model for MAT mirrored that of Stalin's iron-fisted government, so too did the stunning manner in which Kedrov rid himself of Knebel mirror the erratic style of the Stalinist purges. At the end of the 1949 season, an administrator matter-of-factly informed Knebel that Kedrov was willing to work only with those who considered themselves his "students." At first amused, Knebel wryly observed that, being "the same age, his comrade, and his colleague," she could hardly call him teacher.

Yet, when she arrived for work the next season, she learned that her salary had been suspended, that she had not been assigned to any new productions, and that all the plays in which she regularly performed, including *The Cherry Orchard*, had been pulled from the repertory.[17]

One might argue that Kedrov could simply not stomach competition from a woman whose talents were as great as or greater than his own. "Being a woman director is not easy," Knebel wrote. "There are not many of us."[18] Her words understate the hostility she must have faced when she moved from acting into the male-dominated endeavor of directing. Once, when MAT director Vasily Sakhnovsky was corrected for saying there were no women directors, he retorted: "Women who direct are not women!"[19] The same prejudiced attitude would later condition even the praise that Knebel received. She had "a mind that was truly not a woman's mind"[20]; she displayed the "masculine traits" of clarity and structural integrity.[21]

Post-World War II Soviet nationalism had made it extremely easy for Kedrov to rid himself of Knebel. By 1949, Stalin had initiated bitter anti-Semitic campaigns against so-called "cosmopolitans."[22] On the grossest level, these campaigns facilitated Kedrov's move against Knebel, since her Jewish father had been the preeminent publisher of children's books in pre-revolutionary Russia. Anti-Semitism had already hit her hard in 1940, when her brother Nikolai was arrested as an enemy of the people.[23] In the atmosphere of Stalinist Russia, the branding of her brother as a traitor meant that she, too, had become dangerous company. Following her brother's arrest, "people would avoid meeting her in the corridors of the MAT, so that they would not be obliged to say hello," recalled a former student.[24] That she should also become a casualty of Soviet anti-Semitism may have seemed only inevitable to Kedrov and his camp.

But in the highly competitive battle that developed between Knebel and Kedrov, more was at stake than male pride and Stalinist nationalism. As the new head of a major theatre that received heavy governmental subsidies, Kedrov was bound by Soviet policies on the arts. Moreover, as a loyal Communist, he supported the policies without question. His selection of ideologically correct, but artistically weak, plays during this period best demonstrates his overall political complicity.[25] The different stories that Kedrov and Knebel told about Stanislavsky's last experimental studio are even more revelatory of the era's politics. The political machine was at work in Kedrov, who bent Stanislavsky's experimental work to Soviet injunctions on the arts, while Knebel resisted, thus making her a dangerous thorn in Kedrov's side. He may have fired her for her gender and her Jewish roots, but he also fired her for her passionate commitment to Active Analysis.

On the artistic front, Stalin cracked down on any form of art that that ran counter to Socialist Realism. His postwar artistic decrees tightened into a stranglehold, and provided Kedrov with this artistically pernicious justification for ousting Knebel. Since her staging of *As You Like It* in 1940, she had publicly espoused Active Analysis, which operates through the exploration of dramatic conflict, whereas new governmental injunctions on the arts had made conflict itself politically subversive. To understand how such an absurdity might be reasonably argued, one needs only review the principles of Active Analysis and Socialist Realism side by side.

Active Analysis is more than an acting technique; Stanislavsky developed a theoretical model that links drama of any style and genre to embodied performance. By invoking the Aristotelian notion that drama is an imitation of an action, Stanislavsky redefines a play as a score of actions. He sees dramatic language as encoding action, just as musical notes record melody. In Active Analysis, a play is read in the same way as a musician reads a musical score, with each detail determining potential performance. Next, by adapting structuralism to drama,[26] Stanislavsky locates the basic structural element of action in the event, which occurs when an impelling action collides with a counteraction. Actions may connect directly, producing sharp conflict, or bounce off each other obliquely resulting in a subtler drama. The play's tone, style, genre, and thematic issues emerge from the specifics of this interaction. Like vector analysis in physics, which describes the direction, force, and quality of motion, Stanislavsky conceives of performance as a dynamic interplay of actions and counteractions,[27] and hence, as conflict.

Socialist Realism enjoined artists to reflect a varnished Soviet reality that had successfully transcended class. In the late 1940s, when Stalin cracked down especially hard on the arts, critics and playwrights reacted by proposing a theory of "conflictlessness." In the allegedly perfect society created by Stalin's five-year industrial, agricultural, and economic plans, conflict was deemed irrelevant and, in its place, only competition between the better and the best was appropriate in Soviet life and art.[28] "Conflictlessness" willfully ignored not only the "conflictual processes" of history,[29] but also the complexities of social and personal relationships upon which dramatists have historically relied. As a result, by 1949, with conflict banned, Active Analysis could be nothing less than politically suspect.

With Knebel gone, Kedrov was now free to develop a politically acceptable version of Stanislavsky's last legacy. First, he called it "The Method of Physical Actions," citing manuscript pages that Stanislavsky had penned shortly before his death[30] in order to provide his mentor's *imprimatur*. By emphasizing the actor's physicality, this label beautifully suits Marxist materialist expectations. In contrast, Knebel called her competing interpretation "Active Analysis," in order to reflect the full psychophysical range in the technique. The actor uses both body through "action" and mind, even spirit, through "analysis."[31] As she cautioned, "While the specific meanings of [her own and Kedrov's] words may seem close, their substance leads to diametrically opposite conclusions."[32]

Second, Kedrov taught that in this new Method, Stanislavsky had finally found an accurate, scientifically based approach to acting that dispensed with his mentor's early idealistic, but misinformed, approaches. Thus, Kedrov aligned himself with the teleological expectations of communism.

Both he and his government agreed that history (whether it be of the country or of an art form) naturally leads to a perfect moment, beyond which evolution need not go. In contrast, Knebel saw Active Analysis as an approach that "absorbs everything that was discovered earlier; it absorbs Stanislavsky's entire life and work. Without understanding this, you can not understand what is new in this discovery."[33] In short, for Kedrov, the Method of Physical Actions meant rejecting prior processes of work; for Knebel, Active Analysis was an evolutionary step forward that depended upon what came before, and which would continue to evolve in the future.

Third, Kedrov suits his practice to the phrase "Physical Actions" by turning psychophysical actions and counteractions into simple sequences of physical motions. To leave a room, the actor walks forward, reaches out a hand, turns the knob, opens the door, and exits. The actor's score focuses directly on this physical map. In contrast, Knebel views Active Analysis as "a gymnastic system for both body and soul."[34] She promotes a holistic approach toward performance in which physical motion creates trajectories of desire which loop back again and reshape motion. The character who wishes to escape an uncomfortable meeting may still walk forward, reach out a hand, turn the knob and exit, but the actor does so by embodying complex, human conflicts produced by actions colliding with counteractions.

In her 1967 memoir, Knebel describes the liminal moment she experienced when she admitted to herself that leaving the MAT was the necessary condition that made her future contributions to theatrical art possible.

> Very slowly and gradually did I come to realize that what was most important and dear to me were not the walls of M.A.T., but what I had taken from within them. Having lost my home, I found it within myself . . . And only after I understood that, with all my soul, with all my being, did I feel free and able to work.[35]

She vowed to keep alive what she called the "secret cult of knowledge" about Active Analysis,[36] a vow that proved far from trivial. Throughout the 1950s, she admitted that she was mocked as the "village idiot"[37] for her unflagging commitment. Indeed, she risked more than mockery; she risked Soviet imprisonment, as well. But without her stubborn persistence, the holistic technique would surely have died a political death.

Like the absurdist writers of the 1920s who took refuge from Soviet control over the arts in children's literature, Knebel took a job directing for Moscow's Central Children's Theatre (CCT) in 1950, and became its Artistic Director in 1955. Theatre for young audiences had become an established institution of the Soviet government by the 1940s, fully subsidized and professionally staffed with well-trained adult actors. Yet, because these theatres staged fantasy and fairy tales, they could often escape the confines of realism in ways unavailable to other companies. They could also "react earlier than others to changes in the theatrical weather."[38] CCT thus launched a number of stellar theatrical careers, Knebel's chief among them.

Knebel significantly raised the level of sophistication in the CCT's repertory, often commissioning new works by playwrights who would later become major voices after Stalin's death. As she explained, "I strove to speak with children through the language of great art without the babbling condescension, which in those years, when the 'theory of conflictlessness' was blossoming, could be heard loudly."[39] In making this decision, Knebel came into her own. Her productions of the classics (such as Griboyedov's *Woe From Wit* in 1951 and Molière's *Bourgeois Gentilhomme* in 1954), stage adaptations of novels (including Gogol's *Dead Souls* in 1952 and Dickens' *Oliver Twist* in 1956), fairy tales (such as Ershov's *The Little Humpbacked Horse* in 1952 and the Chinese *Magic Blossom*, with a script devised entirely by actors' improvisations in 1958), and contemporary plays of true merit made Knebel's seemingly modest children's enterprise into one of the most popular theatres in Moscow, even among adults.

More pertinent to this study, she built a strong company of actors by using Active Analysis under the radar of governmental control. Many from her group (for example, Oleg Efremov, who would become Artistic Director of MAT during the 1980s) reinvigorated Russian acting under her tutelage.

Having survived the harshest years of Soviet control at the CCT, Knebel turned earnestly to teaching and writing in the 1960s, when a thaw in Soviet control over the arts allowed her the opportunity to share her secret knowledge more openly. She began teaching full-time at Russia's State Institute of Theatrical Art (GITIS) and became chair of the directing program in 1961. By the time of her death in 1985, she had written six books and more than a hundred articles. These last endeavors turned Active Analysis from an underground cult into a widely accepted and well-respected process for theatrical training and rehearsal throughout Russia.

By century's end, Knebel was generally acknowledged as Stanislavsky's true heir. Anatoly Efros, whose reinterpretations of the classics stunned audiences in the 1960s and 1970s, baldly stated that, although he had studied the Stanislavsky System for years, "I actually understood what this method was in practice only when I came into contact with Maria Osipovna Knebel at the Children's Theatre."[40] His sentiment was widely shared. At the centenary of MAT in 1997, the contemporary avant-garde director, Anatoly Vasiliev, named her as a major influence on him.[41]

While the theory of conflictlessness was relatively short-lived, it played a major role in the culture of disinformation that had manipulated Stanislavsky's image since the 1920s. Because of Knebel's unflagging promotion of Active Analysis, the politically correct Method of Physical Actions lost support in Russia during the 1960s. Yet, in the U.S., Kedrov's fragmentary piece of the puzzle is still often taken for the whole, with Knebel's work still largely unknown. Consider how many current textbooks on acting reference The Method of Physical Actions without mentioning Active Analysis. A few among them are Doug Moston's *Coming to Terms with Acting: An Instructional Glossary* (New York: Drama Publishers, 1993), the ninth edition of Charles McGaw's classic *Acting is Believing* (with Kenneth L. Stilson and Larry D. Clark, Belmont, CA: Thomson Wadsworth, 2007), and Paul Kassel's *Acting: An Introduction to the Art and Craft of Playing* (New York: Pearson Education, 2007). Readers might consider whether the books they regularly use do the same.

Even current theatre scholars of the highest caliber disagree about the importance of Active Analysis in Stanislavsky's work. While Jean Benedetti recognizes the Soviet reduction of Stanislavsky's late work, he uses "The Method of Physical Actions" to refer to the play's "active analysis on the rehearsal-room floor," thus combining the two into one. At the same time, to counter the Soviet interpretation, he reminds his readers that "Physical action is the foundation on which the entire emotional, mental and philosophical superstructure of the ultimate performance is built."[42] Bella Merlin and I agree that there is a significant difference between the two techniques. The Method of Physical Actions, even when practiced psychophysically, stops short of drafting performances as dynamic interplay of actions and counteractions. As Merlin states, Active Analysis goes farther than The Method of Physical Actions, because it taps "all the available avenues of investigation—mental, physical, emotional, and experiential—[which are] harnessed together holistically."[43]

Perhaps the key to our confusion about Active Analysis lies as much in gender politics as in Stalinist repression. None of Knebel's six books has been published in English,[44] while Vasily Toporkov's account of Kedrov's work, *Stanislavski in Rehearsal*, has been translated twice into English (first in 1979 by Christine Edwards [New York: Theatre Arts Books] and again in 2004 by Jean Benedetti [London: Routledge]). Consider the fact that in the 1970s, when literary critics sought to bring new visibility to female writers of the past, they began by interrogating the informal process of canon formation in university curricula, which had selected for greatness primarily male authors.[45] I see a comparable process of selectivity in the theatrical canon. The major female voice in Russian for Active Analysis remains silent in English.

TIME, FORWARD![46]

The twenty-first century is the right time to get beyond the Soviet culture of disinformation that has clouded American knowledge of Stanislavsky's work since the 1920s. In postmodern America, the historical paragon (still often taken for Stanislavsky the Seeker) seems a tarnished statue of a hero, whose thinking registers as too patriarchal for feminist actors and theorists, too essentialist for scholars of performance studies, and too absolute for contemporary theatre artists in a multi-cultural and unsure age. When Shapiro went to study with Knebel in the 1960s, he learned that the "boring" Stanislavsky he thought he knew actually offered surprisingly vital and vigorous theatrical ideas. Shapiro found himself "unexpectedly taken prisoner for life."[47] Perhaps, if American artists and scholars could encounter the hidden Stanislavsky too, they might yet experience the same jolt of excitement that Shapiro describes.

In my view, contemporary artists and theorists are primed for this jolt, because they are unknowingly exploring territory that Stanislavsky charted. His psychophysical experimentation with Yoga and his interest in modern dance deserve a closer look by those seeking new approaches to the actor's physical training. His probing of the actor's dual consciousness might spark interest in those who try to capture the fragmented nature of the contemporary world where coherence and logic seem irrelevant. His insights into the cognitive processes of performance seem to anticipate the latest discoveries in brain science.[48]

I have focused this article on Active Analysis precisely because this approach provoked a creative jolt in me. I use its principles and terminology to unleash the imaginations of professional actors in my A/ACT workshop in Los Angeles, to ground my approach to reading and directing plays, and to teach my undergraduate students at the University of Southern California about the performative dimension of written drama. Active Analysis takes me to the heart of theatre as an embodied form of art. Moreover, when I watch actors adapt its principles to their auditions and professional work, and when I see the ease with which my students adopt its basic assumptions, I am all the more convinced of Stanislavsky's continuing relevance.

In the twenty-first century, the Stanislavsky myth need no longer be taken for the man. The Soviet Union has fallen, communist archives are now accessible, and a significant body of scholarship corrects misinformation about his System. As early as 1973, Burnet Hobgood examined anew its "central conceptions."[49] Laurence Senelick first exposed discrepancies in the Russian and English versions of Stanislavsky's autobiography.[50] I (in 1984) and Jean Benedetti (in 1990) have discussed the censorship of Stanislavsky's acting manuals in Russian and their abridgement in translation.[51] In 1991, Anatoly Smeliansky published the first hard evidence of Stanislavsky's internal exile under Stalin.[52] In 1998, the first edition of my book, *Stanislavsky in Focus*, analyzed the complex mosaic of forces, both cultural and political, that had obscured many of his most forward-looking ideas.[53] In the last decade of the twentieth century, Russian scholars published the remaining treasures in the MAT archives.[54]

Yet, despite contemporary curiosities that move in sympathy with the System, and more than twenty years of clear-sighted publications, Stanislavsky in the U.S. has yet to break fully free from the constraints of Soviet disinformation. Many theatre professionals and scholars still think of him as the "Father of psychological realism," and of his early experiments on "emotional memory" as his primary technique. Many acting students still associate his name with the Method before anything else. Another quick glance at current acting textbooks suggests how they contribute to the persistence of the myth. Many, like McGaw's ninth edition (cited above), list recent sources in their bibliographies, but make few or no substantive changes in their descriptions of Stanislavsky's career and work.

How can we move beyond the culture of disinformation that surrounds Stanislavsky's System? Some might argue that we have already done so whenever we admit that the American Method and the Stanislavsky System are not one and the same. But such acknowledgement without adaptations to practice is lip service only. Given the fact that reliable information now exists about Stanislavsky's previously suppressed practice, why not challenge ourselves to experiment with his lesser known and previously suppressed techniques?

NOTES

1. I wish to thank the coeditors of this anthology for their invitation to publish here, and R. Andrew White, Associate Professor of Acting at Valparaiso University, for his comments on my first draft. All translations from Russian in this chapter are my own unless otherwise noted.
2. Charles Marowitz, "Getting Stanislavsky Wrong," *American Theatre*, 29:3 (March 2007), 57, 56–9. See also all the "Letters to the Editor" about Marowitz's article in *American Theatre*, 29:4 (April 2007).
3. Anne Bogart, *A Director Prepares: Seven Essays on Art and Theatre* (New York: Routledge, 2001), 37.
4. I examine the details of the historical processes which shaped perceptions of Stanislavsky in the U.S. and U.S.S.R. in my book *Stanislavsky in Focus: An Acting Master for the Twenty First Century*, Second Edition (London: Routledge, 2008). The context for the first section of this chapter relies on this earlier research. My discussion of Active Analysis derives from my current research, supported in part by grants from the American Society for Theatre Research and the National Endowment for the Humanities.
5. M. Gus, "V bor'be za realizm" [In the Battle for Realism], *Sovetskoe iskusstvo* [Soviet Art], 6:412 (1938), 4.
6. M. O. Knebel', *Vsia zhizn'* [All of Life] (Moscow: VTO, 1967), 280–282.
7. Knebel', *zhizn'*, 265.
8. Lee Strasberg, "The Actors Studio," Sound Recording No. 339A, 1956–1969, Wisconsin Center for Film and Theatre Research, An Archive of the University of Wisconsin, Madison, and the State Historical Society of Wisconsin, Madison, Tape #A12, 2/16/1965.
9. Hapgood published her abridged translations as *An Actor Prepares* (1936), *Building a Character* (1949), and *Creating a Role* (1961) with New York's Theatre Arts Books. The first to challenge the hegemony of Hapgood's work is Jean Benedetti, who has translated Parts I and II of Stanislavsky's *Rabota aktera nad soboi* [An Actor's Work on Himself], as *An Actor's Work: A Student's Diary* (London: Routledge 2008).
10. In Chapter 6 of the second edition of *Stanislavsky in Focus*, I discuss the mechanisms of censorship and Stanislavsky's specific writing strategies in detail.

11. Adolf Shapiro, *Kak zakryvalsia zanaves* [How the Curtain Opens] (Moscow: Novoe literaturnoe obozrenie, 1999), 133.
12. See Chapters 7–10 in the second edition of *Stanislavsky in Focus*. For Yoga in the System, see also R. Andrew White, "Stanislavsky and Ramacharaka: The Influence of Yoga and Turn-of-the-Century Occultism on the System," *Theatre Survey*, 47:1 (2006), 73–92. Dennis C. Beck, "The Paradox of the Method Actor: Rethinking the Stanislavsky Legacy," *Method Acting Reconsidered*, ed. David Krasner (New York: St. Martin's Press, 2000), 261–282, deconstructs the myth of Stanislavsky, especially in regard to the assumed identification of actor with role. Ashley Wain, in his dissertation, *Acting and Essence: Experiencing, Essence, Presence and Archetype in the Acting Traditions of Stanislavsky and Copeau* (University of Western Sydney, Australia, 2005) studies both Yoga and dual consciousness in the System. I know of no specific study on modern dance's impact on the System as yet. Active Analysis is the subject of my next book.
13. My description of Active Analysis is taken from Maria Knebel's writings, especially *O deistvennom analize p'esy* [About the Active Analysis of Plays] (Moscow: Iskusstvo, 1982) and classes conducted by her assistant, Natalia Zverova, at Moscow's Russian Academy of Theatrical Arts (formerly GITIS).
14. Irina and Igor Levin, *The Stanislavsky Secret* (Colorado Springs, CO: Meriweather Publishing, 2002), 17–18, briefly discuss this period of disinformation.
15. This type of codirection is common in Russian theatres, but the distinction is hard to make in English since both Russian terms are best translated as "director." Nikolai Khemlev, whom Knebel' considered among the best of MAT's actors, was her codirector. Knebel', *zhizn'*, 347.
16. Knebel', *zhizn'*, 485.
17. Knebel', *zhizn'*, 477.
18. M. O. Knebel', *Poeziia pedagogiki,* [The Poetry of Pedagogy] (Moscow: VTO, 1976), 248.
19. Goncharov in V. I. Liadov, ed., *O M. O. Knebel'* [About M. O. Knebel] (Moscow: Iskusstvo, 1991), 31.
20. Krymova, in Liadov, 61.
21. Z. V. Vladimirova, *M. O. Knebel'* (Moscow: Iskusstvo, 1991), 204.
22. This Soviet period was called "Zdanovism" after party boss Andrei Zhdanov, who set in motion the strict political controls of the time. For information in English on this period, see Evgeny Dobrenko and Thomas Lahusen, eds., *Socialist Realism Without Shores* (Durham, NC: Duke University Press, 1997) and Marc Slonim, *Soviet Russian Literature: Writers and Problems, 1917–1967* (New York: Oxford University Press, 1967), 277–292.
23. Krymova in Liadov, 88–90; Petrova in Liadov, 100.
24. Petrova in Liadov, 100.
25. Inna Solovyova, "The Theatre and Socialist Realism, 1929–1953," in *A History of Russian Theatre*, Robert Leach and Victor Borovsky, eds. (Cambridge, UK: Cambridge University Press, 1999), 355. See also Chapter 6 in *Stanislavsky in Focus* (Second Edition) for more on Kedrov. Knebel', *Poeziia*, 356.
26. Stanislavsky was specifically influenced by Russian Formalism, a type of literary criticism developed in the 1920s, and a precursor to later Structuralism. Formalists judged works of art on craft and structural integrity without regard to the author's social or political views. This type of criticism was banned by Stalin as early as the 1920s. Usage of the term "formalism" was generalized under Stalin and came to mean anything artistic that was not Socialist Realist. See Slonim, 101–102; 275.

27. When the leading French theorist, Patrice Pavis, proposes examining performance's lines of vectorization in *Analyzing Performance*, trans. David Williams (Ann Arbor: University of Michigan Press, 2003), he seems unaware that he is following Stanislavsky's lead into the realm of Active Analysis.
28. The best discussion on "conflictlessness" in English is Matthew Cullern Bown, "Conflictlessness," *Socialist Realist Painting* (New Haven, CT: Yale University Press, 1998), 221–301.
29. I borrow this term from Joan Wallach Scott, *Gender and the Politics of History* (New York: Columbia University Press, 1999), 5, 7, 9, 25.
30. Kedrov cites his sources in an article entitled, "To Preserve the Legacy of Stanislavsky Means to Develop It" ("Khranit' nasledie Stanislavskogo— eto znachit razvivat' ego," *Ezhegodnik MKhAT-a: 1951–1952*, [Moscow: MKhAT, 1956], 99–116). To buttress Kedrov's revision, the journal *Teatr* published his sources in September 1950 (No. 11) as K.S. Stanislavskii, "On Physical Actions: From Unpublished Materials" ("O fizicheskikh destviiakh: iz neopublikovannykh materialov"), 48–52. Some of these materials were later translated by Elizabeth Reynolds Hapgood in Constantin Stanislavski, *Creating a Role* (New York: Theatre Arts Books, 1961).
31. M. O. Knebel', "Vysokaia prostata" [Supreme Simplicity], *Teatr*, 9 (Sept. 1968), 48.
32. M.O. Knebel', "Razmyshleniia," [Musings], *Teatral'naia zhizn'*, [Theatrical Life] 13 (June 1984), 12.
33. Knebel', "Vysokaia prostata," 47.
34. Knebel', *zhizn'*, 271.
35. Knebel', *zhizn'*, 484.
36. Knebel', "Vysokaia prostata," 46.
37. Knebel', "Vysokaia prostata," 46.
38. Shapiro, 136.
39. Knebel', *zhizn'* 484.
40. Anatolii Efros, *Repetitsiia—liubov' moia* (Moscow: Panos, 1993), 139. This book has been recently translated into English by James Thomas as *The Joy of Rehearsal*, New York: Peter Lang, 2006.
41. Anatoly Smeliansky, *The Russian Theatre after Stalin*, Patrick Miles, trans. (Cambridge, UK: Cambridge University Press, 1999), 215.
42. Jean Benedetti, *Stanislavski and the Actor* (New York: Routledge, 1998), xiv–xv.
43. Bella Merlin, *The Complete Stanislavsky Toolkit* (Hollywood: Drama Publishers, 2007), 197.
44. Only two of her articles have been published in English: a much abridged version of "Vysokaia prostota" ("Superior Simplicity" in Sonia Moore, ed. and trans., *Stanislavski Today: Commentaries on K.S. Stanislavski* [New York: American Center for Stanislavski Theatre Art, 1973], 44–47) and "Vital Work with my Eminent Students" (in Miriam Morton, ed. and trans., *Through the Magic Curtain: Theatre for Children, Adolescents and Youth in the USSR* [New Orleans: Anchorage Press, 1979], 107–135). One of Knebel's books has appeared in Spanish, *La Palabra en la Creacion Actoral*, Madrid, 1998. Director Anatoly Vasiliev has published two of her books in abridged forms in a single volume in France: *L'Analyse-Action* [Active Analysis], Paris: Actes Sud-Papiers, 2006. Bella Merlin has had unpublished translations made for her personal research. Scott Phillips and Vladimir Rovinsky are reportedly working on a translation of *Analysis in Action* (www.setc.org/publications/symposium.asp; accessed 12/23/2005).
45. For a brief explanation of this history, see "Canon/Canon Formation" (37–38) and "Liberal Feminism" (169–170) in *The Columbia Dictionary of*

Modern Literary and Cultural Criticism, Joseph Childers and Gary Hantzi, eds. (New York: Columbia University Press, 1995).

46. I borrow the title for this section from the 1932 Stalin-era novel by Valentin Kataev.
47. Shapiro, 135.
48. See, for example, Rhonda Blair, *The Actor, Image, and Action: Acting and Cognitive Neuroscience* (London: Routledge, 2008).
49. Burnet M. Hobgood, "Central Conceptions in Stanislavsky's System," *Educational Theatre Journal*, 25:2 (1973), 147–159.
50. Laurence Senelick, "Stanislavsky's Double Life in Art," *Theatre Survey*, 26:2 (1981), 201–211.
51. Sharon Marie Carnicke, *"An Actor Prepares/Rabota aktera nad soboi:* A Comparison of the English with the Russian Stanislavsky," *Theatre Journal*, 37:4 (1984), 481–494; Jean Benedetti, "A History of Stanislavski in Translation," *New Theatre Quarterly*, 23 (August 1990), 266–278.
52. Anatolii Mironovich Smelianskii, "The Last Decade: Stanislavsky and Stalinism," *Theatre*, 12:2 (Spring 1991), 7–13.
53. Sharon Marie Carnicke, *Stanislavsky in Focus* (New York: Harwood, 1998; Second Edition, London Routledge, 2008).
54. See, for example, the most recent K. S. Stanislavskii, *Sobranie sochinenii* [Collected Works], 9 vols. (Moscow: Iskusstvo, 1988–1999), and the three volume study on Stanislavsky's relationship with Nemirovich-Danchenko by Olga Radishcheva, *Stanislavskii i Nemirovich-Danchenko: Istoriia teatral'nykh otnoshenii* (Moscow: Artist, Rezhisser, Teatr, 1997–1999). There are a host of others, too numerous to mention here.

2 Actor Training Meets Historical Thinking

Jonathan Chambers

A few years ago, I taught a beginning acting course at Bowling Green State University. As is typical in academic theatre departments, the primary course objective was to introduce students (both majors, putatively interested in careers in the theatre, and nonmajors, drawn from a variety of academic disciplines) to the "basic techniques of acting" such as they had presumably been set forth by Stanislavsky, and, in turn, reinterpreted, reconceptualized, and reorganized by others who followed.[1] Although the students in my class were not required to read in translation Stanislavsky's work (or for that matter, the primary texts by noted teachers of acting who worked in the tradition of Stanislavsky, such as Boleslavsky, Strasberg, Adler, and Meisner), they were asked to develop skills and, moreover, to identify, in the work of other performers, those skills that were fundamentally (albeit, perhaps, tacitly and/or indirectly) linked to the precepts of "the System."

Naturally, my desire to comply with the spirit of this course objective was an important factor when it came to choosing a text. That choice was complicated somewhat by a departmental expectation that the course would also help students develop script analysis skills. As I weighed these factors, I was certain of one thing: I would follow my long-held practice of avoiding Elizabeth Reynolds Hapgood's English language translations/adaptations of Stanislavsky's acting manuals, *An Actor Prepares* (1936), *Building a Character* (1949), and *Creating a Role* (1961).[2] Recalling my own experience years before as a beginning acting student assigned to read those canonical texts and apply their approaches, I was quite certain that the students in my class would find the language difficult, the layout confusing, and authoritative tone off-putting. Of course, my choice to forgo the use of Hapgood's texts has subsequently been validated by the work of Sharon Marie Carnicke, particularly her study *Stanislavsky in Focus*. In that paradigm-shifting work, Carnicke meticulously traces the convoluted publication and translation history of Stanislavsky's work, including the Hapgood translations/adaptations which, despite presenting Stanislavsky's ideas in a significantly abridged and adapted form, "became the definitive statements of Stanislavsky's views in the West for nearly fifty years—the

'ABC's' of acting."³ Thus, in weighing the need to introduce students to the "basic techniques of acting," against my aversion to Hapgood's texts, and taking into consideration the necessity of developing the students' script analysis skills, I at last chose from the many texts available Charles Waxberg's *The Actor's Script: Script Analysis for Performers*.⁴

Once the course began, I spent the first few weeks focused on introducing students to the principles of System-based acting. Along the way, I not only incorporated the methods set forth in Waxberg's text, a study that takes as its central force the principle precepts of Stella Adler, but also drew lesson ideas and explorations from Michael Chekhov's *To The Actor: On the Technique of Acting*, Robert Cohen's *Acting One*, and Melissa Bruder's *A Practical Handbook for the Actor*.⁵

After about a month, the students and I discussed at length scripts from which they might draw material for their final scenes. In the course of the conversation, one of my more ambitious students asked if, for his final scene, he and three of his classmates might work on a cutting from Sarah Kane's *Crave*, an opaque, poetic script that troubles the representational/presentational divide, is seemingly set outside "normal" time and place, and has four archetypal characters identified only by letters of the alphabet. I must admit that initially I thought the idea was impractical and unreasonable. To be sure, the student's suggestion completely disregarded the two primary guiding principles I had provided for choosing material. First, the scene involved four, not two, characters. Second, it was not material connected to the realistic tradition (i.e., the convention of illusionistic realism, which situates the stage as environment as opposed to platform, is structured around linear action and logical syntax, and takes a normative tone). Still, a part of me wanted to honor my feelings of assurance by allowing these students to gravitate toward material they found intriguing when choosing scenes. Moreover, as the students made their case for tackling the challenging script, it occurred to me that, in the attempt to apply the methods and approaches we had been studying to a decidedly nonrealistic script such as *Crave*, there might be a valuable learning experience. In particular, I thought how engaging in this sort of work might not only help these students gain a more nuanced understanding of preparing a role System-atically, but it might also lead them to identify and, perhaps, question the powerful assumptions, histories, and ideologies that underpin the commonly held conceptions of "good" (and, for that matter, "bad") acting. Then, too, I hoped they might learn to question the often-encountered claims that such approaches are infinite in their scope and range, and that realism is a neutral (i.e., ideologically free) mode of performance. I therefore threw caution to the wind, and told them to push forward with their plan.

As I reflect on that acting course, now a few years removed from the experience, I recall how the students working on *Crave* did, indeed, over the course of the five-week rehearsal period, slowly begin to view System-based acting as a *particular* mode of performance that is shaped by *particular* concerns and contexts, and, moreover, came to regard realism as a *particular* style of representation that forwards (and perhaps even structures) a *particular* view of the world and its functions. Likewise, in terms of my own development as a teacher of acting, the profundity of that experience has been a driving impulse behind attempts I have undertaken since to develop more formalized ways of helping students critically consider and, indeed, question the espoused neutrality and universality of that now conventional mode of acting.

A handful of key resources deeply informed my initial attempts to think through these concerns. Those sources, in turn, proved vital to the development of strategies I have since incorporated into all beginning acting courses I teach. Perhaps the text most formative to my thinking was Colin Counsell's fine study, *Signs of Performance: An Introduction to Twentieth-Century Theatre*. In his chapter, simply titled, "Stanislavsky's 'System,'" Counsell offers a general summary, and apt and lucid critique, of the often-disregarded limitations of Stanislavsky's approach to acting as it is commonly understood. Counsell argues:

> Champions of the System tend to be fierce in their defence of its neutrality, asserting that it does not lead to a particular style of performance but is simply a practical means of creating characters suitable to any theatrical form. But while it is true that System-atic acting is varied, its variety is not infinite and it does display consistent characteristics. Behavioral detail, 'plausibility', a sense of profound psychological depth, a marked linearity or smoothness to the performance as a whole— these are the hallmarks of Stanislavskian work, and if we view them as the signs of 'good acting' *per se* it is largely because the System has been at the heart of orthodox western performance training for a substantial part of the twentieth century. Stanislavsky's ideas have become the accepted 'common sense' in performance, seeming 'self-evident', so that actors not infrequently employ the Russian's basic concepts without knowing that they do so.[6]

In the balance of the chapter, Counsell critically evaluates Stanislavsky-derived ideas, focusing specifically on the often used methods set forth in the three Hapgood translations/adaptations, and the prevailing attitudes guiding those ideas. Centering his analysis on the always present ideological forces operating in Stanislavsky's work, Counsell adroitly ties "the System" to the larger enterprises of "realism" and humanism—"Realism and the bourgeois individual are symbiotic concepts"—and, in turn, works to demonstrate how the ideas inherent in both realism and humanism are most appropriately viewed as interlocking and complimentary products of a particular cultural context and historical moment, and, thus, discursive formation.[7]

The bulk of Counsell's stimulating and forcefully argued critique is a demonstration of how the mid-twentieth-century, English-language versions of Stanislavsky's texts, and, I would suggest, the variant though allied practices offered and taught by others who followed in their wake (creating, as it were, derivative or by-product approaches), are haunted by the "discourse of humanist individualism."[8] In short, then, Counsell argues that System-atic ideas and methods are historically specific, discursive objects that, "far from neutral, reproduce constructions of the human subject and the world it inhabits." Relationally, realism is not, as is often professed and believed, "a style without a style," but is a particular mode of artistic expression rooted in a specific historical moment.[9]

As it did for me when I first read it, I am certain that Counsell's discussion of the tendency, on the part of many, to elide the history of Stanislavsky-derived ideas and to regard realism as "a style without a style," will sound familiar to many who teach theatre in both liberal arts and preprofessional contexts. Indeed, while it is true that many among us who have spent years studying and teaching theatre have long taken the view that realism *is* a style and that the System *has* a history, it has nonetheless been my experience that undergraduate students new to the study of acting specifically and theatre more generally, rarely think about such things. Moreover, as Counsell's argument implies, by continually positioning the study of System-based acting as the beginning point or default for the craft, the notion that the realistic performance that approach proffers is persistently reinforced as "normal" and "good."

There are, of course, many scholars who take serious issue with the claim, such as the one made by Counsell, that realism is ideologically driven. The counterview, which underpins my pedagogical efforts discussed in this essay, is further informed by the work of Louis Althusser, who in arguing that "[i]deology has a material existence," set forth the premise that ideology forms subjects and is unavoidable in that it is inherent in practices and rituals that make up material culture.[10] Thus, building on Counsell's and Althusser's arguments that material culture is inescapable from ideology and that everyone is constituted as a subject of the system, I began to think about the necessity of encouraging my students to view realism as a style that sometimes knowingly, but more often than not unknowingly, aligns with the winners in ideological struggles, masks its fictionality under a pretext of factuality, imitates (or seeks to imitate) reality without really questioning it, and in so doing "collaborates in the work of ideology."[11] As such, I began the process of creating methods for imparting to my acting students a more nuanced understanding of art (including realism and the affiliated System-based modes of performance) and encouraging them to think critically about how such activities are as much about invention and creation of truth and reality as they are about discovery and unearthing of truth and reality.[12]

   It warrants mentioning, however, that while the ideas of Counsell and Althusser played an instrumental and determining role in shaping my pedagogical practice, I also endeavored to stay aware of how such predilections (postmodern, poststructural, neo-Marxist or otherwise) are also ideological. To that end, I often reminded myself that while encouraging students to understand realism as prescribing one sense of the world and its functions, I too would be inserting into the classroom a particular point of view. In so doing, I sought to remember the words of Robert Anchor: "Realism *is* ideological, but so is every form of opposition to it."[13]

   In addition to the work of Counsell and Althusser, my thinking about the need to lead students to a more finely tuned understanding of realism and the historical specificity of "the System," was also influenced by the work of Richard Hornby, specifically his text *The End of Acting—A Radical View*. Echoing and reinforcing Counsell's remarks and, perhaps, Althusser's as well, Hornby argues that it is imperative for actors to understand "and see realism for what it is—not stylelessness, nor the basis for other styles, but simply one acting style among many."[14] In some respects, Hornby's adversarial tone, categorical dismissal of work that takes issue with the authority of the dramatic text (or, for him, the regrettable advent of "antiliterary prejudice"), and near vicious attacks on Strasberg—whose approach still "shackles American acting"[15]—and Artaud—who held an "outlandish attitude"[16]—are somewhat off-putting. Nonetheless, in my endeavor to create strategies that would lead students to think more deeply about their work in the acting studio, I found considerable value in Hornby's implied assertion that student–actors are better served when they are reminded that the craft has a history. Moreover, I found wisdom in his ardent call to encourage students to resist the pull of esoteric and mystifying notions of "feeling" and "emotion," and instead critically engage the dramatic text by considering how that object is a product of a particular historical moment, and as such was and is shaped by specific material conditions.[17]

   Taken together, then, Counsell's and Hornby's historically savvy remarks on realism and on Stanislavsky-derived ideas, as well as Althusser's claim that "[i]deology has a material existence," served as the foundation of the historicist strategy I developed and have subsequently used in the introductory, undergraduate acting studio over the course of the last few years. This historicist strategy takes as its primary objective the questioning of the unacknowledged attitudes and assumptions operating within the widely practiced and taught, System-based acting processes. To my knowledge, the pragmatism (or eye toward use–value) that guides the historicist strategy I outline below is largely missing from the literature on the System proper and System-based acting writ large. Indeed, while much has been written on the application, history, scientific underpinnings, and ideological attitudes intrinsic to these approaches, few have addressed the particulars of these concerns in the context of the academic acting studio and the effect such approaches have on the material bodies and minds of student–actors. Hence, in the balance of this essay, I will focus first on further detailing the ideas and impulses that underpin my historicist intervention, and second on ways one might go about using historical thinking as a jumping-off place for examining the authority these approaches hold in the context of the liberal arts, undergraduate acting studio. By extension, I will suggest that in encouraging students to question the authority of such acting approaches, one might also lead them toward a critical consideration of the received idea that realism is a neutral (i.e., ideologically free, acultural, and ahistorical) mode of expression.

Before outlining the particulars of this strategy, I believe it is significant first to explain my use of two key terms, "the System" and "System-atic," and second, to clarify my position in relation to the subject. Regarding the former, throughout this essay I employ the term "the System" when referring to the ideas and methods typically ascribed to Stanislavsky, and "System-atic," "System-based," and "System-influenced" to refer to the broad tradition of approaches related to and, indeed, founded upon his ideas and methods (while trying to remain cognizant of the relevant details that separate one approach from another). For this reason, in the course of my discussion I take Strasberg's Method to be a System-atic or System-based approach. Additionally, it is important to note that my use of the term System-atic is somewhat different from Counsell's (whose work I cite as foundational to my thinking), who employs the term in reference to what we have come to think of as Stanislavsky's ideas and method proper.

Regarding my position in relation to the issues I am discussing, as do many others who work in the arts within the academy, I find myself at the intersection of practice and theory, and accordingly, my work charted here arises out of two interconnecting contexts related to those domains. On the one hand, my ideas emerge from my own experiences (or actions) as an actor and teacher of acting. Moreover, it is, perhaps, important to point out that my teaching experiences have been within institutions that situate the study of theatre in general (and acting in particular) as part of a liberal arts education. Consequently, the usefulness of my remarks for those who teach in preprofessional training programs might be nominal. That said, and on the other hand, my remarks are also informed by my study of much of the literature by and about Stanislavsky's System and a variety of System-influenced approaches (although, in terms of Stanislavsky's own work, always mediated through translation and adaptation) and speculation about his ideas regarding the process of acting. Thus, those who hold the view that too much thinking about the craft disrupts inspiration might also find little value in my remarks. While I recognize the presence of these two strands in my approach, I also acknowledge the symbiosis of the acts of "doing" acting and "contemplating" acting in my own work. As such, my thoughts as set forth here are perhaps best viewed as an effect of the interplay of *praxis* and *theoria*.

With those caveats in place, my strategy of historicization begins with a central postulation about System-based acting. In sum, I contend that all such approaches, which are widely taught in liberal arts and professional actor-training programs in the United States, are framed by and, in turn, recreate humanist attitudes and assumptions.[18] Broadly defined, humanism is expressed in the belief that all people have inherent and transcendent worth, are endowed with the capacity to pursue and attain freedom, and are committed to humanity's progress.[19] While it is true that System-based ideas and methods are wide-ranging and flexible, I nonetheless hold that all such approaches are products and producers of a common universe of discourse that takes as its primary goals the advancement of humanist thinking and the situating of that mode of thought as normative (if not ideal).[20]

In light of this view, although it may reasonably be asserted that the work attributed to Stanislavsky differs in many important respects from the work of Strasberg, they are both nonetheless irrevocably tied to the larger humanist enterprise. As such, it may be argued that an awareness of the differences that divide the social democratic form of humanism, which held sway in many parts of Europe and the larger West during Stanislavsky's lifetime and emphasized the *shared* experience of all humans,[21] from the neoconservative form of humanism, which held sway in the United States during Strasberg's lifetime and emphasized the *private* rights of each individual,[22] is perhaps key to understanding some of the marked differences in their approaches. Indeed, an understanding of these contextual and ideological distinctions may help illustrate why and how Strasberg's Method, which seems to set as a principle the near deification of the individual (and, arguably, seeks to stage her or his private tortures and triumphs), has held such force in a country like the United States that was founded on the belief that all people held "certain unalienable Rights," including the right of "the separate and equal station to which the Laws of Nature and of Nature's God entitle them."[23]

More broadly speaking, however my central assumption regarding the humanist imprint on System-based acting approaches has led me to consider and, in turn, seek to contest not only what humanist discourse has allowed (and continues to allow) and what it has marked (and continues to mark) as off-limits in the context of the undergraduate acting studio (that is, how it is a *product* of the aforementioned discursive formation), but also to try to help students see that this allowable knowledge about acting is also directly, but more often indirectly, implicated in maintaining and legitimizing humanist thought (that is, how it is instrumental in the continued *production* of certain types of knowledge).[24] As one final point regarding the large shadow cast by humanism, it warrants mentioning that the tradition of liberal arts education, arising as it did in the fourteenth century, parallels the advent of humanist ideology. As such, it seems more than coincidental that the method of acting taught at present-day institutions that declare their ancestral connection to the liberal arts tradition is also linked to the maintenance of the humanist enterprise.

In an effort to address these complex and potent histories, attitudes, and assumptions, such as they relate to the undergraduate acting studio, I have attempted to invest my own pedagogical practice with a heightened sense of historical awareness. I contend that the inclusion of historical thinking as a primary framing device provides beginning, undergraduate acting students with important tools—not only ones that enable them to question and contest the notion that "basic," "good," or "valuable" acting is indisputably System-atic in its orientation, but also ones that facilitates a view that such actor training, and the realistic performance it proffers, is founded upon the highly regulated and, perhaps more importantly, culturally, historically, and ideologically specific techniques attributed to Stanislavsky and his various progeny. Needless to say, a dynamic impulse driving the development of my historicist intervention is the contention, set forth by Counsell, that even those students who do not study Stanislavsky's System such as it has been handed down to us in a formal or proper sense are nonetheless usually expected to engage with his ideas and methods on an elemental level, are obliged to vigorously apply those ideas and methods in their acting work, and, moreover, are required to demonstrate their mastery of them in their pursuits to be "good" actors.[25] That is to say, then, that more often than not, actor training in the academy in the United States judges as "good" those performances that carry the markings of "realism," and, moreover, that the method for achieving said performance is by way of masterful command of what is known as the System or an analogous approach.[26] Thus, with this historicist strategy I have sought to question introductory actor training such as it often exists in the context of undergraduate, liberal arts education, by drawing on and, in some respects, expanding, Thomas Postlewait's observation that "[h]istorical thinking—not just historical knowledge—is one of the cornerstones of our discipline," and as such "[h]istorical thinking should operate throughout the course sequences in theatre studies."[27]

To that end, my strategy summarized here takes as a starting point Fredric Jameson's call "always [to] historicize."[28] In the spirit of Jameson's appeal, I would like to suggest that teachers of acting bring nuanced historical thinking into the beginning acting studio and, moreover, find ways of encouraging in novice acting students a more finely tuned understanding of the operations of history. This historicist impulse finds its foothold with first encouraging students to view themselves as both agents and subjects in the world, who are living in a particular moment in time and under specific material, cultural, social, and political conditions. Building on this general move toward historical awareness, I believe it is imperative that we ask students to consider the notion that "everything has a history"—academic institutions and disciplines, artistic and cultural practices, aesthetic and philosophical movements, political systems, social structures, and, yes, even themselves as individuals and groups of peoples—and, as such, every-thing changes as time passes.[29] In the beginning acting studio, my move toward building historical awareness begins with the simple act of calling students' attention to the history of the craft they are studying. However, I believe an important and necessary step beyond the mere inclusion of historical knowledge and toward infusing the acting studio with historical thinking involves encouraging students to view themselves as subjects and agents in the world who have made, and will continue to make, history.

It is important to note, however, that while I seek to invest the class-room with a historicist perspective, I also try to remain sensitive to the arguments made against statements such as "everything changes as time passes." Regarding such objections, I believe it is fair to say that while some hold that artistic choices and conventions may be viewed transhistorically and/or entirely in aesthetic terms, the Neo-Marxists and New Historians whose arguments ground mine (i.e., Jameson, Tony Bennett, Mark Cousins, Stephen Greenblatt, and Catherine Gallagher) rethink those choices and conventions entirely in terms of historical practices and norms.[30] Given this almost singular focus on history, certain critics have taken issue with the totalizing nature of "always historicize (e.g., Linda Hutcheon's and Douglas Kellner's nuanced critiques of Jameson)."[31] In the end, then, I try to remain cognizant and encourage in my students a cognizance of the effect of centering *history* as the only significant factor in cultural, liter-ary, and artistic analysis, and also work to remind my students that such thinking is also of a certain historical moment and, as such, leads to certain visions of the world and its workings.

An equivalent to my proposal to historicize the acting studio is found in James Peck's account of his endeavors to endow the undergraduate directing studio with a historicist perspective. In his essay, "History in the Directing Curriculum: Major Directors, Theory and Practice," Peck summarizes his attempts to "[inject] history into the directing studio" when he writes:

> I try to help the students enrolled in [my studio directing course] Major Directors encounter [artists such as Meyerhold, Brecht, and Mnouch-kine] not as objects of history, but as subjects and at times even agents of it. In so doing, I hope the students learn to think of themselves as artists who are historical subjects and who can aspire to become his-torical agents. Students need to encounter historical perspectives in the studio classroom because by doing so they grapple with the possibility that art-making is a historically significant practice.[32]

I believe the same may be said regarding the beginning acting studio. Indeed, in my own experience, I have encouraged students to think of themselves as citizens of the world living in a particular material context, and thus sub-ject to the influence of a number of cultural, sociopolitical, and economic forces. In turn, and as I lead them through a consideration of the principles of System-based acting, I remind the students that people in the historical past—including those who forged the principles they are studying—were similarly and differently subjected to such forces. More importantly, however, I encourage them to view themselves as agents of change. That is to say, I hope that through my endeavors to historicize the acting studio I might lead students to see that the choices they make (both onstage and off), as agents in the world, help constitute the world.

Accordingly, when reviewing the syllabus on the first day of class, I strive to convey and model this historicist perspective by calling students' attention to the principles guiding the catalog course description. In more specific terms, I engage them in a critical and close reading of the implications and assumptions of the primary learning goal expressed therein: "Creating contemporary characters in realistic situations." In turn, I offer a brief overview of the social and political contexts that gave rise to realism in the West during the nineteenth century, discuss how that historically specific movement prompted profound changes in design, dramaturgy, and acting, and, in turn, point up the ways in which the practices they will be studying during the term are linked to that particular tradition. While I do not overwhelm them with references to Foucault or Jameson, I do suggest that what one perceives as "real" and "realistic" is not only historically and culturally specific, but is made or allowed to seem that way via rote practices and the enacting of systems of exclusion. I often find it helpful in this preliminary discussion to note Brecht's well-known and accessible call for a more elastic and allowing rendering of the idea of realism. In particular, I draw student's attention to Brecht's declaration that:

> We must not abstract the one and only realism from certain given works, but shall make lively use of all means, old and new, tried an untried, deriving from art and deriving from other sources, in order to put living reality in the hands of living people in such as way that it can be mastered. We shall take care not to ascribe realism to a particular historical form of novel belonging to a particular period. [. . .] Our conception of realism needs to be broad and political, free from aesthetic restrictions and independent of convention.[33]

Using this as a point of reference, in the balance of the term I look for opportunities to continue to draw students' attention to the elasticity of realism by highlighting the dynamism of the approaches they are studying. For instance, early in the term I endeavor to help students see how what is regarded as Stanislavsky's approach evolved and changed in relation to his own experiences, passions, and contexts, and that the methods of the System, such as he envisioned them, were not meant to be frozen in time. While I do not seek to provide an exhaustive account (at least in this course) of how the ideas developed, I do find it useful to call the students' attention to accounts, such as the one provided by Vasili Toporkov in *Stanislavski in*

Rehearsal, which, in part, charts this dynamism.[34] In turn, and as we continue to explore and discuss precepts drawn from Stanislavsky's work as it is typically understood, I endeavor to remind students that the contexts governing their lives in the present cannot help but shape their reading and consumption, and structure their understanding and experiencing, of those ideas and methods. More broadly speaking, and drawing this strategy full circle, I hope that students leave my course at the end of a term with a view that they might actively engage in the reading of other texts they encounter (including the catalog descriptions guiding other courses they take), and view such texts as historical items and ideological apparatuses that have political consequences.

By the same token, throughout the term I strive to make students aware of the complex and convoluted history of various System-based acting approaches. Taking my cue from Carnicke, I endeavor to help students see how the System was adapted and altered in the United States in an effort to serve particular ends (e.g., how the socially conscious work of the Group Theatre fit well within the era of the Popular Front in the 1930s,[35] or how the ardent individualism of the Actors Studio was a fitting approach in the decades immediately following World War II[36]) and that, correspondingly, realism as the preferred mode of theatrical expression became rooted and used as a standard in United States theatre through a series of connecting and analogous developments. Routinely, I call their attention to the ways in which these approaches, and by extension, realism, have been granted the status of "normal." In short, then, I work to help them see that such normalization is nourished and sustained, not through the threat of direct physical force or overt intimidation, but through the tacit force of legitimizing certain practices while, at the same time, establishing others as aberrant.

Taking a slightly different tack, throughout the term I also look for opportunities to highlight the ways in which such approaches assume and construct dramatic characters as coherent, unified identities, which are unceasing in the pursuit of an objective; or, as Counsell terms it, as perpetual "desiring machines."[37] I frequently remind them how in real social life individuals are called upon to adopt many different discursive and behavioral personae. Similarly, I look for opportunities to point up how characters created through these approaches lack the discontinuity that occurs in actual life.[38] In relation to this, and borrowing heavily from Counsell's argument, I ask students to view the common System-based processes of naming an objective, identifying obstacles, and verbalizing supporting actions/tactics as a *made* thing that assumes/creates an unceasing drive of action, and suggest that this is linked to humanist notions of personhood which are, in fact, historically specific.[39] In turn, I ask them to imagine a construct wherein this might not be so. Moreover, I encourage them to see this active pursuit of objective as a flawless and logical pursuit, one that does not match the fragmentary and contradictory experience of actual life.[40]

In the simplest of terms, one way of exploring some of the aforementioned ideas in the beginning acting studio involves encouraging students to view System-based approaches as historically specific styles. In a Styles class, I urge students to view the stylistic marks of the Restoration or the Elizabethan period as particular effects that can be applied and taken off at will; in the same way, I encourage students in my beginning acting course to view realism and System-inflected acting as an exacting manner of shaping action in the theatre that brings with it specific outcomes. While this is certainly a useful way to introduce some of the issues I am interested in having the students explore, I have found that two other strategies often evoke in them a more nuanced understanding in historical terms.

First, I ask students to abstract and apply a governing principle of System-atic performance to their work, and then, in turn, encourage them to consider critically the effects of that principle. For example, as is common in beginning acting courses, I often have students complete an "action run-through," wherein they focus fully on the beats and actions they have identified and around which they structured their roles. In my version of the action run-through exercise, I ask students to preface each line of dialogue by saying aloud the action that will be played (i.e., "I want to [action verb]"). While this type of exercise is beneficial in helping students comprehend the process of naming of "beats" and identifying "actions" and "through-action," for the purposes of drawing their attention to the authority of those approaches, I always follow the action run-through by asking them to reflect briefly on how such thinking structures the reading and acting of the play in logical and consecutive ways. In so doing, I endeavor to draw their attention to the humanist and historical assumptions implied in a single principle of System-based acting, and help them see that application of the principle will proffer certain interpretations of the text. For example, after completing this exercise with the students working on *Crave*, we had a lively and informative discussion of how their interpretations of that text, born from the process of naming beats and identifying objectives, imposed a throughline and logic on the script that might well have worked against its/Kane's intent. My point was not, of course, to suggest that their interpretation was wrong, but rather to illustrate that the process of interpreting scripts using System-based methods is not without consequence.[41]

Another way I have tried to encourage my students to think critically is to broaden the field of play when they are selecting material for scene study. Building on the experience I had with the students who worked on *Crave*, I have now made it my practice to allow students in the beginning acting course considerable latitude when choosing their scenes, allowing them to work on material that is not necessarily connected to the realistic tradition. Regardless of the nature of the scenes they have chosen, I ask students to apply the System-atic tools discussed and explored in the course, and meticulously to document their journeys through that process, as well as their thinking about the script and the characters they are playing. As one might imagine, there are always some methods that feed the students' work in profitable ways, no matter what the material is (and what proves useful shifts from scene to scene). For example, the students rehearsing *Crave* found ways of making logical sense of that densely layered script by exploring Stanislavsky's notion of "communion" such as it is commonly understood and experimenting with the exercises known as Circle of Attention and Object of Attention. That said, there are always other parts of the process that amount to trying to fit a square peg into a round hole. It is at these moments of disconnect that the limits, fissures, and historical nature of the approaches becomes most clear. Typically, it is in these moments of unease that questions begin to pour forth: How does one create a singular, consistent, multifarious, and coherent character when the script denies such logics? What if the fractured or archetypal character I am playing eschews the plausible? What should I do if my character is not engaged in the unbroken and unceasing pursuit of an objective? And, perhaps most importantly, if System-based acting is supposed to model the process for "good" acting, and yet the script I am working on thwarts such thinking, is the performance it proffers (and, by extension, the theatre it represents) "good"? In short, then, I believe that by shaping assignments so as to encourage such questions, I help students start to recognize the limits of these conventional approaches; begin to see how such approaches are deeply culturally and historically specific and, hence, ideologically empowered; and, in turn, critically evaluate the unacknowledged assumptions operating within those processes.

As a teacher of acting in the context of the liberal arts institution, I have developed this (still-in-process) strategy of historicization in an effort to encourage in my students a more nuanced consideration of the methods they are being taught to employ. The guiding force behind the development of this strategy is my belief that I am ethically bound to help students see the limitations and assumptions of the method they are being asked to master. Indeed, I feel strongly that to teach System-based acting approaches, without simultaneously helping students recognize and understand the attitudes and assumptions that frame those processes, is a disingenuous enterprise. Having noted this, I do want to make it clear that I am not calling for an end to the teaching of the System or System-based approaches to performance, any more than I am calling for an end to the use in class of realistic scripts. All the same, while the profession, the market, and the academy will very likely continue to demand that students have at least some command of System-atic acting, I suggest that strategies such as the one outlined in this essay will, in part, answer the call forwarded in this same volume by Lissa Tyler Renaud—the "need to give our actors an intellectual life"—by helping instill in them an astute, critical, and historically savvy understanding of the claims and assumptions that accompany such acting.

NOTES

1. Bowling Green State University, "Course Descriptions," Office of Registration and Records, http://webapps.bgsu.edu/courses/result.php. The complete course description for THFM 241: *Acting: Principles* at BGSU reads, "Basic techniques of acting applied to creating contemporary characters in realistic situations; imaginative, emotional, and sensory responsiveness."

2. Constantin Stanislavski, *An Actor Prepares*, trans. Elizabeth Reynolds Hapgood (New York: Theatre Arts, 1936); *Building a Character*, trans. Elizabeth Reynolds Hapgood (New York: Theatre Arts, 1949); *Creating a Role*, trans. Elizabeth Reynolds Hapgood (New York: Theatre Arts, 1961).

3. Sharon Marie Carnicke, *Stanislavsky in Focus* (Amsterdam: Harwood Academic Publishers, 1998), 77.

4. *The Actor's Script: Script Analysis for Performers* (Portsmouth, NH: Heinneman, 1998).

5. Michael Chekhov's *To The Actor: On the Technique of Acting* (London: Routledge, 2003); Robert Cohen's *Acting One*, Third Edition (London: Mayfield, 1998); and Melissa Bruder's *A Practical Handbook for the Actor* (New York: Vintage, 1986).

6. Colin Counsell, *Signs of Performance: An Introduction to Twentieth-Century Theatre* (New York: Routledge, 1996), 25.

7. Ibid., 46.

8. Ibid., 39.

9. Ibid., 24.

10. Louis Althusser, "Ideology and Ideological State Apparatuses," in *Essays on Ideology* (London: Verso, 1984), 39.

11. Raymond Tillis, *In Defense of Realism* (Lincoln: University of Nebraska Press, 1998), 50.

12. Robert Anchor, "Realism and Ideology: The Question of Order," *History and Theory* 22:2 (1983), 107–108.

13. Ibid., 108.

14. Richard Hornby, *The End of Acting—A Radical View* (New York: Applause, 1992), 214.

15. Ibid., 5.

16. Ibid., 51.

17. Phillip Zarrilli's cogent review of Hornby's text in *TDR*, 38:1 (Spring 1994), 177–182, informs my reading.

18. Counsell, 26.

19. Ibid., 26, 46, 50, and 77. See also Jeaneane D. Fowler's *Humanism: Beliefs and Practices* (Brighton, UK: Sussex Academic, 1999).

20. Ibid., 25.

21. Ibid., 49–50.

22. Ibid., 76–78.

23. One of the ironies here is that while many of the first generation Method Actors held liberal, radical, and even revolutionary political views, they did so while practicing a form of acting that tacitly forwarded an conservative view of the world and its functions (Counsell, 77–78). While a detailed accounting of this irony is beyond the scope of this chapter, suffice it to say Althusser's ideas on ideology once again help illuminate my thinking on this subject. More precisely, for Althusser there is no realm that exists outside of ideology, and moreover ideology has a material existence. As such, all attempts to extricate or retrofit the realist form and the concomitant System-based acting practice to include an invalidation of that governing capitalist and bourgeois ideological apparatus will ultimately fail because the form is inherently encoded with

capitalist and bourgeois presuppositions. For a convincing Althussarian critique of realism, see Catherine Belsey's *Critical Practice* (London: Methuen, 1980). Cogent counterarguments are offered in Tillis's *In Defense of Realism* and Timothy James Prenzler's "Ideology and Narrative Realism: A Critique of Post-Althusserian Anti-Realism" (PhD diss., Griffith University, Australia, 1991). Prenzler's study can be found at http://www4.gu.edu.au:8080/adt-root/public/adt-QGU20051116.101351/index.html.
24. Obviously, my thinking here takes its cue from the work of Michel Foucault, particularly *The Archeology of Knowledge* (New York: Pantheon, 1972) and *The Order of Things* (New York: Vintage, 1973).
25. Counsell, 25.
26. Once again, I reference the BGSU catalog course description for THFM 241: Acting—Principles, where "basic" skills are located as synonymous with realistic acting.
27. Thomas Postlewait, "Theatre History and Historiography: A Disciplinary Mandate," *Theatre Survey* 45:2 (2004): 186.
28. See Jameson's, *The Political Unconscious: Narrative as a Socially Symbolic Act* (Ithaca: Cornell University Press, 1982).
29. I borrow the phrase "everything has a history" from J.B.S. Haldane's study of the same name (London: Allen and Unwin, 1951).
30. For overviews of these scholars' ideas see Bennett's "Texts in History: The Determinations of Readings and Their Texts" and Cousin's "The Practice of Historical Investigation," both in *Post-Structuralism and the Question of History*, edited by Derek Attridge, Geoff Bennington, and Robert Young (New York: Cambridge University Press, 1989), as well as Greenblatt and Gallagher's *Practicing New Historicism* (Chicago: University of Chicago Press, 2000).
31. See Linda Hutcheon, *A Poetics of Postmodernism: History, Theory, Fiction* (New York: Routledge, 1988); Douglas Kellner, *Postmodernism/Jameson/Critique* (Washington, DC: Maisonneuve Press, 1989); and Kellner with Sean Homer, *Fredric Jameson: A Critical Reader* (New York: Palgrave Macmillan, 2004).
32. James Peck, "History in the Directing Curriculum: Major Directors, Theory and Practice," *Theatre Topics* 17:1 (2007): 34–35.
33. Bertolt Brecht, "The Popular and the Realistic" (1936), in Richard Drain, *Twentieth Century Theatre: A Sourcebook* (London: Routledge, 1995), 189–190.
34. Vasili Toporkov, *Stanislavski in Rehearsal* (New York: Routledge, 2004).
35. Carnicke, 38–46.
36. Carnicke, 46–51.
37. Counsell, 33, 39.
38. Ibid., 30–31.
39. Ibid., 39.
40. Ibid., 37–39.
41. Ibid., 40.

3 The Politics of Western Pedagogy in the Theatre of India

Chandradasan

To investigate the politics of actor training—and indeed, of theatre training as a whole—one has to look into the other aspects of theatre with which the training is associated. Training in itself is not the end; rather, it is the means to produce and propagate an aesthetic and an ideology. Basic questions such as why, how, and where the theatre takes place all originate in the training process itself. This becomes all the more important when the training is formalized into a system. The rigid shell of the systematic scheme of training in an institution holds the practitioner captive. The training is not just dedicated to informing the craft, but is in itself impregnated with an embryo of the end result.

Long before the emergence of the "modern theatre," India had its own theatrical tradition—now referred to as the "the theatre of roots." The performance traditions of India included the Sanskrit plays in the classical stylized form, set to a well-codified system/methodology laid out in *The Natyasastra* by Bharata,[1] as well as a wide variety of folk traditions spread out across the entire country, and which are less systematized. The Sanskrit performance tradition places the emphasis on the actor, who is complemented by the trio of *Geetha* (music), *Nritha* (dance), and *Vadya* (percussion).[2] The folk theatre is very open and flexible, and has a wide spectrum of performance styles, functions, and forms; these include ritual plays, devotional performances, the folk popular forms, dance dramas/dramatic dances, etc.[3]

In India, the idea to set up an institution for theatre training was first germinated at a seminar entitled "Education," organized by the Sangeet Natak Akademi in 1956. With the financial help of UNESCO, and with a commitment to the cause of helping students realize their aspirations in the field of theatre, the Asian Dramatic Institute at Delhi finally came into existence on January 20, 1958.

This institute was renamed the National School of Drama (NSD) in 1962,[4] and developed into the primary theatre training center in Asia. Ebrahim Alkazi, the leading figure in Indian theatre training and practice, was in charge of its affairs and pivotal in developing the school's curriculum. Alkazi himself was a very creative director of plays and a stringent academician, trained in the theatre discipline at the Royal Academy of Dramatic Arts (RADA) in London. Thus, in some ways, the theatre training in India is derived from the Western model that Alkazi acquired in the West.

Before further discussing training, it may be useful to look at the present state of Indian theatre, as well as its immediate past.

HISTORICAL OVERVIEW: WESTERN THEATRE IN INDIA

The contemporary Indian theatre is complex and diverse. India is a sweeping country wherein each of its twenty-eight states and seven union territories is culturally and linguistically distinct from every other; it is a republic made up of various cultural entities that differ inherently in their natures. But the divergence in contemporary Indian theatre does not spring from the cultural heritages and ethnic variety of this native populace. Instead, the current Indian theatre practice is the edifice of a synthetic construct.

The modern Indian theatre as a genre was initiated by, and under the influence of, the Western colonizer. The British officers and administrators in Kolkota and Mumbai were moved to perform dramas as a form of entertainment. Naturally, members of the "educated Indian elite" who were closer to the British masters supported this leisure pursuit with all possible help, and even participated in the performances. English education offered in the newly created universities added new members to this elite, in turn adding further impetus to the development of this new genre of drama. It flourished in India during the late 1700s, and was a direct result of the cultural expansion of the West.

This new form was modeled on the realistic proscenium theatre then current in London, with characters, dialogue, conflicts, emotional wrangles, humor, and a storyline unfolding in a linear narrative structure. The entire action was simple, direct, and immediate; it was also appealing in that it resembled "real life" but in a contained form. Moreover these earlier productions were in English; it was the gift and fashion of the master, and "new" to the Indian scene. All these factors contributed to the fast pace at which this Western drama established itself and began to take over the performance sphere in India.

The cultural colonizers used the great William Shakespeare and his plays to establish the supremacy of the West over native literatures, as it did in all its colonies elsewhere in the world. Knowledge of Shakespeare came to epitomize the Indian elite and its aesthetics. Indian playwrights such as Kalidasa and Bhasa became secondary and were now considered inferior in the Indian psyche in comparison to the Bard and his dramatic works. Such undercurrents were subtle, but deep.

As it turns out, this sad saga of cultural dependence on performance from the West continued with great vigor, and even intensified after India became a sovereign, independent nation in 1947. Our own drama and theatre—its performance, practice, training, and organization—were consumed by Western know-how and its concerns. As a result, India entered an era of tension in its cultural deliberations, and conflict about basic definitions. Third World politics has always fed on and bred a sort of hallucinatory, misleading jargon. Everything from the West was seen as best, noblest, and most fashionable; every sphere of living was influenced by what amounted to a form of cultural slavery. Kavalam Narayana Panikkar, one of our contemporary playwrights, depicted this situation with bitter irony: the people are shown pleading with the Sun "to rise from that far haven of the West and not anymore from the East from where it came till yesterday."[5] The West ruled all, and the theatre was no exception.

After independence came the NSD and Alkazi with the reinforcement of the Western model and the occidental sensibility. These taught us to adapt a written dramatic text into a performance space (mostly inside a building and mounted on a proscenium) with strong technical support such as scenery, lights, sounds, and other systems (now multimedia projections). Acting was refined to the level of professional excellence, with weight given to subtlety and clarity of execution. Indian theatre was suddenly on a par with its Western counterpart. Theatre technicians and artists became "professionals" who strove to make their work the best. Each of them had to nurture their craft to achieve and maintain "professional standards." Group activities, ensemble work, and social connectivity become secondary in this new aesthetic environment due to its emphasis on craft and commerce.

In contrast, theatre was traditionally a social activity in India, rather than another product to sell. Outside the major cities of Kolkota, Mumbai, and Delhi, selling tickets for a play is a rare practice in India. Occasionally people have been specially invited for a restricted show of some kind; mostly, though, people come and watch a show freely. The audience may be asked to give donations or to support the company indirectly. In the rural context, the villagers even take part in the production process. They may build the set, make properties and masks, cook and feed the actors during rehearsals, and even pool their money towards the production expenses. But entry to the performance is free. It is felt to be a privilege to see a performance.

Under Western influence, we began to look up to the Broadway system of theatrical production, execution, and dissemination, even though it was nearly impossible to implement in our country. We expected our educated urban intellectuals and the middle class to come to the theatre to buy tickets and fill the seats; we began to dream of the box office. We hung on tales of off-Broadway and off-off-Broadway, with their models for experimentation. But all of these were diametrically opposite of the performance traditions, social realities, and aesthetic sensibilities of India.

Then, by the late 1960s, we started to shift towards "Indian-ness" in performance. Discourse on the "theatre of the roots," the indigenous performance traditions and systems, was in the air. The 1970s was the era of looking on Sanskrit performance with renewed interest and declaring the proscenium defunct. The popular "minor forms" and folk traditions were viewed anew as the models for performance. They formed the basis for new performance theories and practices—in accordance with the postmodern tendencies and ideals that were current in the West. "It is indigenous Indian theatre that must radicalize the concept of theatre itself!" was the new cry, even while we expounded on making our theatre modern and universal. Independent Indian theatre wanted to celebrate itself and its freedom of theatrical expression, while simultaneously striving hard to match international theatre practices. Still today, all our reflections on our theatre travel in these two different directions.

While we were engaged in the delicate work of balancing these two impulses—to find an authentic Indian-ness in our performance and to achieve standards recognized by the West—the American funding agencies inserted themselves into the equation.

THE FUNDING MESSIAHS

State sponsorship and support for the theatre were very meager compared to the demands of the new theatre which, if nothing else, required superior technology. To fill the vacuums of patronage and sponsorship, and to give a more "focused orientation" to our theatrical activity, condescending agencies from abroad emerged to fund "specified projects scrutinized and developed under expert supervision." Many of these India-specific projects were focused on indigenous performance traditions, on the search for their potentials in modern performance, on development of theatre pedagogy, on collaborative work between artists from different cultural entities, and so forth.

The effect of these funds, this external patronage, was to entice Indian theatre activists to be less specific, less sharp; they became less bound to the particular time and place of the performance's action, and were encouraged instead to conduct research "into the universality of the temporal experiences."[6] By alienating a native practice from its roots, from the place and context that feed it, and by repositioning it in a more generalized and academic soil, one de-energizes it, takes from it its efficacy and life essence, and ultimately, devitalizes it altogether. The projects encouraged by these funds are mostly productions featuring fake physicality, characterized by a lot of wasted human effort, and with movement bordering on gymnastics and circus. Much of this activity holds only academic interest.

Classic examples of this kind of patronage were the "Theatre Laboratory Projects," so named by the Ford Foundation, one of the most active American funding agencies that operated in India. It was pointed out by many that the Foundation had a "relative (and apparent) disinterest in the urgent task of theatre dissemination."[7] Leela Gandhi of La Trobe University in

Melbourne, in her extensive study on the programs of the Ford Foundation in India, describes the perils of such funding:

> Many of the TLP (Theatre Laboratory Projects) groups worked too exclusively in a "hot-house" environment, rarely connecting the indispensable business of research and experimentation with the obligations of performance. Leaving aside the question of bringing their work to audiences in other regional centers, some groups, especially, were unable to establish regular and meaningful contact even with audiences within their immediate communities . . . And in the absence of adequate infra-structures for dissemination and performance, TLP groups (and other Ford Foundation grantees) ran the risk of museumification: valuable as ephemeral repositories of "pure" rather than "applied" theatre; academic rather than practical or "vital in their focuses."[8]

After a few years of funding and execution of the resulting projects, many theatre people left the theatre. They seemed to have lost a sense of the reason for it, of the meaning of language, of their own efforts and purpose; they had for so long been blissfully lost in a kind of isolated euphoria.[9] Truly the accidental deaths of many anarchists! And the tragedy is that they were the radical youth, who had done powerful and meaningful theatre in their pre-funded days.

It is obvious that the motivation for the American presence, with its funding, pedagogy, and research methodology, was not simply its concern for the theatre scene in India and its improvement. It was part of a larger vision—a vision to establish America and American culture as the true models of the democratic world. Like a cultural messiah, it sought to establish "the US as *the* canonical and archetypal form of Western liberal democratic culture."[10] Patronage and orientalist policies were part of this larger ploy.

The Cold War between America and Soviet Russia also set the stage for a feverish contest to establish intellectual superiority and authority on Indian soil. America found that the USSR was effectively spreading leftist ideology in India through cultural activities such as the distribution of Russian literature at low prices, and by engaging university students and the intelligentsia. To counter this, the U.S. was keen to intervene in the cultural sphere, and among the fields they focused on were theatre and theatre training. There were direct U.S. attempts to lure writers, journalists and intelligentsia to participate in this intellectual war, with its goal of spreading democratic ideology and freedom of expression.[11] These efforts were not specific to India, but operated all over the globe.[12]

Let us say, in summary, that the American system of theatre pedagogy has resulted in what we might call "rampant professionalism,"[13] uprooting the Indian theatre activist from his sense of immediacy and context, instilling Westernized sensibilities and aesthetics in place of Indian ones, making the concerns of the elite and the urban the concerns of the nation, establishing the supremacy of craft and technology over substance and essentials, making communication secondary to abstract experimentation, sidelining the specific and encouraging the universalisation of local traits, submerging rural theatre and its indigenous productivity under academics and pedagogy, replacing the collective ensemble with the creativity of the individual, and altogether making theatre an apolitical activity. The dismay, disillusionment, and dilemmas that prevail in the contemporary Indian theatre are all offshoots of this indirect cultural imperialism; the chaos that has resulted from the puzzles of politics and culture, nationalism and internationalism, tradition and modernity, all can be understood in this context. Indian theatre suffers under the pressure of changing historical, political, and cultural conditions on the global scene.

PARADOXES OF NEO-ORIENTALISM: THE WEST LOOKING TO THE EAST AND THE EAST LOOKING TO THE WEST[14]

"My contention is that Orientalism is fundamentally a political doctrine willed over the Orient because the Orient was weaker than the West, which elided the Orient's difference with its weakness ... As a cultural apparatus Orientalism is all aggression, activity, judgment, will-to-truth, and knowledge."[15]

Even the upsurge in Indian-ness took place under strong Western influence. India's own cultural foundations were reinvented to conform to the demands of Western sensibilities. This new and fertile Orientalism was actually false; it was nothing but Western sensibilities disguised as the Oriental. Many of our myths and folk tales, for example, were retold or fabricated to suit Western sensuality or sexuality according to Freudian and related perspectives. Indian theatre and its characteristics had been rather more than the "presentation," "representation," "show" or exposition of craft, as it was in modern Occidental academics and practices. The Indian narrative and performance techniques that can transcend the barriers of class and caste differences were eclipsed in a new pursuit of the Oriental. The primary rationale for, and characteristics of, Indian theatre—its spontaneity, the informal ambience, its vital and organic nature, the transparency and openness, the invitation to the spectator to join and complete the creative work, and the possibility that the experience in theatre can grow beyond the production—were all effectively marginalized. The traditional Indian theatre practices were relegated and remolded to address the "non-Indians" living in a few Indian cities, or to the academic activities in a handful of universities. The Indian theatre tradition was given over to arty, spectacular, big-budget productions full of abstract images and symbols and slippery "subtext," catering to the fake sensibilities of intellectuals uprooted from the realities of India. Theatre became just another "professional practice"—and the art of preparing a good brochure for a glossy press packet for easy marketing became a liability to true art.

The Orient was all the trend in the West, too. Artaud, Grotowski, Brecht, Brook, Schechner, and Barba all turned to the East. *So why shouldn't we do the same?* we asked ourselves. And we started looking to the host of Indian performance forms, found across the length and breadth of the nation, to use in constructing a contemporary theatre. We approached them not directly, but through the writings, perspectives, priorities, and measures of the Western masters. We studied our own performance traditions and their nuances with Western/American methodologies. It is true that a group of Indian scholars, artists, and academicians, including Kamaladevi Chathopadhyaya, Mulk Raj Anand, Suresh Awasthi, and Kapila Vatsyayana, pleaded for an Indian theatre modeled on the performance aesthetics and traditions of the land.[16] But for the most part they were scholars and theoreticians, not practitioners of theatre, and hence their influence remained at the level of inspiration or instigation. In contrast, those practicing theatre were either American, or Western-educated or inspired Indians or, at times, the visiting Gurus from the West. For example, Richard Schechner toured India many times, and during each of these trips he studied, documented, and theorized about traditional Indian forms of performances, and related them to the constructs and practices of contemporary theatre. At the same time, he took time to teach, workshop, explain, and propagate his theories and concepts of performance. He traveled with his group and showcased his productions created from the very essence of Indian tradition; he directed plays for Indian students and theatre people at NSD and all over the country. Schechner's own writings describe in detail the hardships he had to face during these visits.[17] The Indian theatre practitioners and their performance milieu posed many a predicament—including technical, physical, emotional, and ethical concerns—during his attempts to showcase the results of his contemporary extrapolations of Indian tradition!

In fact, the theatre of the West needed energy from the East to revitalize itself. As Antonin Artaud perceived,[18] Western theatre practitioners felt their theatre was feeble—insufficient to hold the contradictions and conflicts of the life and times. In search of new and vital energy, they began their journeys to the East, inventing new models that became the trends and the scheme for a new era in theatre.

Any cultural interrogation has to be based on the context in which it exists. A rite or a ritual is derived from the inner demands of the social fabric and acquires its uniqueness of form, characteristics, and structure from these. By and large, Western inquiry into the Indian forms has been from an exterior perspective. Westerners have been preoccupied with the external atmosphere created by the forms, and with the possibility of superimposing these on their own performances and experiments, neglecting both the context and inner nuances. Rather than a path of inquiry that travels from outer to inner, investigation should move from inner to outer—from essence to structure—with care taken to validate the presumptions in relation to the context. It should engender discourse specific to the overall situation and to the nature of the event, and not on broad generalizations. But the visiting masters were so fascinated by externals that, in their enthusiasm for a universal model, they ended up with more confusion than resolution.

As an example, we can look more closely into the work of Richard Schechner, who has been attracted to Oriental models of performance, and has done an immense amount of work in this area. He writes, "The possibility exists that a unified set of approaches will be developed that can handle *all* phenomena, classical and modern, textual and non-textual, dramatic, theatrical, playful, ritual."[19]

Schechner's purpose, then, is to develop an all-encompassing treatise and *theory* that can be applied everywhere, a sort of universalizing of *all* performances and occasions. In this pursuit, he travels to the so-called primitive tribes from all civilizations, to all human activity that is ritual, entertaining, dramatic, sports-like, whether collective or individual. He overlaps the parameters of one performance genre onto every other with the help of analysis charts, sketches and corollary observation.[20] Thus, Australian aboriginal performance practice is dissolved into Sri Lankan Shamanism, and then into Indian classical theatre, and then into modern "theatre" and "drama." While it may be an attractive notion to devise a theory that can comprehend the premises of all performance, in reality such a theory entails simplifications and approximations that are fatal to the universality it pursues. Culture is specific to people, time, and place, and the ethos of pragmatic rituals and performances cannot be relived organically through a modern "civilized" occidental body. Performance theory is valid in parts and for certain situations; but it cannot be all encompassing and universal. The theory and the practice diverge.

To collect disparate human activities into a single pot and fuse them together by means of postmodernist alchemy (many times these operations look magical or romantic) is an ideological, political activity. The implications of such activities of cultural dissolution, and such interdisciplinary/ intercultural notions are to be understood as part of a cultural imperialism that works hand-in-hand with political imperialism. And their connotations are deeper, and hence, more disturbing.[21]

TRAINING ORIGINAL TO INDIA: BEFORE COLONIZATION CONFUSED EVERYTHING

As students of Indian theatre know, India had a broad, rich spectrum of theatre practices and a wealth of dramatic literature that goes back to 500 BC or earlier. Dramatists such as Bhasa (475 BC–417 BC?) and Kalidasa (third century AD) were versatile geniuses who created masterpieces of the world's dramatic repertoire.[22]

The Sanskrit tradition of performance was robust enough that we had a complete manual on theatre named *The Natyasastra* (*The Science of Performance*), written somewhere around 200 BC.[23] It covers all aspects of the art of performance, arranged with scientific clarity. *The Natyasastra*, codified by Bharatha, classifies and elucidates all the dramatic elements comprehensively: the dramatic structure, dramatic language, poetry, poetic composition, language and grammar, music, aesthetics, dance, movement and choreography, costuming, makeup, properties, audiences, rituals, theatre architecture, and—not least—actor training, along with the styles, modes, and functions of acting.

The sections on actor training are detailed, even exhaustive. The human body is divided into units (*Angas* and *Upangas*), such as chest, sides, belly, hips, thighs, calves, foot, neck, head, etc. Different sets of exercises are listed for the training of each of these for performance. Each of the facial muscles is given its own movement exercises, and elaborate exercise sequence is specified for the eyes. The emotional states that an actor has to depict in performance are classified into nine *Rasas,* and their subtle variations—the nine Rasas being: *Shringara*, sensual love, beauty, devotion; *Rowdra*, anger, irritation, stress; *Hasya*, joy, mirth, humor, sarcasm; *Bhibatsya*, disgust, depression, self-pity; *Veera*, heroism, courage, pride, confidence; *Karuna*, sadness, grief, pity, compassion, sympathy; *Bhayanaka*, fear, anxiety, worry; *Adbhuta*, wonder, curiosity, mystery; *Shanta*, serenity, peace, calm, relaxation. Different training processes, of course, are offered to accomplish and master each of these.

Similarly, different movement patterns and vocalizations are suggested for depicting different range of character types. Separate chapters elaborate on the gestures of limbs and hands. Different postures, gaits, and movement patterns have their own chapters. *The Natyasastra* delineates and expands on 108 movement patterns (*Charis*) that are possible for a human body. For the voice, the text deals with meter and rhythm, as well as diction, intonation, singing, use of language, and the like; even a discussion of grammar is included.

Such a treatise had produced a very systematic and stylized theatre, and enabled the classical actor to work almost entirely with his body, voice and imagination, without any technical aid other than music and costume. Over time, the whole undertaking of doing a play became refined and specialized, even elite, demanding years of training to master. We are not sure about the structures and modes of performances at the time, but many classical forms have been generated by adapting this acting methodology. We have examples of forms derived from the performative aesthetics of *The Natyasastra* that are still being performed even now. *Kutiyattam*[24] is the oldest living form—that is, performed continuously for a thousand years or more—derived from the rich classical system of theatre discerned in *The Natyasastra*.

TRAINING AND MODERN THEATRE IN INDIA:
CULTURAL POLITICS IN DISGUISE

We now have many universities and other schools of drama that impart training in theatre. But the parent institution is the NSD in New Delhi, and other centers are adapting or imitating the training strategies of this principal school. According to the website of the NSD, "the training in the School is highly intensive and is based on a thorough, comprehensive, carefully planned syllabus which covers every aspect of theatre in which theory is related to practice."[25]

The current NSD curriculum in theatre practice and academics was designed and implemented between 1962 and 1977, during the directorship of Ebrahim Alkazi. As mentioned earlier, Alkazi modeled his theatre education program on those in the West. He is responsible for making Indian theatre studies a disciplined activity with a systematic framework. The structure he developed during his fifteen years of leadership was so complete, clear, and productive that any change has been almost impossible. In his relatively brief tenure from 1977 to 1982, B. V. Karanth tried with only preliminary success to include regional perspectives into the curriculum and aesthetics of the theatre school.

Legions of Alkazi's students and disciples spread his NSD theatre training system to every corner of the country, through the many new drama schools and drama departments of various universities, and also through frequent short-term courses and workshops. The 1970s and 1980s might be called the "era of training" in modern Indian theatre.

If we look closely into the NSD syllabus, we see almost the same ingredients we encounter in the training institutions of America or Europe. The NSD program includes training sessions in acting and other basic performance techniques, movement and physical training, voice and speech culture, improvisation, mime, text and speech analysis, scene work, rehearsals, etc. We also find special courses in Acting for Shakespearean Texts, clowning, mask work, stage combat, and *commedia dell'arte*. For students of technical theatre, courses are offered in carpentry, mask-making, model-making, theatre architecture, concepts and methods of scenic design, costume design, lighting, and stage makeup. The theory sessions have classes in the aesthetics of art and the history of world drama (meaning Greek theatre in particular) and modern Indian drama (including regional language theatre), along with Indian folk texts and adaptations of them. The courses culminate in in-house student productions; for these, advanced workshops in everything from puppetry to computer applications for lighting design are conducted by eminent visiting theatre practitioners.

This entire curriculum is what one would expect in any theatre institute in the world and is not specific to India; it is carried out with meticulous precision and professionalism, making the institute illustrious among theatre centers in all of Asia. But what does this training address? What kind of theatre does it result in? Where exactly do the graduates find work after this? Does this curriculum help them relate to the performance traditions and contemporary realities of Indian theatre in their own context, with its resources, potential audiences, funding realities? Graduates of our drama schools—not only NSD, but all theatre schools throughout India—do not have realistic ideas about the nature or conditions of our performing spaces, our resources and limitations, or even the function of theatre on the Indian continent where they are expected to work and live. They are educated for a production system and technology that are very difficult to practice in India.

The working conditions in India have no parallel with Broadway's or RADA's; the sensibilities and sensitivities of Indian audiences have nothing to do with Western perspectives on art or theatre. Theatre that survives from box office receipts is almost impossible, even in the metros of New Delhi and Mumbai, where there is a middle class that identifies itself as "elite," has Western attitudes, and may attend the theatre once in a while. The student who comes from a small Indian town or village to a drama school is transported into a dreamy Broadway-like milieu, and naturally becomes disillusioned when he later has to encounter the actualities of the performance conditions in India. Returning home, he will face a rustic working environment, with totally different operating conditions, rhythms, perspectives, and priorities, along with very weird economics with which to comply. The unusual technology he encounters there will render his theatre impossible, his philosophies and theorizations invalid. He will land with his well-crafted directorial concept in a very unsafe performance space, and even his planning and rehearsal schedules may be sabotaged by the "nonprofessional" actors and technicians with whom he has to cope.

The final result is that many theatre graduates stop doing theatre at all; instead, they end up in film, television, and other entertainment industries, or emigrate to India's big cities or to foreign countries. This is precisely why only a few products of the NSD have made their marks in the theatre of their own land.

The real deterrent has been the education, aesthetics, and priorities that demand professional execution in theatre. The criteria for this professional excellence were perfection of the actor's craft and the technical stage, to achieve a smoothed-out "aesthetically appealing" product as dictated by Western sensibilities. Thus, in this mad chase for professionalism, theatre has become more and more an urban elite activity, diverging from the rural Indian heartland in both soul and substance. And the tragedy is that the market for such a product is not to be found in India, but rather in distant Western countries.

This does not mean that theatre is impossible in Indian towns and villages. It is very much possible, and its actual potential has not yet been sufficiently tapped. The truth is that the training at NSD or most other theatre schools does not equip an artist to resonate with Indian realities outside the metropolitan areas. And he is also not politically aware enough to adjust himself to those realities. His training has made him a nonpolitical being, since the schooling he has gone through is "apolitical" in nature. And even if he claims to be political, it is an idiosyncratic "radicalism of the university kind," filled with jargon and assertions, not rooted in the rural soil. The existing political and cultural features that mark the histrionic tradition and native sensibilities of real India become secondary in a fictional, pseudopolitical discourse.

TRAINING THAT CAN BE: ALTERNATE SOURCES FOR TODAY

To reconceive an Indian theatre training that is authentic, we have to bear in mind the native theatre context. The training has to equip the student to address the functions and specific demands of doing theatre in India, with its particular social and cultural needs. To develop a model for such training, we have to look around at our own performance traditions and training methodologies. Whenever an alien system is used, it should be adapted to suit the situation in India.

The same care and introspection are needed when we look at our own tradition, including *The Natyasastra*. The structure and practice of the sophisticated and elaborate theatre as delineated in *The Natyasastra* were subject to the social and political structures of that period. Social patterns have changed, and hence the form of theatre as envisioned in *The Natyasastra* may not be valid as such now. Problems of funding, organization, function, method, and the needs of the society will dictate the new theatre.

India's own exhaustive theatre tradition, with its meticulous training for actors, can easily be adapted to suit contemporary demands. We do not need to start from scratch, from an "empty space." And models for this are plenty; we can reflect on the traditional forms such as *Kathakali* and *Kutiyattam*; how they had adapted *The Natyasastra* tradition to create quite effective training systems valid and distinct for those forms.

And the Indian tradition does not end in classical theatre and *The Natyasastra*. Once we move out of the metropolitan limits, away from the urban elite, we can encounter a rich array of varied folk forms that are still in practice; forms which are vibrant, spectacular, rooted to the earth, forms that function as true living theatre. These connect people with the immediate realities of their daily lives, history, and beliefs, and serve to socialize them. These folk forms have facets of entertainment, devotion, ritual, and theatricality, mostly merging one with the other, giving each a distinct character. They are enacted in all sorts of spaces—in the open air, temple grounds, village squares, and fields after harvest—out in the natural environment, often occupying a vast area for the performance. The division between stage and audience areas dissolves to give flexibility to the enactment. The audience members themselves are devotees/spectators, and at times also participants. Most of these forms operate with strictly local conventions and practices that have significance only in that explicit context.

The performance modes involved in these forms include narration of the story, singing, creating characters and dancing, interpreting the action aloud while narrating or while playing a character, along with carrying out the ritualistic conventions. The actor/performer may be depicting anything from everyday characters to birds and other animals, to mythical characters, divinities, gods, demons, monstrous beings, and from abstract ideas to superhuman entities. He may be pretending, commenting, interpreting, and at times transforming into the characters he is playing. At other times, he is a shamanic vehicle traveling between the mortal audience and the extrahuman.

This kind of a performance requires skills and talents that have to be trained and then nourished by the performing community and the general public. Often, performers grow up with the form, receiving continuous and indirect training, along with more formal training in specific skills, before being initiated into performing.

The methodology of acting, the practice of narration, and the features and spontaneity of these forms can provide the springboard for a contemporary theatre activist in molding his theatre and training systems. They can offer profound inspiration and study material for the modern theatre that dreams of the emergence of an energetic village theatre culture rooted in the Indian ethos and tradition, and depicting contemporary Indian realities.

Such theatre is not a purposeful construct in the sense of a "show"; rather, it is a natural entity, an organic activity that is part of life's routines. It is not separate from their lives; the aesthetics and sensibilities are blood-wedded to their immediate experiences and their day-to-day struggles. It is from long tradition, and at the same time speaks to the immediate present. This kind of a theatre is cathartic and returns the audience to a sense of the essentials of life.

Contemporary Indian theatre should be relevant to Indian aesthetics and all-around life. The training for it should empower the theatre person to shake off false notions about himself and his art. It shall instill in him the passion and energy for doing theatre; equip the actor to face the demands of performance with his body and imagination; give the actor the skills to variously enact, comment, critique, narrate, and demonstrate the character to fit the situation; it will even enable him to transcend the theatrical form. Overall, the training for this new theatre needs to redefine theatre as an ensemble activity with shared creativity; redirect vibrant, dynamic actors to the central core; and enable direct communication with audiences. Indeed, the training for the new theatre culture will commit to the audience rather than to the actor's craft and technique for its own sake. The objective of such training will be to create a flexible and sensitive actor, who is politically and culturally conscious, who can stay current with the times, and who has the potential to create a relevant theatre for India.

EPILOGUE

In conclusion, let us remember the great man who knew India to its heart, Mohandas Karamchand Gandhi. He wrote:

> I would say that if the village perishes, India will perish too. [There] will be no more India. Her own mission in the world will get lost . . . We have to concentrate on the village being self-sufficient, manufacturing mainly for its use . . . When our villages are truly developed there will be no dearth in them of men with a high degree of skill and artistic talent. There will be village poets, village artists, village architects, linguists and research workers.[26]

This is also true of the theatre. We have to reinforce the fact that Indian theatre's own traditions are strong enough to address our times effectively, with real contemporaneity and vigor.

NOTES

1. Manmohan Ghosh, *The Natyasastra of Bharata*, trans. and ed. (*Volume I*, Calcutta: Manisha Grandhalaya, 1967. *Volume II*. Calcutta: Asiatic Society, 1967).
2. Kapila Vatsyayana, *Traditional Indian Theatre; Multiple Streams* (New Delhi: National Book Trust, 1980).
3. Farley P. Richard, Darius L. Swann, and Philip B. Zarrilli give a comprehensive description of this aspect of Indian theatre in their book, *Indian Theatre: Traditions of Performance* (Delhi: Motilal Banarsidass Publishers, 1993).
4. The National School of Drama at New Delhi is the first and foremost theatre training institute in India, and considered one of the best in Asia. There is a wealth of other university centers and institutes throughout India; these offer fine theatre education at both the undergraduate and graduate levels. Nevertheless, all these institutes follow, with some variation, the pedagogic approach of NSD.
5. *Mamathil* (*The Mother-Wall*), written and directed by Kavalam Narayana Panikker, performed by Lokadharmi, Kochi, 1991. Unpublished.
6. We have to accept that "temporal experience" is bound to time and place; when attempting to expand it into universal experience, what remains is only the outer form, not the inner essence that created it. Ultimately, research and exploration into "the universality of temporal experience" turn out to be relevant as theatre exercises rather than for performance. These exercises may seem useful and imaginative, but when they displace actual theatrical production and performance, they become a menace. Such exercises were the concerns of most of those internationally funded programs.
7. Leela Gandhi, *The Ford Foundation and Its Arts and Culture Program in India: A Short History* (unpublished document in the Ford Foundation Archives, New York, 2001), 66.
8. *Ibid.*, 66

9. The effect of funding on many of the young and energetic minds emerging as the real torch bearers of the new Indian theatre in their pre-funded days— with productions sharp in content and innovative in form—was agonizingly sad. Such practitioners typically sunk into depression or alcoholism, disillusioned with theatre altogether. After the funding days ended, they were left with no theatre, in real dilemmas and traumatized on personal, social, and aesthetic levels.

10. Leela Gandhi, *The Ford Foundation and Its Arts and Culture Program in India: A Short History*, 66.

11. One such example is *Vishavriksham* (*The Poisonous Tree*), anthologized in the volume of plays and translations by C.J.Thomas, entitled *CJyude Natakangal Natakavivarthanangal* (Thrissur: Kerala Sahitya Akademi, 2004). This play was written and performed in Kerala in 1958 to further attempts to topple the first democratically elected communist government. It served to counter Thopil Bhasi's *Ningal Enne Communistakki* (*You Made Me a Communist*; Kottayam: National Book Stall, 1952), a play widely performed and believed to have been a contributing factor in the election of Kerala's communist government in 1957. The infamous *Vimochana Samaram* (*The Struggle for Liberation*), which prompted the Nehru regime to suspend the elected state government of Kerala, was led by the church (joined with other religious and feudal groups) and with support from the CIA and other American agencies.

12. John Elsom analyzes in detail "the theatre or the lack of theatre" during the Cold War era (1950 to 1990), and "the impact of the Cold War upon the cultures of various countries, taking the theatre as the point of departure, and to speculate whether the Cold War itself may not have been affected by the cultural climates in which it was conducted." John Elsom, *Cold War Theatre*, (New York: Routledge, 1992).

13. The schools of drama and the departments of theatre in various universities in India focused on training the students to be "professionals" through the perfection of their "craft." The accompanying ideology was fundamentally hedonistic and egotistical, or offered abstractions in terms of the aesthetics of art and theatre, and was primarily technology based. In this pedagogical scheme, theatre ceased to be a social act.

14. This segment of the article may be read in relation to the premise of Edward W. Said and his path-breaking book, *Orientalism* (New York: Vintage Books, 1978).

15. Ibid., 204

16. The search for an indigenous idiom of expression in Indian theatre actually started with the productions of Indian Peoples Theatre Association (IPTA) in 1943. The productions of IPTA facilitated the Indian struggle for independence. They took their performances into Indian villages and performed in open-air spaces, on makeshift platforms, in village squares, etc. The whole performance was in a flexible and informal format, and included folk songs, patriotic songs sung to folk melodies, improvised skits, music, and plays. This search for a theatrical form rooted in an Indian performance tradition was followed up in writings, seminars, and other discussions. In his essay, "Post-Independent Theatre and the Plays of Kavalam," T. M. Abraham outlines the history of the development of an indigenous Indian theatre: "In 1944, Baldoon Dingra wrote a book titled *A National Theatre for India*. In 1945, Kamaladevi Chathopadhyaya published her book, *Towards a National Theatre* . . . But the first Indian who thought about a national theatre for India after its independence is the Indo-Anglican writer, Mulk Raj Anand. He wrote in 1951, 'If the concept of Indian theatre is to be realized, it should

be speaking the Indian languages. The folk theatre is to be revived. The folk theatre remains amidst the masses because it has that internal strength. It has the energy of the tradition.' . . . The Central Sangeeth Natak Akademi (The Academy for Drama and Music) was formed in 1953. The Central Sangeeth Natak Akademi organizes a National Seminar in April 1956. The purpose of the seminar was the enquiry about the form the Indian theatre has to accept . . . " (T. M. Abraham, *Svathanthryananthara Natakavediyum Kavalathinte Rachanakalum* [*Post-Independent Theatre and the Plays of Kavalam*] in *Kavalam Natakangal*, ed. Kavil P Madhavan [Kozhikodu: Haritham Books, 2008], 700.)

17. See Richard Schechner, *Performative Circumstances from the Avant Garde to Ramlila* (Calcutta: Seagull Books, 1983).

18. Artaud maintained that the Western theatre was insufficiently strong to break out of the ordinary and touch the primordial essence of human experiences. For him, imagination was reality, aimed to hurl the spectators into the center of the action, forcing them to engage with the performance on an instinctive level and shock them out of their complacency. Such an experience of ecstasy, he said, cannot be achieved by the Western theatre, which is "lunar" in nature. He looked upon the Oriental theatre as the "solar" model, with its masks, sounds, highly ritualistic performances employing precise physicality, gestures and movements that acquire meaning beyond words, shattering the false reality and touching the deeper and most basic emotions in all their intensity.

19. Richard Schechner, *Performance Theory* (New York: Routledge, 1988).

20. Ibid., xiii. Schechner writes in the introductory chapter of this book, "Performance is an inclusive term. Theater is only one node on a continuum that reaches from the ritualizations of animals (including human) through performances in everyday life—through greetings, displays of emotion, family scenes, professional roles, and so on—through to play, sports, theater, dance, ceremonies, rites and performances of great magnitude . . . Also I put historical events side by side with speculative ideas and artistic performances. My method is similar to that of the Aborigines who credit dreams with a reality as powerful and important as events experienced while awake."

21. Read in relation to the ideas of Edward Said and his writings on Orientalism.

22. The exact dates of these master playwrights are not established; their lives have come to us as legends and myths rather than as historical facts, this being a typical Indian way to remember history.

23. The exact dates of Bhasa and *The Natyasastra* are not clearly established. Different scholars propose dates ranging from 500 AD to 500 BC. But a close reading of the Bhasa plays suggest that his period is much before the period of *The Natyasastra*, since he had not followed the rules laid out by *The Natyasastra*. Thus, the period of Bhasa can be placed somewhere around 400 BC and *The Natyasastra* around 200 BC.

24. K.G. Paulose gives a detailed and authentic account of the form Kutiyattam, its origin development and its characteristics in his book *Kutiyattam Theatre, the Earliest Living Tradition* (Kottayam: DC Books, 2006).

25. See http://www.nsd.gov.in/nsd_schoolacademics.htm.

26. M.K.Gandhi, *Village Industries*, (Ahmedabad: Navjivan Publishing House, 1960), 7.

4 Degrees of Choice

Leigh Woods

So Many Acting B.A.'s, So Few Paying Gigs
Headline of Bruce Weber's article in the *New York Times*,
December 7, 2005

From time to time, my teaching colleagues and I bemoan the lives our students stand to lead by pursuing careers in acting. In the amiable way of cohorts, we don't visit the matter often, nor do we approach it in the stark way employed by Bruce Weber and others writing in the same vein.

I was all the more struck, then, when I saw my university listed among the ones Weber names that offer guidance on "the business within the business" of professional acting.[1] Yes, we *do* offer guidance, but seldom do we broach the causes of imbalance between supply and demand for professional actors. Meanwhile, performance degrees have multiplied so much that, according to Weber, "You can get a Bachelor of Arts or a Bachelor of Fine Arts in performance . . . at more than 200 American colleges and universities."[2] Recent downturns in the economy have not seemed very much to diminish the appeal of undergraduate degrees in acting, or of other degrees in which acting stands as a major component.

This means that even students who are able to establish themselves as professional actors are almost certain to face chronic unemployment and marginal livings.[3] One month after Weber's piece appeared, Charles Isherwood, in another *Times* article, "Stage Acting: It's Nice Work If You Can Afford It," observed that professional actors are already helping to subsidize the American theatre. They also play no small part in the teaching of acting across America. Meanwhile, as Isherwood reports, they work in the theatre for less money under ever less favorable conditions.[4] Little has happened over the last years, especially recently, to reverse the trend Isherwood spotted.

AS THINGS ARE

The present state of the acting profession has weighed differently on my department since, first, we added BFA students in the early 1990s, and second, when in 2006 we moved into a building that holds a theatre in the name of our distinguished alumnus, Arthur Miller.

Miller, as much as any American playwright of the twentieth century, treated matters of ethics and justice. He considered social conscience to be the measure of a theatrical establishment worthy of its name. He esteemed actors highly, and actresses, too, of course. He was willing to challenge established practice in the theatre as elsewhere. And so might we, too, be willing to challenge, or at least to question, the way things are.

DILEMMAS

Some soul-searching seems in order at a time when colleges and universities make fewer distinctions than they once did between education, in its purest light, and commerce. Now, facing a balky economy and worsening fiscal conditions, theatre departments will tend to stick with the status quo in the ways we groom and multiply our actors-in-training.

We train student majors knowing that most of them will never be able to earn a living from acting. The students accept our training on these terms in ways that are easy to construe as informed consent. When we were students, we offered something of the same sort of consent ourselves, with results that affected the course of our own lives and of others' lives, too.

THE RISING NUMBERS

The sheer demand for actor training, as with instruction on musical instruments or in singing, fosters complacency among us teachers. Why should we change what we're doing so long as students flock steadily to study with us—more of them, at times, than we have space for in our classes, or in the majors that require those classes?

The apparently bottomless demand for actor training has, in Bruce Weber's word, helped "democratize" a profession long colonized in line with its peculiar demands.[5] In step with the times, the spread of actor training has followed an explosion of electronic media that has exposed dramatic and comic performances to more viewers across ever wider spaces. This robust interest has to be a good thing for acting teachers, and for the practice of acting in the long run, though not so much for professional actors in the short haul.

The fact that acting is taught, by and large, using methods friendly to, if not derivative of, the stage, lets us celebrate, and our students sample, the power of live performance. Our allegiance to the living theatre is expressed in the ways we organize our classes and in the priorities we assign there.

Many of us teachers function, in this sense, as loyalists to the stage as much as we do to the profession of acting, insofar as a distinction between the two can be made. Our places in the academy help us imagine and, in some degree, inhabit an ideal realm, a safe space in which our students can learn and grow.

But even our wisest counsel and most highly principled idealism cannot carry acting students far beyond the places where they earn their degrees. Not only do they join an overpopulated workplace, but in the professional theatre, as indeed with film and television owing to the effects of globalizing, more actors are working under unusual conditions or trying to meet demands their training has not prepared them for.

The practice of acting continues to mutate in ways that make it more widely admired and richly experienced. But this very fact makes it harder to train actors to fit every need. So it is that, even with more actors joining the profession, there are not many of them to serve for all uses, places, and seasons.

Many actors, of course, develop a professional adaptability, often with some assistance from their training. And adaptability is something that can serve actors in different workplaces from the ones we teachers and administrators, and our students, tend most to idealize.

OTHER DEGREES, FOR BETTER AND WORSE

While I pursued an MFA in acting in the early 1970s, I watched as competitive environments tightened with the influx of the first corps of actors who had earned graduate degrees in this new specialty. Over time, the MFA became the degree of choice for actors like me, who may have had a career in acting in mind but also wanted the option to teach in higher or in secondary education without having to earn a doctorate.

The MFA is appealing as a self-appointed terminal degree, and it has been one of the academy's more effective responses to the difficulty in acting for a living. Academic appointments have also served as a subsidy, or enhancement, for working members of the acting profession who hold MFAs. But the graduate degree has also proliferated across the academy in ways that have anticipated the boom that undergraduate degrees in acting have enjoyed more recently.

The sheer number of places where the MFA has taken hold has wrenched the dozens of programs offering the degree into tiers that confer preeminence on schools that have offered the MFA the longest or in closest proximity to the largest urban centers. Some elite MFA programs exercise the same selective recruitment and preferential casting that apply in the professional theatre and more harshly, if anything, in films and television. This is changing, yes, but slowly.

The advent of MFAs in acting has also perpetuated the *guru* model for acting teachers in a sort of sacred ring that connects one blessed site to another. In the spirit of competition, the MFAs have spawned a cohort of teachers who separate themselves into something like the star systems in force among professional schools of theatre. The *guru* mentality, in turn, tends to mystify training and render it more cloistered and opaque.

Taken collectively, MFA acting programs have also contributed to some belief, among sterner academics, that persons who hold the degree, by having come to dominate the professoriate in many departments, degrade the academic enterprise by valorizing the preprofessional mission while teaching theatre studies classes beyond their expertise.[6]

In fairness, the growing surplus of trained and university-educated actors has also been a boon for the academy, and nothing less for a professional theatre reeling from funding cuts and withered by competition from television and motion pictures. But the same chronic oversupply of actors scarcely favors the prospects of present undergraduates, nor of those who have earned or will earn an MFA in acting.[7]

Nor has the oversupply of holders of any degree in acting led, as often as might have been hoped for, to the founding of new companies. Meanwhile, we continue to train actors largely for the known opportunity in what marks a profoundly conservative, and in some ways wishful, reading of circumstances. And many of the issues that cropped up with the success of MFA degrees are now rearing their heads with the recent spate of undergraduate degrees in acting.

To be sure, the MFA has added quality and substance to the practice and instruction of acting across the land, and in foreign countries, and by no means in the academy only. The MFA has given higher priority, not to mention currency, to pedagogy and to theorizing about acting, while actors-in-training have gained by studying with artful scholars, as well as with artists themselves. The MFA has loosened older networks of apprenticeship, conservatory training, and plain old cronyism that required fewer teachers to serve a more cohesive, clannish, and inward-looking profession.[8]

BFA and BA degrees in acting, however, even as they have helped support a number of us who hold MFAs, have not proven so flexible or so friendly to acting for its own sake. The economic motives that have driven the creation of undergraduate degrees have scarcely eased, nor do they show signs of easing as I write this.

INSTITUTIONAL CONTEXTS

Broader trends in society and in higher education have also contributed to multiplying degrees in acting. Intermittently since the late 1940s, with the passage of the GI Bill, and progressively since the 1960s, colleges and universities have shed their former obligations *in loco parentis*. College students, the consensus runs, deserve some discretion in choosing what to study.

And we wish our students well, of course, wherever their lives and training take them. As far as that goes, the study of acting is no more intrinsically limiting or impractical than many another undergraduate major.

Indeed, the case can be made that young actors have learned to work together under pressure, and that this may prove to be of value to them and others during their working lives, wherever those unfold. "Let experience be the guide," we say gently to ourselves and, sometimes, to them.

Part of college students' challenge in weighing their options as undergraduates owes to the lack of worldliness that most of them bring to their training. Their idealized notions of the lives actors lead find reinforcement in the leisure that college life allows.[9] Romantic theories about the sanctity of art, imbued with antibourgeois tendencies that growing up middle-class seems to inspire, leave many students spoiling to fly in the face of what they have been warned, more than once and in utter honesty, are the odds against their ever making a living as actors. They hear it, but it does not faze them, or at least not too much during their first couple of years of study.

THEN AND NOW

If we teachers are over forty or thereabouts, our undergraduate educations had us widening our options, in most cases. The problem now lies in the fact that so many undergraduate actors seem to be narrowing their options in proportion with the formal demands of whichever degree in acting they earn.

Laying on requirements is part and parcel of what have come to be called, loosely, "preprofessional degrees." BA degrees in theatre, to be able to claim something like competitive parity with the BFAs, ramp up the portion that acting takes up among their own formal requirements, if not quite in the same vaulting proportion. These trends have shaped degrees anchored more narrowly in performance than ours were from being framed under more expansive definitions of the liberal arts.

Under our tutelage, student–actors undertake creative lives that, when things go well, gain depth and appeal as the students' training and maturity advance. Students will commit more of their time to actor training, and to productions, even when these come at the expense of their other studies. They will spend extra hours in rehearsals instead of in the lab or the library. Or, they will compromise the rigor of their college experience, and will even finesse the meeting times of the courses they choose, to leave their evenings free for training, rehearsing, and performing. They will burn the midnight oil, and more of it, perhaps, than students do in other disciplines for lacking such regular and agreeable after-hours pursuits.

And whether it is nocturnally or otherwise, our students will apply themselves to productions with great enthusiasm. We are proud of them for it. We and others literally applaud them for it. It's a heady experience for them. It disposes them to keep acting, come what may. In this sense, they are ripe for whatever measures we might devise to help them keep acting.

ASSESSMENT AND ACCESS

In acting classes, judging from the few in-house studies I've seen, we grade our students pretty generously, as a rule. High grades inspire in them the feeling that they have been well chosen and are progressing nicely, as often they are. It nourishes in them the premise that we, the veterans, think they have a shot at making it. Under these conditions, it is easy for them to feel flattered. The same conditions confirm in us the feeling that we are training them well, as often we do. In this sense, awarding high grades aggrandizes us, too.

Add to this the fact that faculty directors will often recast students they consider more talented. While this can be tempting indeed, the practice mimics the Darwinian-like dance of acting for hire. Repeatedly being cast can also give students a clearer picture of where they stand than their classes might do. In this way, casting offers a more accurate preview of students' lives as professional actors. But when it does this, it sidesteps learning among the student cohort, taken as a whole.[10]

Our students' desire to take the stage (and just as intensely these days, to stand in front of cameras) shows us succeeding on a fundamental level. We offer discreet encouragement to students we see as most likely to catch on as professionals, or who seem to be the most driven to do it. Their interest in acting for pay grows stronger as they see themselves cast regularly and flourishing. The effects are electrifying and addictive, as we ourselves will remember. The cast parties can be sweet.

The theatre at any level is a pricey and labor-intensive endeavor, and artists need to justify themselves more during harder times. Our departments can usually cite demand for our offerings, and for actor training in particular. We take pride not only in the hearty turnout for our classes, but in the happy evaluations we get from students unused to the pure joy of acting and, in larger institutions, of learning in close quarters under the direct observation of faculty, many of whom are tenured.

We acting teachers are, by and large (if I do say so myself), a versatile and humane lot. Many of us have taught at more than one institution, and not only in the academy. Most of us have gotten our feet wet, at least, as professional actors, and at least a few of us have found careers that have taken us well beyond that.

Even with that, we may feel at a disadvantage when we find ourselves set down among a community of scholars who publish. Our sense of our exceptionality, the isolation it encourages, and the hermetic conditions of making theatre can breed a passion in us that inspires loyalty in our students. When we are measured purely by our inspiring them, we stand up pretty well, I'd say, as judged across the academy.

How can we infuse our students with the means and the vision to carry on as actors beyond their time with us? Ways of facing this question may vary from one institution to another.

CLOSER TO HOME

At the University of Michigan, in the early 1990s, we instituted a BFA in acting. My colleagues and I were worried by quotas, which were assigned over our heads then and have been ever since, for the number of acting students we were to admit. The targets challenged not only our faculty's notion of the demand for professional actors, but our estimate of our energy and resources.

It would have been hard, under conditions of financial stringency that applied then, to say "No." So we said "Yes," however grudgingly. We've continued to say "Yes" in the face of a dispiriting economy in our state, which is unlikely to improve any time soon. Meanwhile, we have also drawn a sense of mission from making training for our student–actors as challenging and serviceable as it can be. We are continually gratified by the enthusiasm our students bring to their studies. The work brings satisfaction all around.

Quickly, in our case, and after that through consolidation of a series of academic appointments, the BFA became our leading degree in the number of students it enrolled and the revenues it accrued. The students we have recruited have grown in raw talent and, in virtually direct proportion, in the hope they cherish of working as professionals.

In light of the tuition generated, any incentive for jurying BFA actors out of our program vanished. We have continued to turn out more actors, not fewer. The cash cow we helped bring to life keeps dragging its standard, udder-like, behind it.

While I was teaching classes in acting and in theatre studies,[11] I noticed a differential response that seemed to grow more marked at first—although it has abated somewhat since. The acting students, and the majors especially, showed real passion and dedication in their practical training. But many of the same students, in more conventional academic courses, did not apply themselves very well. Some of them regarded cognate studies of drama, history, and critical theory as a distraction from what they liked to think of as their true calling.

Perhaps my teaching was insufficient. It was certainly ill-adapted to a shift that saw vocational motives gain force across the academy, at some cost to the liberal arts.[12] I saw students who felt they had made a worthy choice by following their bliss. It seemed to me that many of them craved validation before they had learned what lay in the way of acting at its best.

I watched as students pined or grew disaffected when their dreams for the future, fed by sterling grades in performance classes, were not met with being cast for our most prestigious, heavily budgeted faculty- or guest-directed shows. A few parents of acting majors would lodge the odd complaint when their progeny failed to win a role in one of the showcase productions. What were they paying for, they wondered—and their offspring wondered as well—when the students couldn't find their ways onto our main stages? For what it's worth, anecdotal accounts tell me that our experience at the University of Michigan is not altogether exceptional.

WORKING THE MISSION

How can we encourage undergrads to make the most and best of their education and training? How can we help them find flexible, fulfilling, and ongoing work as actors? How can we instill in them something that will carry them on beyond the satisfaction they may take from being knowledgeable viewers?

One sure way of expanding students' horizons, and our own, lies in weaving the art of producing more deeply into the curriculum. The earlier that fledgling actors take on basic tasks of mounting a production—not just in the tasks of stagecraft but in conceiving, promoting, and publicizing collective ventures—the readier they'll be to meet opportunity, or to work up opportunities from scratch. We teach students to collaborate as it is, and collaboration is a precious commodity, especially in workplaces that undergo rapid and drastic changes, as can be seen in the ones around us now.

Luckily, in colleges and universities, we don't have far to look to offer students a wider experience. Students might, with a little practice and supervision—and some of that, perhaps, for credit—learn to recognize opportunities to showcase their skills, and not necessarily those opportunities that are limited to our own or to any other single institution.

Young actors might easily begin to teach, under supervision, on the way to doing it on their own. This would let them offer bits of their craft to students less advanced than themselves, or to primary, middle, or high schoolers, to children in after-school programs, or to senior citizens, or to working adults in evening classes.[13] Theatre departments that facilitate this kind of outreach by single students, or by groups of them, earn goodwill from the communities they serve and build audiences accordingly. There are lots of people who would like to study acting, and we could try—and our students could—to find pockets of interest, and to meet them.

Acting can be reconceived as a kind of common language spoken, potentially, by many. This ideal would enlarge on Bruce Weber's notion of democratizing the acting profession, and it would exploit the popular interest in acting—and for reasons that transcend the allure of stardom. Initiatives that stir instruction will feed talent into the teaching and casting pools. Broader instruction informs a wider appreciation of what actors do, rather than of who they are; and that would be no small thing. Over time, widening instruction in acting could inform notions of who actors are, what they have to offer, and what they should make of themselves.

STARTING SMALL

Here follow ten measures (feel free to add your own to the list) toward making actor training more flexible and accountable, and having broader application. Given the glacial pace at which most colleges and universities move, you may want to choose first the one or two projects that fall beneath or beyond the notice of curricular committees, or that take advantage of local conditions within or beyond the institution you serve.

1) In recent years, one of my colleagues has sponsored a touring group that shows bits from Shakespeare's plays, woven into a quick lesson about the playwright and his work. This company, in support of a local Shakespeare festival and with a troupe that has changed as students graduate, has plied a local circuit of primary and secondary schools that feed our department and university.

It is easy to imagine extending such a venture to disadvantaged groups or to others who are least mobile. Theatre departments could win institutional credit for helping diversify the student body while showing themselves, their students, and their home institutions, to advantage.

2) It would be convenient, and wise, for theatre departments to volunteer their and their students' services toward assisting, polishing, coordinating and, in some cases, reworking commencement ceremonies and other more and less formal institutional and community events.[14] This would offer another way for students to apply themselves where they would be welcomed, and make useful contributions and, potentially, do so across lines of age, class, ethnicity, and gender.

We could, by leading such initiatives, help students to identify, and to help streamline, public events distinct from productions staged in theatres. This outreach would get our students thinking about how best to make nontheatrical dramatic occasions as lean, portable, and festive as possible, and as broadly based and fully participatory, as well. Students can apply something of what they learn to the staging of productions they undertake with us, and later, and to events at entirely other kinds of sites after graduating.

3) To tap the seemingly boundless interest in acting that prevails at colleges and universities, theatre departments can draw greater numbers of future doctors, lawyers, businesspersons, and teachers by offering more classes in the rudiments. Catering to preprofessional groups stands to build interest across the campus and into the wider world. This initiative can sometimes fall into step with the missions of schools of education.

At larger universities, the professional schools of law, medicine, business, and education harbor groups of faculty and students who see their work as apposite to, as variations on, or as permutations of, acting. Wherever actors-in-training might help teach interested parties, or show topical pieces to learned, professional, or advocacy groups, they could be helped to do it and credited for it in one way or another.

4) As I mentioned earlier, the more experience undergraduates gain as teachers, the easier it will be for them to continue acting beyond graduation, and maintain feelings of worth and self-esteem if they should never gain fame or fortune. Furthermore, the teaching of acting, as anyone who has taught it knows, tends to perpetuate the teacher's desire and opportunities to act. It may do the same for students who begin to teach with us.

I have had good luck with letting graduate students assist me in undergraduate acting classes as apprenticeships toward teaching classes on their own, with my oversight. It would be easy to try this approach with undergraduates ranked by training, maturity, and interest. Courses, or more feasibly, workshops in the teaching of acting, will give students skills to help them effectively engage beginners. Along these lines, one colleague of mine has trained students in stage combat in ways the students have used to serve amateur and professional companies, and as a way of supporting themselves. They have to begin somewhere. Where better than in our own departments?

The more we teach undergraduate acting classes that have students appraising each other's work, and their own, the more the training can be demystified when we, the teachers, are secure enough to allow it. The more we encourage students to distill their own standards of quality and aspiration, the better informed and more generous we leave them in how they transmit and apply their acting.

5) Acting techniques can easily be adapted to the instruction of subjects other than theatre. Where schools of education hold classes or workshops on teaching, let our theatre departments offer our expertise, and when appropriate, our students, to help facilitate dynamic exchanges in the classroom. This is an important civic function, feeding democracy by helping make a meaningful education available to one and all.

In any case, acting students make eager, knowledgeable, and savvy viewers. In that capacity, they can help those studying to become teachers find ways to make themselves as compelling as they can be in the classroom, to the benefit of students for years to come.

6) Collaborations can be struck across academic departments to perform classroom presentations that would speak to interdisciplinary or multidisciplinary interests.[15] This could be done at scholarly conferences, or at other sites within or beyond the academy. Collaborations might also be formed between student–actors and school-, community-, recreation-, profession-, and worship-based groups. The rubric "theatre games" has been used, perhaps because it sounds less artsy and bohemian than "acting" does, at least to some.

In the British Isles and in Europe, "applied drama" and "applied theatre" have, over a generation and more, introduced playmaking techniques to social and political organizing and to community building.[16] I have found Augusto Boal's methods difficult to apply to local organizing; they require skills at improvising and facilitating that would challenge many a seasoned actor or director. Others who try Boal's practices on behalf of those he calls "the oppressed" may be able to grasp what I have not. I have seen groups of faculty and students at my university and at others nearby, who cater to incarcerated populations, for instance, by helping to realize prisoner-generated productions and events.[17]

7) In the way of local action, my university has sponsored a performance group, funded outside my department but drawing occasionally on present and former acting students. The group gives rough-and-ready performances for dormitory residents and freshman orientees, improvising partly around subjects such as drug and alcohol abuse, date rape, sexism, and racism. The same group has not, so far as I know, extended their work beyond the academy, though it is easy to imagine their doing so. Rarely are there too few issues of importance to be raised and discussed in public forums.

8) We can help actors devise ways to make productions simpler, cheaper, and more conveyable. Faculty designers will sometimes balk at this. But just as productions at professional theatres price themselves out by exceeding by too much the cost of moviegoing, so can productions in the academy become bloated, especially in light of tightening instructional budgets.

Lavish productions tend also to bring on imitations of themselves from students. Their aesthetic is shaped by the kind of well-appointed, handsomely funded, effectively subsidized stagings that strive to recapitulate ones seen at the upper end of the professional theatre. It's nice to be able to execute a showpiece, but it needn't eclipse other priorities. Performances that are less costly, more mobile, and restrained in their use of technology will recommend themselves more during harder times, or under the modest circumstances in which artists so often live.

Theatre can flourish using minimal means, as it has done often over its long history. It can resist the pressure to attract ever larger crowds to support ever greater visual effects. One Broadway is enough, thank you very much. Lean can be good.

Performances that have been stripped in ways advocated by Jerzy Grotowski in his vision of "poor theatre"[18] might help reduce the academic acting teachers', and the theatre's, chronic anxiety about economic conditions that are difficult to predict, much less alter. A less heavily encumbered stage, at whatever level, will prompt ingenuity, not least when it comes as a means of promoting cultural change. A more spare visual style will encourage student designers to study the eloquence of minimalism. It may also spawn a more self-sufficient, muscular acting adapted to lighter investiture. Think Shakespeare.

9) In addition to tracking alumni who have established themselves as, or are on their way to becoming, working actors, let theatre departments keep in touch with *all* alumni/ae, especially in the years just after graduation.

By soliciting the immediate postgraduate experiences of former students, we can credit, commend, and recommend a wider range of activity at relatively low cost. We can ease some of the stigma students are apt to feel when they don't choose professional acting, or fail to find themselves in it.

For every agent or casting director we invite to speak to or audition undergraduates, let us bring in someone who works at a nonprofit theatre, or has started her own company, or who applied his training to some use other than, or in addition to, professional acting as we know it.

10) Our sponsoring online directories or interactive alumni chat rooms can help students, past and present, network in ways that may spark collaborations of the sort they will have been trained to imagine, model, and take on.

CONCLUSION

So long as we acting teachers allow our students to believe that our definition of their success hinges on their landing a place at a regional theatre, or on Broadway, or in a commercial film or sitcom, we do a disservice, however unwittingly, to the vast majority who will never do such things. The same students might, in the greater scheme of things, apply themselves to some ideal of the greater good that includes, but exceeds, the arts. Call me a dreamer, but I think it's better than waiting for the phone to ring.

We acting teachers uphold a tradition that extends back at least as far as the Sanskrit masters and the ancient Greeks. Over millennia now, instructors in our field have labored under greater pressures than we face from our institutions of privilege in what is even now a position of comfort for most of us in higher education across North America.

To honor our predecessors, especially the ones who took their motives from civic life, let us help our students broaden their talents and their dreams. Let them contribute to events that coexist with, as well as serve or feed, the professional theatre and commercial television and films. Let them refine a sense of community that reflects on and honors the times in which they live. We can, if we will, nurture abilities in our student that will spring from their first true calling, but not serve art only, or the academy.

NOTES

1. Bruce Weber, "So Many Acting B.A.'s, So Few Paying Gigs," *New York Times,* December 7, 2005, B8.
2. Weber, "So Many Acting B.A.s," B1, 8.
3. I heard the film actor Jeff Daniels speak to a group of University of Michigan students in the late 1980s about how hard it was for him to deal with the quixotic and often arbitrary workings of professional acting, even at a time when he was establishing himself as one of the film industry's most employable thirtysomethings. He talked candidly about how quickly he and other actors could give way to depression when they found themselves out of work. See also my interview with Daniels in *Playing to the Camera: Actors Discuss Their Craft,* eds. Cardullo, Woods, et al. (New Haven: Yale University Press, 1998), 247–262.

4. Charles Isherwood, "Stage Acting: It's Nice Work If You Can Afford It," *New York Times*, January 15, 2006, 7 (Arts and Entertainment).
5. Weber, "So Many Acting B.A.'s," B8.
6. Joseph Roach, "Reconstructing Theatre/History," *Theatre Topics* 9:1 (1999), 6–7.
7. Ian Watson includes a brief history of MFA degrees in acting, and of BFAs, and catalogs some of the advantages and drawbacks of these degrees, in his "Actor Training in the United States: Past, Present, and Future," in *Performer Training: Developments Across Cultures*, ed. Watson (London: Harwood Academic Publishers, 2001), 76–78.
8. As more MFA actors have earned the degree, the standard for hiring them at institutions of higher learning has often risen to require greater amounts of professional experience or teaching, and sometimes publications.
9. I find myself hoping that, someday, students may arrive in my classes more worldly than I was at the *end* of my college years. I had visited New York by then, but it was not until I moved there, was studying for an MFA, and saw the lives actors lived, that the sternness of the challenge became clear to me. I'm not suggesting that living in New York, Chicago, or Los Angeles is the only way to test the business of professional acting. But as teachers—especially those of us who teach at a distance from the largest, most entertainment-saturated cities—we ought to address the naiveté that many students bring to their study with us. Their interests will always be served by our giving them as much information as we can about the lives professional actors live, and as much stimulus as we can toward having students diversify their skills in light of what promises to remain a challenging labor market in many fields, including acting.
10. Faculty directors sometimes incline toward the same competitiveness that they themselves have felt in the professional theatre, and this is sometimes independent of their success there, or lack of it. Some faculty directors favor more conventionally and conspicuously talented students for the sake of winning raises, promotions, or tenure for themselves, or in a more altruistic way, to feature their students and their departments to advantage. These motives, even the more selfless ones, stand at odds with the ideal of giving every acting student equal opportunity based on equal application and, as is often the case, equal grades, more or less. It is ironic that one of the downsides of our success in drawing acting students should have created the same disparity, in departmental productions, between opportunity and the number of aspirants for being cast, as exists among professional actors.
11. Through the 1990s and into the 2000s, I was teaching doctoral students, some of whom were actors, but few if any of whom were still aiming for a career in acting. I was also teaching undergraduates, including BAs in theatre and in other departments, and BFAs in performance, directing, and design and production.
12. Increases of tuition, even at public institutions like mine, have forced students and parents into considering a college education as more of an investment. If anything, and counterintuitively, this has seemed to put a higher premium on students being cast in college and university productions, even in the face of general assumptions that those students may never be able to support themselves as actors. Even the frankest acknowledgement of this likelihood can raise expectations of being cast in departmental productions, and with that rises the level of resentment, and the sense of betrayal, that comes when the student doesn't get cast.
13. My first teaching of acting did not come until I had finished the MFA in acting (Columbia, 1972). I was lucky, then, to work with a gang of sixth-grade

girls at the Spence School on New York's East 91ˢᵗ Street, who were more game than any group I could have imagined for playing a broad spectrum of roles—men or women, boys or girls, animals, insects, spirits, foodstuffs: the works. Their enthusiasm and imagination made me want to teach acting longer, and do it better. Many thanks, more than thirty years later, to Dustin Heuston, the headmaster who hired me, and to the faculty and staff at Spence who were patient with me in my long-haired phase.

14. Websites for Community Arts Network (www.communityarts.net) and for Imagining America (www.imaginingamerica.org) hold information about a host of activities that apply the performing arts to community organizing and political persuasion. Books that catalog and reflect on community-based performances in the U.S. include Robert H. Leonard and Ann Kilkelly's *Performing Communities: Grassroots Ensemble Theatre Deeply Rooted in Eight U.S. Communities*, ed. Linda Frye Burnham (Oakland, CA: New Village Press, 2006); Jan Cohen-Cruz's *Local Acts: Community-Based Performance in the United States* (New Brunswick, NJ: Rutgers University Press, 2005); Sonja Kuftinec's *Staging America: Cornerstone and Community-Based Theatre in the Americas* (Carbondale, IL: Southern Illinois University Press, 2003); and Will Weigler's *Strategies for Playbuilding: Helping Groups Translate Issues into Theatre* (Portsmouth, NH: Heinemann, 2001).

15. See Gavin Bolton, *Acting in Classroom Drama* (Stoke-on-Trent: Trentham Books, 1998); Bolton's "Drama in Education and T[heater]I[n]E[ducation]: A Comparison," in T. Jackson, ed., *Learning through Theatre* (London: Routledge, 1993), 39–50; and Bolton and Dorothy Heathcote's *So You Want To Use Role Play! A New Approach* (Stoke-on-Trent: Trentham Books, 1999).

16. For discussions of theatre and drama applied to categories such as "The Practice of Citizenship," "Community Narratives," "Social Intervention," and "Human Rights," see Helen Nicholson, *Applied Drama: The Gift of Theatre* (New York: Palgrave Macmillan, 2005).

17. See the following books by Augusto Boal: *The Aesthetics of the Oppressed*, trans. Adrian Jackson (London: Routledge, 2006); *Legislative Theatre*, trans. Adrian Jackson (New York: Routledge, 1998); and best-known, *Theatre of the Oppressed*, trans. Charles A. and Maria-Odilia Leal McBride (New York: Urizon Books, 1979). See also note 14 for a short list of sources that addresses community-based performances in the U.S.

18. See Jerzy Grotowski, *Towards a Poor Theatre* (New York: Simon and Schuster, 1968).

5   Training Artists or Consumers?
Commentary on American Actor Training[1]

Lissa Tyler Renaud

Now, [it] goes to one of my core beliefs, and I'm happy to say I think this is a belief shared by the U.S. Government, that culture resides within people, within their community, the individual artist and the individual artist community.

Dana Gioia, Chairman of the National Endowment for the Arts
Speaking at the UNESCO Cultural Diversity Convention[2]

I think . . . it's high time there was a formal program established that invited the best theatres we have in our country to its artistic capitol. I would imagine you'll have a thrilled and positive reception.

Harold Prince, Director, Producer, New York, NY
On the website for the new American National Theatre in
New York[3]

American actor training seeks to thrive in the tension between the two opposing impulses in arts policy expressed in the chapter's opening quotations—one celebrating artistic "difference" across the country, and one seeking to bring the disparate arts communities under the single banner of "America"; that is, one a de-centralizing impulse, the other, centralizing. In the U.S., actor training tries on the one hand to respond to market needs to serve the most students (de-centralizing, spreading out, dividing), and on the other hand to gather the students together under the umbrellas of a few prominent methods or teachers' work (centralizing, unifying, consolidating).[4] As American actor training negotiates these extremes, there are repercussions both for acting students and for the American theatre.

My own perspective on this conversation has developed from teaching in university programs and running a professional theatre studio in the San Francisco Bay Area continuously over a thirty-year period. In the U.S., academic acting programs seem for the most part to be unaware that the country has a great many active private studios, or to dismiss them as commercial or vanity affairs. For their part, the private studios tend to think little of university programs, assuming them to be conservative and sheltered from professional realities. At best, academic actor training and studio training view each other with suspicion; their relationship is not talked about, and they are typically marketed separately, as if they were separate fields. But this belies the fact that they dovetail well in the skills they can offer, and that people wanting to train as actors often move between studio and academic training. For example, my students may have been on their way from the university to studio training, or supplementing one with the other, or finishing a studio program and going on to an M.F.A. program. My own experience has been that any of these various ways of training is a path to professional acting work in America.

As a result, writing on the subject of "American actor training" in its broadest sense, I cannot say definitively what it is. If you put ten U.S. theatre professionals in separate rooms and ask each of us what American actor training is, you will surely get more than ten different answers to choose from. In fact, we won't even agree on the meanings of these individual words: American. Actor. Training.

Using these three words as a framework, we can do three things: (1) ask whether one national theatre agenda such as other countries have is either possible or necessary in America, (2) look at trends in the theatre profession buffeted by commercial demands, and (3) take stock of training that needs to adapt—not only to technology but also to larger cultural changes. An evaluation of existing trends may also allow us to suggest some trends to bring about.

* * *

AMERICAN

Is an "American" Actor Training Possible or Necessary?

When we use the word "American" in the context of the theatre, what do we mean? Are we talking about theatre for the descendants of the first European settlers, or of those who fought in the War of Independence? Many have strong opinions about this. Do we mean theatre for the majority populations, or for the populations that have the most access to the media? The answer would seem obvious to some. We might mean theatre for the hundreds of minority populations—not only for the citizens of ethnic minorities, but also for the illegal immigrants, and for other marginalized groups such as the physically disabled, the queer, the incarcerated, the poor, on and on. These are the priorities for many in the theatre. We have all heard America referred to as "the melting pot." But it is something of a serious joke for us now to say that we are really more of "a salad bowl." That is, we are all in the same bowl, we are covered in the same dressing . . . but we don't really mix.[5]

It is significant that America has—or perhaps can have—no national theatre, just as there is no national school of the arts that expresses the nation's
agenda for actor training.[6] There are periodically theatres or schools that
think of themselves as such—but you won't get everyone to accept that
they are *national*. There are many possible examples to choose from, and
each with a different agenda. Here are just a few: there has been a National
Theatre devoted to "top-quality live stage attractions" in Washington, DC,
since 1835,[7] and another American National Theatre and Academy char-
tered by the U.S. Congress "to advance non-commercial theatre in America"
in 1935.[8] More currently, an American National Theatre for "the advancement of the writing of new plays and musicals"[9] had its Founders' Celebration in New York in 2005; also in 2005, the great Baryshnikov created a
nationally-minded arts center in Manhattan, "with the mission to develop
and host interdisciplinary performance art"[10]; at its inception Baryshnikov
remarked, "An art center in New York right now? . . . I think that's what
this city and this country need."[11] These two recent projects are challenging,
dynamic, admirable. But they are both in New York, and the United States is
3,000 miles wide. One can see professional plays in cities across the nation.
Is New York in a better position than Washington, DC, to be American?
Lots of people outside of New York and Washington do not think either
one is America, or can represent the entire nation artistically. *American
Theatre Magazine* is essentially a New York magazine that has a wider base
for including the "regional" theatres.[12] The same is true of the actor training at the American Conservatory Theatre: although founder William Ball
believed deeply that this combined conservatory and theatre was American,
no one in New York thinks this San Francisco acting school is American. It
is just . . . Northern Californian. It doesn't matter whether it is Washington,
DC, or Chicago or Miami or Los Angeles claiming to be American; from a
New Yorker's perspective, they will always be speaking for themselves.

NEA Chairman Dana Gioia spoke further on his remark quoted above:

> One of the key things, for example, in America about culture is lan-
> guage. I was raised speaking a dialect of Italian in Los Angeles with a
> Mexican mother. I had a different sense, I think, of what culture would
> have been for somebody in Boston or New York or Florida, you know,
> or Minnesota. And if you think about that, a Mexican and Italian
> marrying in Los Angeles, living in a Mexican neighborhood, I went to
> a school in a city where half the people were Japanese. That culture is
> migratory, it's dynamic, it transcends national boundaries. It belongs
> to individuals and also to minorities.[13]

Your definition of *American* will determine the kind of theatre you
think we should be producing, and the actor training you think should
be available. British Shakespeare? Southern Tennessee Williams? Political
street theatre, folk theatre, popular theatre, ethnic, new, or experimental?

Multi-cultural or multi-media? As time goes on, none of these provide Americans with a core, inviolable sensibility for an American theatre.

* * *

ACTOR

What is an Actor in a Profession Buffeted by Commercial Demands?

It is said that, because of science and technology, our world has changed more in the past century than in the previous one hundred centuries. The actor's world has changed that drastically in the last quarter of a century. Twenty-five years ago, we still knew what an actor was. His job was pretty much the same as the job of the actor who worked in production with Aeschylus, Shakespeare, or Chekhov. We recognized the actors' skills and challenges when we read about them in Cicero, Racine, and Shaw.

But today, for many actors, that old world has been swallowed up in new technologies, media, and globalization. For these actors, the venerable definition of the theatre as one actor and one spectator is dim in their memories. Moreover, many of today's actors may never have learned that definition of the theatre. In fact—having grown up with TV and the movies, they may never have been in a theatre. Today, knowing what an actor does is as complex as making sense of our new world.

In June of 2004, in San Francisco, I was asked to organize and moderate a statewide panel on actor training. The process I went through struck me as a metaphor for our confusion over the word "actor."

I gamely set about gathering my panelists. I planned to have one representative from each of several overlapping areas of actor training—one teacher for acting, one for voice, one for movement, one for theatre history, and perhaps one or two others. But it was impossible to contain the task, and my job grew at an alarming rate. In this way, I felt firsthand that there was no one definition of what an actor did, or of what constituted necessary training for an actor.

To find my one acting teacher, for example, I had to choose between contacting the head of the new acting conservatory, or the director of that old independent studio, or the owner of the famous commercial studio, or the man who runs the popular community theatre classes. Should I invite the Stanislavsky specialist or the Meisner? The one who teaches Shakespeare, on-camera, improvisation, or youth theatre? All of these train actors, depending on what they think the word "actor" refers to.

First I contacted a respected repertory actor, thinking a working professional might talk about the usefulness of his training. He seemed to think his training had not been useful. One "acting" teacher turned out really to be teaching dialects. Another well-known acting teacher asked to be on the panel, but then had a job offer in Los Angeles and left.

Then, looking for the one panelist on voice training for the actor, I had to decide between teachers of singing or speech, classical or experimental, dialects, voice-over, mic technique, commercial voice acting, broadcasting, or voice for video games. Beyond these, there were proponents of several competing vocal "techniques" to select from. Likewise, finding the one movement teacher meant choosing between various schools of mind–body exploration— dance, gymnastics, mime, improvisation, stage combat, and clowning.

The theatre historian I called was out of town . . . on a directing job.

Of course, when the time came, we had a splendid gathering of prominent actor trainers from throughout California. One of Strasberg's students came to talk about her longtime independent teaching career, and this was balanced by the director of the brand new Irish theatre. The traditional dialects teacher was balanced by the cutting-edge voice-over trainer. And when the head of the new conservatory didn't come at the last minute, the on-camera studio director asked to step in to cover film and television for us. I was also graciously asked to talk about my interdisciplinary acting program.

But when each of us spoke, there was no question that we were not talking about the same "actor." One person meant the artist who knew dramatic literature; one meant the person off the street who knew how to handle a close-up in a dog food commercial. One meant the actor who was on a quest; one meant the "talent" who was hoping for a television series. Some thought an actor should specialize in one medium; some thought an actor could only make a living if he could work in all media. Some thought the trained actor would be working around the world; some imagined him never leaving the recording booth. The only thing we had in common was that we each thought we were offering those skills that were most critical for the actor. Whatever that was.

* * *

American actors are well-respected around the world. Directors abroad often talk about the discipline, energy, imagination and all-around professionalism they encounter when working with an American actor. Actors abroad seek out opportunities to work with American actors. The Actors Studio in New York broadcasts interviews with highly-visible actors, and this program is followed religiously by professionals and the general public alike across the United States.

Indeed, there are many aspects of the actor's world that form an impressive picture. At the same time, without throwing into question any of those aspects, there are several points to remember regarding the context the American actor works in. To form a complete picture, one point we have to include is that the actors just described constitute the barest fraction of the actors who are working or looking for work. Another point is that this recognition is really for film actors, rather than for stage actors, whose names few people know. We can compare the award ceremonies for film and stage actors: the Oscar Awards for film had their lowest viewership on record during the height of the Iraq War in 2003—only 33.1 million viewers—but were even lower in 2008, with only 32 million.[14] Even so, in 2004 the Oscars for film were still far ahead of the Tony Awards for theatre, which had their lowest rating to date that year; in 2005 the Tonys had 6.6 million watchers, and it went up to 7.8 million in 2006; in 2008, though, it fell lower than the previous low ever, which was in 1977.[15] In any event, it comes as no surprise that neither film nor theatre claims the audiences that sports do: in 2004 neither award ceremony relevant to the actor's work claimed the 40 million viewers who turned on the Lakers basketball game the same night as the Tonys; in 2006 the NBA finals were ahead of the Tonys; in 2008 the Super Bowl had an audience of 97.5 million.[16]

A third point to consider when we are thinking about the talented American actor, is that whether film actor or stage actor, he is probably not making a living wage. In 2002, around 4,500 members of the Actors' Equity Association (AEA), the stage actors' union, earned between $1 and $2,500, which might cover annual subway fare. Moving up the pay scale, around 1,400 members earned up to $10,000 a year, which is just under the national poverty line. Ninety-six members of the profession in the entire country made $150,000 a year, while the average cost of a single family home in Los Angeles is around $650,000.[17]

We may imagine that film and television provide a better living for the actor. This is not so.[18] Here are the dismal 2003 statistics from the Screen Actors Guild: "70% of the guild's members earn less than $7,500 a year as actors, while less than 2% earn more than $250,000 annually. Only about 8% of the guild is considered middle class—[that is,] those who earn more than $40,000 a year, which leaves about 20% of the membership earning $7,500–$40,000 annually from acting. At any given time, 70% of SAG members are not working at the craft."[19] For those who are *in the know*, "not working at the craft" means "unemployed."

* * *

TRAINING

How is Actor Training Adjusting to Larger Cultural Changes?

It is a feature of the U.S. actor-training landscape that actors who are working or looking for work may not have any training.[20] American actor training—which goes on in large and small conservatories, in private and public universities and high schools, in a vast array of independent studios and academies, in professional and community organizations, and in the devoted teacher's living room (and often in combinations of these)—is regularly portrayed in the media as unnecessary for success in the acting field: actors in the public eye are still told to refrain from referring to any formal training[21]; stories of non-actors being "discovered" still proliferate; the public, as well as many a university administrator making decisions about theatre programs, still has the idea that training is in opposition to the actor's "spontaneous" or "natural" performance.

In this setting, inside academic programs and out, the marketing of actor training nationally is very related to the marketing of the "Hollywood Dream Machine" as a whole. There is a sprawling and lucrative industry that thrives on people—trained and untrained—who think an acting career is made primarily through buying things. We certainly cannot say that this buying is all that goes on for actors in training, but it is absolutely pervasive. Theatre, film, or television hopefuls will each need to buy a headshot session with a photographer, who will also sell them hair and make-up services. They will need resumes written by resume specialists, and then printed by resume printers. They will need to purchase special cards to send to agents, attend workshops with casting directors, join professional organizations, buy books on career development, and have cell phones so they can always be reached by the agent who suddenly needs them. And while they are buying all of these things, it is understood (and accepted) that they will be living in chronically temporary housing so they can leave on a moment's notice for that plum role, and working in low-paying jobs in return for the flexibility to take time off without warning to appear at auditions.

One might respond that every profession has a support industry that grows up around it. The athlete, the architect, the mechanic—all make heavy financial commitments to their fields of choice after they complete training. What is so different in the acting field—and so different from fields outside of entertainment—is that this buying often goes on *instead of* the training. People who have never had any acting training, or had miscellaneous or introductory training, are being encouraged to participate in a profession that cannot possibly hire them or pay them back for their financial devotion.

There are, at the same time, the savvy students who know that ongoing training is an important part of having an acting career. There is a vast array of short-term—often expensive—classes available to them. These classes are often called "workshops." In a workshop, the implication is that participants will get the salient points from six or ten years' worth of actual study, but in six or ten weeks—or, more commonly, six or ten hours. People can take specialized classes or workshops of the kind we mentioned above: camera techniques, audition techniques, voice-over, dialects, acting for commercials, puppeteering, stage combat and improvisation—or the class that was advertised at a high-profile theatre offering acting classes, "Attaining Wonderfulness."

Again, we might say that such specialized study is a normal part of a professional's continuing education—staying current, expanding one's skills. And again, the problem for the training actor is that these "workshops" are there for them *instead of* any of the consistent training they need to prepare for a viable acting career.

Northern California's leading theatre organization is called Theatre Bay Area. Over the years, Theatre Bay Area asked me to hold various kinds of work sessions for both union and non-union actors looking for work at the regional level nationally. These were union and non-union actors who had trained all over the U.S., in respected undergraduate, graduate and conservatory programs, many of which were on the East Coast. Just as the top acting schools across the country are full of actors trained in the San Francisco Bay Area, the Bay Area is full of actors trained in those top acting schools. Over time, I have seen a profound shift in the way these actors think about their training.

When I started giving those sessions, an actor would typically tell me where or with whom he had studied. This is, of course, how many a professional actor introduces himself in most countries of the world. After some years, I found that the typical U.S. actor would instead tell me only what workshops he had taken. By the early 2000s, the typical American actor was telling me only what *experience* he had had; I often heard that an individual going into professional auditions had studied years ago—most often in an academic program—and had done only "some shows" and audition workshops locally in the many years since then, and believed these had kept them "conditioned" to work professionally. Most recently, I have also seen a trend for actors to find very short-term "coaches" to teach them pre-fabricated audition performances, or even to form groups to "critique" each others' audition pieces so as to bypass having a teacher altogether. Indeed, a large segment of potential actors are simply not looking for the traditional acting mentors or teachers. Somehow, not university study, nor workshops combined with experience, have given these people "respect for acting" training.[22]

* * *

In the U.S. cultural environment, so saturated with competitive marketing, it is natural that theatre training has also been commodified. Academic and conservatory theatre programs work to keep abreast of advertising trends, packaging their offerings with pull quotes, shiny brochures with stylish photos, and hi-tech websites. [23] University training programs may assure prospective students that training is "quickly grasped," "fast" or "accessible"[24]; independent programs may list celebrities said to have studied there, and promise "industry access." Behind the advertising, hundreds of noble acting teachers struggle awkwardly in plain rooms to help their students breathe fully, love language, and see each other as meaningful.

Where "awkward struggling" is not marketable, Methods are. Methods, while articulating a teacher's approach, can also organize the bumpy, complex undertaking that is actor training into linear how-to packages. Dynamic teachers who work by combining myriad sources of inspiration are reduced to teaching in the "method" of a teacher who has passed away but has valuable name recognition. Ambitious teachers, who themselves have drawn from multiple disciplines and influences, paradoxically create "techniques" for students to follow exclusively. Methods also help programs hire their teachers, since those who can claim expertise or certification in a particular body of work are relatively known quantities in a field where independent approaches to teaching can be hard to evaluate.[25] Indeed, the convenience of methods for marketing purposes far outweighs the protestations of many acclaimed teachers that no single method can be made of their work.[26]

Books about methods often play an important part in actor training, figuring in course syllabi, as well as serving many an aspirant as substitution for professional instruction.[27] Books that give quick overviews of a range of high profile methods are popular, culling a few straightforward ideas from among the contradictions and other difficulties that may challenge a reader interested in a gifted teacher's work. These may also be practical as "buyers' guides": Richard Brestoff's *The Great Acting Teachers and Their Methods* follows an introductory survey of methods with training school profiles, including phone numbers and prices.[28] Some books double as advertising: Arthur Bartow's *Training of the American Actor* is addressed to the beginning NYU acting student and parents confused by NYU's wide offerings in actor training, with a preface including the startling claim that his book on NYU covers "the ways American actors are universally trained."[29]

Writings on actor training can also become a troubling force in the field, in spite of serious work done by both writers and editors. Volumes on Stanislavsky's method abound, although it is common knowledge that the versions we have been using of his texts in English are truncated, muddled, and misleading somewhat beyond serviceability.[30] Ian Watson's excellent article in Hodge's *Twentieth Century Actor Training* is entitled "Training with Eugenio Barba," but explains in a footnote that there hasn't been space to say anything about the vocal training integral to Barba's work.[31] In the same volume, Lisa Wolford explains that her expert article, "Grotowski's Vision of the Actor," doesn't include the vocal work we know to be inextricable from Grotowski's thinking about training.[32] While offering invaluable information, such adjustments made for the realities of publishing or for other practical reasons may also give many naïve readers a sadly partial impression of the real work of these major figures, and of what it means to prepare one's self for work in the theatre.

These issues of whether and how to get professional training affect not only actors, but also directors. A distinctive condition of the American actor's world is his auditioning for, and working with, directors who have no qualifications. It used to be assumed that directors were trained, either through professional apprenticeships of one kind or another, or through professional or academic programs. Today, it is not uncommon for "directors" to be actors who have simply decided they would rather put others through the audition process than do the auditioning themselves.

In both conventional and experimental theatre training, actors are taught to comply with a director, regardless of the director's competence or conduct. For the 2004 conference held by the Association for Theatre in Higher Education (ATHE), Ellen Margolis posed the challenging question:

Do teachers in a conservatory setting have an obligation to indoctrinate students into the traditional power relationship seen in the professional theatre? I think not. The movement against the Vietnam War in the 1960s had the slogan: What if they gave a war and nobody came? Along with giving acting and directing students tools for respectful and cooperative creative work, we can certainly ask them at least to consider: What if they gave an audition and nobody came?

It is commonplace to hear that the audition process as it stands is unpleasant but that there is really no other way to cast. In fact, simple gestures can create an equitable balance of power for auditions. For example, directors can post their resumes for the actors on waiting room bulletin boards or websites—along with their artistic philosophies and concepts for an upcoming show. These things would be so easy to do that one may be led to think directors don't do them for actors—only for prospective employers—because it is not customary, because they don't want to, and, of course, because the actors do not insist.

* * *

CONCLUSION: LOOKING BACK TO MOVE FORWARD

What are Some Useful Trends to Foster for the Future?

In the spirit of the saying, "there is no future without a past," I begin to consider what might be next for American actor training by first looking back. Taking the long view of the history of Western theatre, we can clearly see specific periods that have exploded with theatrical energy. For instance, Sophocles, Seneca, Shakespeare, and Shaw all saw such periods. They were characterized by advances in dramaturgical thinking and in the design elements, as well as in the practice of acting.

I wonder if ours will be known as one of the great periods of Western theatre. Or perhaps only a little great. Certainly thriving—but focused on experimenting rather than enduring. Energetically, the theatre is still absorbing the shock of the appalling wars of the twentieth century. Artistically, we are still feeling the impact of the advent of cinema. Dramatically, we are still trying to extricate ourselves from the idiosyncratic ideas of Sigmund Freud.

In spite of everything, whether you think the center of theatrical creation is the playwright, director, designer, or actor, for the audience the core of the theatrical event itself remains one actor and one spectator. The quality of the actors working in our theatres will play a critical role in determining how our theatre is remembered. Since this quality is rarely achieved organically through apprenticeships in our time, I have concluded that formal training—not fragmented "experience," but formal study, whether in a recognized program or with a skillful independent teacher—is critical in our time to keeping the theatre vigorous.[33]

Our challenge now is to train a generation of actors who do not know what an artist is. That is, we are asking young people to specialize in one art form when they do not have a general understanding of the arts, or the larger role they play in our society. They do not have a coherent sense of the actual work of an artist in any discipline. Regarding how to provide acting students with that "sense," my own thoughts echo, in many respects, ideas expressed eloquently by colleagues, in and out of the press—and diverge quite a bit in other respects. In any case, there are three ideas fundamental to my own perspective, and I respectfully gather them here to add them to the general discourse.

1. An intellectual life

In the first place, we need to give our actors an intellectual life—by which I mean broadly "the life of the mind." For years, for a variety of reasons, our training has put enormous emphasis on the exploration of emotion and uninhibited impulse, under the influence of popular psychology and at the expense of an aesthetic education. The results acting students can achieve without an informed aesthetic sense at the helm are not inspiring. In 1966, the eminent Richard Schechner interviewed the equally eminent Moshé Feldenkrais on actor training. Schechner asked: But if the actor becomes too self-aware, isn't he in danger of losing his spontaneity? Feldenkrais replied: "If you look at it properly, what we mean by spontaneity is just to be an idiot. How on earth can an actor be spontaneous?"[34]

Towards this end, I believe that theoretical studies must be the cornerstone of a professional actor training program, no matter what kind of theatre one is striving for. If our goal is to foster meaningful inquiry into the theatre as a whole, we have to give our students the intellectual tools to make the inquiry. If we are going to keep the theatre of the past alive, we will need actors who can compellingly perform those texts—and to learn how, students need a conceptual framework to support them.[35] Likewise, if we are going to create a viable theatre of any kind for the future, we need to teach our students now to recognize—and enter into, even if only to reject—the lively and elegant theoretical debates of the past 3,000 years.

2. An interdisciplinary foundation

Furthermore, our students need an interdisciplinary foundation for theoretical as well as practical studies. Before they begin to specialize in the particular field of acting, they need to understand the technical concerns and humanistic values intrinsic to all the arts.[36] For my thinking on this point, I always turn to the profoundly original Wassily Kandinsky (1866–1944)—painter, dramatist, teacher, and administrator. Although some may think his interdisciplinary ideas utopian beyond serviceability, in fact Kandinsky founded some of Europe's most renowned, inclusive associations and programs for arts study, and his ideas on education stimulated new vitality for the arts of his day as well as ours.[37]

Kandinsky wrote this blunt statement at the Bauhaus in 1928:

> Specialist training without a general, human basis ought no longer to be possible. Every kind of teaching today—almost without exception—lacks any "worldview" of an internal nature, any "philosophy" to establish the meaning of human activity. It is remarkable that young people today are still trained as specialists, who may be . . . useful in their external lives, but who are rarely capable of representing any purely human values.[38]

And perhaps blunter still: "A school that is incapable of conveying to the student in a planned manner [a broader philosophical basis] is not entitled to call itself a 'school'—least of all if it aspires to recognition as a university."[39]

Seeing the acting teacher's task from Kandinsky's point of view, we would do well to help our students see the contradiction in the notion of a "theatre specialist": What does it mean to "specialize" in one field made up of so many others? Theatre, after all, is nothing without architecture and history, without music, art, dance, and language, or without an all-inclusive discussion of human dignity.

3. Knowledge of the early European avant-garde

In addition to making intellectual and interdisciplinary training priorities, for a long time I have been pre-occupied with bolstering the position of the historical avant-garde in actor training. I believe that the theatre of our time will never fully flourish until we have made our peace with French and Spanish Surrealism, Italian Futurism, German and American Dadaism. These are still treated in dramatic literature like messy teenagers we love, but would rather not meet; in acting classes, students typically learn nothing about how to perform them. But this brilliant and exasperating body of work had firm roots in the sensibilities of the past, and also suggested ways forward. It is the conceptual, interdisciplinary bridge our students are missing between classical thought and values, and the theatre of their own difficult times. The development of our acting students will remain stalled until, with or without their teachers' help, they find their way back to that bridge.

As it is, we ask acting students simply to make the leap from Ibsen to Arthur Miller, and from Chekhov to Pinter, as if the decades of chaos and development between them never happened. In acting classrooms, one would never know that the noise born of the Industrial Revolution reduced the early twentieth-century theatre to silence. The songs of the rhapsode, the verses of Shakespeare, the poetic cadences of Romanticism no longer expressed life with the noisy, superficial rhythms of the industrial machine. When the sounds of war drowned out language as we knew it, the early avant-garde expressed a new anger and created a new beauty. The theatre today is suffering the consequences of having neglected these, and our training dooms our students to parochial outlooks in an increasingly internationalized cultural landscape.

The Japanese architect Suzuki Ryoji spoke to this problem: "The real avant-garde only existed at the beginning of this century, and we still haven't digested all of their ideas. I don't think the brilliance of that time has been fully appreciated yet. The avant-garde movement was interrupted by political forces that arose at that time, so we still don't know all the ideas its proponents may have had in mind."[40]

The modernist impulse captured by the avant-garde movement at the opening of the twentieth century has much to offer our students today, at the opening of the twenty-first. Its project was the first international art movement in history, using performance as a common ground for culturally and linguistically diverse artists. Its proponents, educated in the European classics, had a passion for the ethnic and traditional cultures of Africa and Asia, for experimental texts, innovative spaces and technology. Knowledge of their work can be an important part of giving U.S. actors the sophistication in training they will need to participate internationally in the coming years.

Whether the role of our theatre is to reflect our country's "vastness and diversity," or to emphasize "shared values" and commonalities,[41] in our time, choosing an approach to acting is no longer a matter of preference, but of cultural politics. As the field of actor training finds its place in the changing world ahead of us, the internal and external market pressures will surely become stronger and more complex. There will also doubtless continue to be a role for those committed to bringing dignity to actor training—intellectually, artistically, and humanistically—insisting on Kandinsky's "broader philosophical basis" in actor training, in universities, conservatories, and beyond. There is still time to make ours one of the great periods of Western theatre.

NOTES

1. Portions of this article are versions of speeches I have given in Canada ("Actor Training: Training Actors or Consumers?"), Korea ("American Actor Training") and India ("America's Actor Today; Kandinsky's Internationalism Tomorrow," keynote speech). The portions given in Korea were also printed in the 10th Anniversary Symposium booklet (Seoul, Korea: Korean National University of Arts Press, October 8, 2004), 28–45. In English and Korean; trans. Sung Soo-Jung.
2. Dana Gioia, "UNESCO Cultural Diversity Convention: The U.S. View," Foreign Press Center Roundtable, Washington, DC, September 27, 2005, http://209.85.173.132/search?q=cache:G6Jw-osd8fEJ:fpc.state.gov/

fpc/54039.htm+www.fpc.state.gov/fpc/54039.htm&hl=en&ct=clnk&cd=1
&gl=us&client=firefox-a.
3. See http://www.americannationaltheatre.org/.
4. Surely these centralizing/de-centralizing impulses are at the core of our country's nature. About this, Professor Emeritus of Dramatic Art and director
Robert Goldsby remarked in correspondence: "The opening quotes by Dana
Gioia and Harold Prince echo the original arguments between Hamilton and
Jefferson: one bank or many." In the introduction to *1915: The Cultural
Moment*, editors Adele Heller and Lois Rudnick point to related issues that
pre-occupied artists and intellectuals in the early years of the twentieth century: "How do we create a body of art, literature, and cultural criticism
that responds to personal vision but also speaks to more than an academic
elite and privileged few? How do we build a vital national culture that at
once provides a coherent source for our identity and incorporates the sometimes conflicting cultures of men and women and of diverse ethnic and racial
groups?" (New Brunswick, NJ: Rutgers University Press, 1991), 2.
5. Rustom Bharucha's notion of the "intracultural" in India may give us a
tool for thinking further about this "not-mixing" in the U.S.: "The 'intra'
highlight[s] the deeply fragmented and divided society of India that the
multi-cultural rhetoric of the state refuses to acknowledge." See Rustom
Bharucha, introduction to *The Politics of Cultural Practice: Thinking
Through Theatre in an Age of Globalization* (Hanover, NH: Wesleyan University Press, 2000), 9.
6. As this book is in final stages of preparation, there is a suggestion surfacing
in the media to create a national Secretary of the Arts position. At this early
juncture, those in favor think such a position would mirror the Ministers
of Art or Culture that other countries have appointed for centuries. Those
against the idea feel the NEA has already shown that the government knows
little about fostering the arts. In any case, such a Secretary would likely
shape—deliberately or indirectly—a national position on actor training,
playing a role unlike any we have in government today.
7. See http://www.nationaltheatre.org/location/timeline.html.
8. See http://www.nationaltheatre.org/backstage/ntcorp.htm#mission.
9. See http://www.americannationaltheatre.org/about/ANTInfo.doc.
10. See http://www.nysun.com/article/69731.
11. Jennifer Dunning, "Baryshnikov Hatches Grand Plan for a New Arts Center," *New York Times*, Arts Section (December 19, 2002). Also on the web
at http://query.nytimes.com/gst/fullpage.html?res=9C06E2DD133DF93AA
25751C1A9649C8B63&sec=&spon=&pagewanted=all.
12. See the February 2008 issue of *American Theatre Magazine*, which features
a conversation between luminaries of theatre criticism in New York and New
Haven, and then includes an article on critics in Denver, San Francisco, and
Nashville. In recent years, the magazine has also cast an eye increasingly to
theatre overseas. Published by Theatre Communications Group, New York.
13. Dana Gioia, "UNESCO Cultural Diversity Convention: The U.S. View,"
http://209.85.173.132/search?q=cache:G6Jw-osd8fEJ:fpc.state.gov/
fpc/54039.htm+www.fpc.state.gov/fpc/54039.htm&hl=en&ct=clnk&cd=1
&gl=us&client=firefox-a.
14. See http://www.cbc.ca/arts/tv/story/2008/02/26/oscars-lowestviewership.
html?ref=rss. Also see http://www.nydailynews.com/entertainment/mov-
ies/2008/02/26/2008-02-26_may_be_blood_over_new_oscar_tv_low.
html.
15. See http://query.nytimes.com/gst/fullpage.html?res=940DE4DB1438F93AA
35755C0A96E948260.

16. See http://en.wikipedia.org/wiki/List_of_most-watched_television_broadcasts #Most-watched.

17. Steven DiPaola (National Director of Finance and Administration for Actors' Equity), writes in "The 2005–2006 Theatre Season: An Analysis of Employment, Earnings, Membership and Finance": "To keep things in perspective before looking at Employment and Earnings in greater detail, Equity members worked an average of 17.2 weeks during this past season, with median earnings of $7,040." See http://www.actorsequity.org/docs/about/AEA_Annual_Study_05–06.pdf. The Occupational Employment Statistics for 2006 (posted in October 2007) list an actor's median hourly wage as $11.61, nearly half the wages of a postman ($21.32) or a school counselor ($22.85)—but, unlike these other jobs, for the actor no annual wage statistic could be calculated because the work is too seasonal. See http://stats.bls.gov/oes/current/oes_nat.htm#b27–0000.

18. In 1996, 80% of members of the Screen Actors Guild (SAG) made less than $5,000. More than 29% of SAG members reported no earnings from acting in 1996. For those who had earnings, 72% of their income came from commercials and television. Jim Emerson, "Actors and Actresses" in *Direct Magazine* (Jan. 1, 1999), *http://directmag.com/mag/marketing_actors_actresses/*.

19. Today, according to the U.S. Department of Labor, "of the nearly 100,000 SAG members, only about 50 might be considered stars. The average income that SAG members earn from acting, less than $5,000 a year, is low because employment is sporadic. Therefore, most actors must supplement their incomes by holding jobs in other occupations." Labor Department site, http://stats.bls.gov/oco/ocos093.htm#earnings.

20. Acting training separate from other more general education is relatively new. Charlie Hensley recently reminded readers of this point, which is widely made in the relevant literature: "Once, even the most rudimentary public education in America included Latin, Greek, rhetoric, memorization, elocution and an immersion in classical literature. Armed with these, any ambitious young actor could go on to learn the elements of stagecraft in the company of more experienced, professional colleagues." "For Working Actors, the Readiness is All," in the Special Training Section of *American Theatre* (January 2008), 52.

21. An exposé of the entertainment industry's secrecy about the training and coaching of its actors would be very welcome. Anecdotally: a student of mine read an interview with a British actor who had refused a spot on a U.S. talk show after learning he would not be allowed to refer to any of his training. A colleague heard a young movie star begin to refer to her dialect coach and then correct herself to say she was just naturally good at dialects. Anecdotes aside, anyone can glean from the online Wikipedia entries for stars in music, film, and TV that a deliberate policy reigns to obscure both their backgrounds and ongoing training. For many years, I asked students to research the professional training and other preparation of their favorite actors; it proved a relatively straightforward task to reconstruct at least the basic training backgrounds for actors of every country except, very often, America.

22. These forays into the current acting profession without sustained training are balanced by an opposite trend that can be observed for students to stay in an acting class for years without any intention of having a career in acting or in any related field. This phenomenon is beyond the scope of this article, but raises, for example, issues of acting training as therapy, and of a teacher's connection to the profession.

23. Stunning photographs of mediocre shows have become the norm in theatre marketing generally. In a training context, the phenomenon of "visual

advertising" has brought with it some troubling ethical questions, since there is so often a big difference between the quality of the production's visual elements, designed by professionals—and the quality of the overall shows, performed by students, who have every right to be uneven. If nothing else, advertising photos mislead students about the level of work they will achieve in a two- to four-year program. Students also routinely see striking photos of shows they have seen themselves and know to have been unsuccessful. When a very high-profile director was in town, my students were astonished to compare the photos, overall marketing, and press for a show they knew had been cancelled due to its unpopularity. In fact, for one of the cancelled performances, my students themselves had been the *only* ones to buy tickets.

24. I am grateful to the anonymous reader who offered the following remarks on this point: " . . . The politics of academia, with its tenure system . . . forces faculty to toe the party line. 'Academic fields are dominated by fewer than 100 powerful people' (*Chronicle of Higher Education*, April 25, 2008, p. A40). The powers in theatre at our universities have generally a bias against actors and acting training . . . Academia is one of the most politically saturated fields in the world . . . The economics are hardly hidden; university endowments are flaunted as symbols of success and the capital of an M.F.A. program (or any university program) is the first thing used to attest to its merits . . . [L]ook at the economics of universities and colleges in totem. [You] will find that the institutions are no different than any corporation: multi-billion dollar institutions that thrive on capital and capitalism."

25. Some time after writing this passage, I received this online posting by respected Toronto voice teacher, Eric Armstrong, in which he speaks to the special case of hiring: "My problem with exclusive methods is in their use of jargon, and in their exclusivity, which is reinforced by a jargon that no one else uses. I firmly believe that a well-trained teacher with an 'eclectic' approach to voice has more tools in her repertoire; however, to be able to become that trainer you must learn how to integrate methods that claim to be complete, competing packages, exclusive, and the solution to everything. As an 'eclectic' teacher, I believe that there are many paths that 'lead to heaven' because there are many learning styles and many different approaches that work in different contexts . . . Ultimately, it doesn't really matter to me what method a trainer starts with (though I do have my preferences, especially when I'm looking to hire a colleague), so long as they start with SOMETHING." From a post on the "Vibration" thread on the discussion group for teachers of voice and speech at vastavox@uci.edu (March 17, 2008). The archives are closed to the public; quoted with the authors's permission.

26. Sanford Meisner spoke for many a teacher when he wrote, "I decided that a creative textbook about acting was a contradiction in terms . . . I came to realize that how I teach is determined by the gradual development of each student." See the prologue, *Sanford Meisner on Acting*, written with Dennis Longwell (New York: Vintage Books, 1987), xviii. Related in thinking, in the preface to the second edition of David Magarshack's translation of *Stanislavsky on the Art of the Stage*, he dismisses "methods" altogether: "A real artist creates his own individual art and is capable of digesting any 'method.' It is only the second-rate actor who becomes what is generally known in the profession as a 'Method actor'" (New York: Hill and Wang, 1961), 2.

27. In the January 2008 issue of *American Theatre Magazine*, see John Istel's "How to Act Better," 104–107, a survey of five new books on acting teachers, including one with interviews of fifty teachers.

28. Richard Brestoff, *The Great Acting Teachers and Their Methods* (Lyme, NH: Smith and Kraus, 1995), 169–187.
29. Arthur Bartow, *Training of the American Actor* (New York: Theatre Communications Group, 2006) xi. Acting teachers and program administrators with high visibility often seem unaware that the independent acting studio remains a vital fixture of U.S. actor training. Large and small studios with eclectic approaches serve thousands of acting students around the country each year. Many studio directors base their studios on their original findings and explorations; others combine existing approaches in creative and unique ways. In 1999, for several lecture- and workshop-packed days, the Symposium for Theatre, Film and Television Professionals in Las Vegas brought together a score of the nation's dynamic studio teachers who had formed a series of impassioned online discussion groups. Through these exchanges, teachers shared and sharpened their work; I was lucky to be among them. Members of this teaching community (myself included) went on to form the Network of Cooperating Studios (NCS), with member teachers in Baltimore, Denver, Kansas City, Los Angeles, Oakland and at Ole Miss. The NCS, active from 1999 to 2002, exchanged workshops and students, carried out joint projects and sponsored visitors from Thailand, India, New York, South Africa, Trinidad, and Washington, D.C. This activity, while having no presence in the media, attracted the warmest interest of fellow teachers and students in the U.S. and abroad.
30. See "The Publication Maze," Chapter 4 in Sharon Carnicke, *Stanislavksy in Focus* (The Netherlands: Harwood Academic Publishers, 1998), 70–91. Carnicke has written extensively on this subject. See also R. Andrew White, "Stanislavsky and Ramcharaka: The Influence of Yoga and Turn-of-the-Century Occultism on the System" in *Theatre Survey* 47:1 (May 2006). Jean Benedetti's new translation of a significant part of Stanislavsky's writings, entitled *An Actor's Work: a Student's Diary*, was published by Routledge in 2007.
31. Ian Watson, "Training with Eugenio Barba" in Alison Hodge, *Twentieth Century Actor Training* (London: Routledge, 2000), 222, Note 1.
32. Lisa Wolford, "Grotowski's Vision of the Actor," ibid., 194.
33. Again from Magarshack's "Preface to the Second Edition," ibid.: "The idea of an Actors' Studio divorced from a theatre would have appeared bizarre to Stanislavsky. However, considering the chaotic state of the theatre in England and in the United States, any place where an actor can get some training is not to be dismissed ... "
34. This exchange is from Moshé Feldenkrais, Kelly Morris, ed. and trans., "Image, Movement, and Actor: Restoration of Potentiality." It first appeared in *Tulane Drama Review*, Volume 10, Number 3, Spring 1966. It is now online at http://www.feldnet.com/Default.aspx?tabid=83.
35. Thanks are due to the anonymous reader who remarked: "[A] passionate belief in giving actors more of an intellectual life is clearly desirable. Most European actors have such a framework before they get into acting and most American actors do not, and obviously they need it if they are going to act onstage in classical plays in front of sophisticated audiences."
36. Many feel that the considerations in preparing actors for film and television are substantially different from those for the theatre. It certainly bears remembering that there is a range of opinions about what constitutes appropriate training for the various media.
37. The training program at my studio, the Actors' Training Project, was infused with Kandinsky's teachings, where they proved highly effective: the studio served as a cornerstone of both professional and commercial actor training

in the San Francisco Bay Area from 1985 to 2004, before moving to overseas institutions for some years.

38. From Lindsay and Vergo, eds., "Art Pedagogy" in *Wassily Kandinsky: Complete Writings* (Boston: G.K. Hall and Co., 1982), vol. 2, 723–724.
39. Ibid., "The Value of Theoretical Instruction in Painting," vol. 2, 704. For much more on the application of Kandinsky's interdisciplinary thinking to theatre training, see my unpublished doctoral dissertation, "Kandinsky: Dramatist, Dramaturg and Demiurge of the Theatre," (U.C. Berkeley, 1985).
40. Architect Ryoji Suzuki [Suzuki Ryoji], in an interview with Christopher Knabe and Joerg Rainer Noenning, eds., *Shaking the Foundations: Japanese Architects in Dialogue* (U.S., U.K., Germany: Prestel Art Press, 1997), 49.
41. See Jane Alexander's *Command Performance: An Actress in the Theatre of Politics* (Cambridge, MA: Da Capo Press, 2001), her revelatory account of her years as head of the National Endowment for the Arts (1993 to 1997), when Newt Gingrich opposed the NEA as head of Congress. Alexander credited Congresswoman Sheila Jackson Lee (D-Texas) with making saving remarks during a critical vote in the House: "She spoke eloquently about art being in the eye of the beholder and about the country being vast and diverse" (293). President Clinton later offered support for the arts in a State of the Union address, stressing not diversity but a collective national identity: "The enduring worth of our nation lies in our shared values and soaring spirit . . . I believe we should stand by [the NEA] and challenge . . . all Americans in the arts and humanities . . . to make the year 2000 a national celebration of the American spirit in every community, a celebration of our common culture . . . " (300).

6 Changing Demographics
Where Is Diversity in Theatre Programs in Higher Education and National Associations?

Donna B. Aronson

Challenges in higher education today include issues related to teaching, research, internationalization, expanding technology and modes of instructional delivery, interdisciplinarity, institutional governance, and changes in demographics (including issues of access and equity), to name just a few. Theatre faculty and departments must move outside their comfort zones and join in the national conversations related to these issues. These national issues affect theatre departments in higher education. We need to participate in the conversations on our campuses, at disciplinary conferences, and with those involved with higher education in general. We need to keep up-to-date with *The Chronicle of Higher Education* and other publications which report on the state of our profession. It is difficult to realize that, whereas at one time theatre departments may have been at the forefront in higher education—particularly in the areas of pedagogy and creative teaching, today we have fallen behind. Nowhere is this more evident than in theatre's demographics. The need for change can be addressed at both the local/institutional level and the national/association level.

OTHER STRATEGIES/IMPLICATIONS OF CHANGING DEMOGRAPHICS

Higher education in the U.S. faces many problems as it seeks to fill needs associated with the changing demographics of the early twenty-first century.[1] Due to the growing inequities inherent in U.S. society, colleges and universities must be prepared to recruit, accept, and support increasing numbers of students of color.[2] A number of national programs have sought to enhance K–12 education for students of color. Nevertheless, many in higher education would argue that, although preparation is crucial to matriculation into college for at-risk students or students of color, the success of these young persons requires something beyond an adequate K–12 curriculum.

Through my work with the Association for Theatre in Higher Education[3] and as the Dean of Humanities, Arts, and Social Sciences at a small, private, Catholic, Hispanic-serving university, I have become acutely aware of the growing number of undergraduate students of color, low number of graduate students of color, and the small pool of qualified faculty of color. Students, particularly undergraduate students, need diverse role models as they prepare to work in a diverse world. Students identify with faculty role models who look like them and come from similar backgrounds. Faculty members from varied racial and cultural backgrounds expand the discourse in the classroom. Recruitment and retention of a diverse student body may stagnate in the absence of a diverse faculty and administration. There are few students of color in graduate programs graduating with the intention to teach. We must encourage talented students of color to complete their graduate education and join the academy.

Colleges and universities have struggled over the past twenty-five years with changing demographics and racial incidents. As student populations become more diverse, the expectation for programs shifts. Theatre departments must address casting and production assignment policies to ensure inclusion. Many institutions of higher education have developed multiple strategies for encouraging inclusion and multi-culturalism on campus. Theatre programs have addressed the same need to involve minority populations, with the added dimension that their success or failure is made visible to their communities through their theatrical productions.

Demographic reports suggest that, by the middle of this century, the size of the minority population in the United States will be equal to or greater than that of the Anglo population. Such projections have raised concerns about access and equity for students of color in higher education settings.[4]

ONE UNIVERSITY'S STORY

Changing demographics and predictions of a growing diverse student population are a certainty. For some faculty and departments this is already a reality; for others, it is only a matter of time. When I interviewed for the director of theatre position at the University of the Incarnate Word (UIW) in the Spring of 1989, I was quite impressed with the institution's overall diversity. At that time, it was over 40% Hispanic and 4% African American, representing the community of San Antonio. However, when I arrived on campus, it was clear that institutional diversity was not reflected in the Department of Theatre Arts. In fact, of the thirty-five majors there was one African American major and one Hispanic major. As I came to know the program, I realized that the department did not have clear objectives related to diversity in recruitment, or to casting and production policies. This was not a problem of our department alone, but was true of many theatre programs across the country.[5] When I left the department in 1999, the department was over 85% students of color with the majority of those being Hispanic. This change resulted from targeted recruiting and an open casting policy. Opportunity for students to work on productions on or off-stage was open to all. Additionally, the production season was expanded to expose students to plays from diverse cultures and periods.

The UIW Theatre Arts Department offers the Bachelor of Arts degree. The program was established in the mid-1960s with a "resident company" offering productions and classes. The "company" focused on providing entertainment to San Antonio. They were quite successful and well-thought of in the community. When I arrived in 1989, I paid close attention to the speeches given by the president and others regarding the goals of the institution. The president stated his objective to grow the student body and have it reflect the diverse population of the community. The college's mission spoke of serving the "poor and needy of San Antonio and South Texas." At the time of my hire, the Vice President for Academic Affairs and the Dean spoke of bringing the department to an "academically viable position" within the college. This meant that as a new Chair I had to evaluate the curriculum, the faculty, the production season, and the recruiting of majors. The university holds regional accreditation with the Southern Association of Colleges and Schools. The guidelines of the Southern Association of Colleges and Schools at that time required a terminal degree or a master's degree with eighteen hours in the discipline for faculty teaching at the undergraduate level. The theatre faculty included a number of long-time members of the resident company who were excellent actors, but did not hold the required qualifications for regional accreditation; the production season did not have a strong correlation to the curriculum; and the student body was not diverse.

At one of the first department meetings, I presented a number of policies for the department; the most challenging were a color-blind policy for casting and assignment of production responsibilities, and a rotation of plays that included a "multi-cultural" production. The faculty went along with the new policies. However, with few students of color, it was easy to avoid the issue.

RECRUITMENT

UIW was lucky to have an institutional fund for performing arts scholarships shared by the Departments of Art, Dance, Music, and Theatre Arts. Texas has a number of annual events that bring students from all over the state to audition for scholarships—the Texas Educational Theatre Association and the Texas Thespian Association. This allowed me quickly to view over one hundred students annually. During those meetings, I met and spoke with high school teachers and counselors from across the state. We discussed my visiting their schools to allow me to speak with other students and drama teachers at various high schools in the South Texas Valley, about five or six hours from San Antonio. The Valley high school teachers work hard to get their students into college. The overwhelming majority of the students in the Valley are first-generation Hispanic students. The high school teachers welcomed my interest and invited me to visit their schools. One teacher worked with me to invite the teachers and students from five area schools to come to their campus to meet with me. The first trip I made alone. I met with a number of students and faculty. I watched their auditions and toured the facility. I spoke with the students about the difference between a BFA and BA degree. At dinner with a number of teachers and students at a local Mexican restaurant, we arranged for them to bring students to San Antonio to visit our theatre and meet the students and faculty. We arranged the visit on a Friday afternoon when our department met together for "practicum." By the next fall we had four new students from the Valley. Regular trips to the Valley with other theatre and music faculty drew more students. Once the "pipeline" was created, we had regular interest in the department. This continued for several years.

Following discussions with the Office of Admissions, we began to bring a recruiter from that office with us to the annual conferences. They brought university information and set up a display table. The counselor sat with us at the table when we called back students to talk about our program. Respected by the Office of Admissions, the theatre faculty members were called upon to travel with them to various college events around the state of Texas. We also worked with the Office of Financial Assistance to get the best financial aid package for the theatre students. Eventually, members of the theatre faculty were visiting the arts magnet high schools in San Antonio, Houston, and Dallas to audition and meet with potential students. High schools in Texas provide a richly diverse pool of graduates. Throughout these different efforts to connect with potential students for the department, we awarded our scholarship funds primarily to students of color.

CASTING AND PRODUCTION ASSIGNMENTS

The new policy for color-blind casting and assignment of production assignments was agreed to by the department faculty. There did not appear to be a problem in the assignment of production assignments. Students who were qualified took positions of responsibility. However, it soon became apparent that some directors were not actually complying. This issue came to a point of conflict when I cast a Hispanic student to play the daughter of two white members of the resident company in a production of Israel Horowitz' *Year of the Duck*. The couple challenged the casting since it would not be realistic to have them play the parents of this young actress. The production went on as cast. But this situation accelerated the personnel issues related to academic qualifications. This was not an easy transition, however; focusing on the greater good for the department, the students, and the institution, the resident company was dissolved in the mid-1990s. The department continued to produce summer productions for the next few years with some community actors and students, but the productions showed an improved connection to the academic program.

The nontenure-track faculty line shared by two resident company members became one tenure-track line, and a new person was hired. That person held a terminal degree in theatre. Changes in departmental faculty can be very difficult to handle in a small department. Concentrating on the goal of a diverse theatre program, which was academically challenging, was a key to riding out the rough times.

CHOOSING A SEASON

For many years, the department chose plays based on the director's choice and suggestions from the resident company's loyal audience. Some productions were repeated due to popular demand. The proposal to change the way plays were selected was accepted in the first year of my tenure as director of theatre. The proposal allowed for a variety of genres and historical periods to be covered, and for one of the four shows per year to be a "multicultural" play. We did a variety of plays in this production slot, including ones relevant to Hispanic and African American culture and (a cultural leap for a Catholic institution) Elie Weisel's *Trial of God*.

In the beginning, we could not fully cast Hispanic or African American productions with our majors and therefore cast members of the university community. At one point, we were doing a production of the Milcha Sanchez-Scott play, *Roosters*, and I realized that we were able to cast the play realistically with our majors. This was a turning point. However, the students soon made it clear that they did not want to do Hispanic plays regularly—they wanted to do Shakespeare, Molière, Miller, etc. Ongoing discussion involving the students and faculty led us to reevaluate the outcomes of the production program and its place at a small, private, Catholic, Hispanic-serving institution. We came to greater clarity about the service that the department provides to the university and the wider community, as well as to the curricular needs of the major. Here again, the restating of the goal of a diverse program in a diverse university was central to accomplishing the goal.

EDUCATING FOR DEMOCRACY

The best education is interdisciplinary, rejecting the boundaries of individual disciplines and educating for democracy. Theatre is a prime location to join theory with praxis. Speaking on education, Michael Apple eloquently states:

Our work is a form of cultural politics. This involves all of us working for what [Raymond] Williams called the 'journey of hope' toward 'the long revolution.' To do less, not to engage in such work, is to ignore the lives of millions of students and teachers throughout the world. Not to act is to let the powerful win. Can we afford to let this happen?[6]

Academic and arts disciplines within educational institutions, then, can become locations of cultural political action. As the student population shifts to a diverse, and in many cases first-generation group, theatre faculty must strengthen their awareness of theorists outside of their disciplines.

Critical education theorist Paulo Freire wrote about the potential of education to raise the social consciousness of those oppressed by the societies in which they live. In *Teachers as Cultural Workers: Letters to Those Who Dare Teach*, Freire states, "A humanizing education is the path through which men and women can become conscious about their presence in the world. The way they act and think when they develop all of their capacities, taking into consideration their needs, but also the needs and aspirations of others."[7] Freire's *Pedagogy of the Oppressed* similarly speaks to the potential of education to do more than just transmit knowledge. Freire's work, a potent testament to the power of education to raise the cultural capital of otherwise marginalized individuals, has influenced a great many scholars in many disciplines. In *Teaching to Transgress: Education as the Practice of Freedom*, bell hooks pays homage to the Brazilian theorist and practitioner: "When I entered my first undergraduate classroom to teach, I relied on the example of those inspired black women teachers in my grade school, on Freire's work, and on feminist thinking about radical pedagogy."[8] In her "playful" dialogue on Freire, hooks further explains:

> Paulo was one of the thinkers whose work gave me a language. He made me think deeply about the construction of identity in resistance. There was this one sentence of Freire's that became a revolutionary mantra for me: 'We cannot enter the struggle as objects in order to become subjects.' Really, it is difficult to find words adequate to explain how this statement was like a locked door—and I struggled within myself to find the key—and that struggle engaged me in a process of critical thought that was transformative. This experience positioned Freire in my mind and heart as a challenging teacher whose work furthered my own struggle against the colonizing process—the colonizing mind-set.[9]

It is clear that hooks understands education as a process of liberation. Hooks proposes "engaged pedagogy" as a means of transforming curriculum so that it "does not reflect biases or reinforce systems of domination" and allows students and teachers to take risks that make the classroom a site of resistance.[10] According to hooks, the classroom must be a democracy, a place where all students feel safe to participate and share responsibility for contributing to the learning that takes place. She suggests that students of color generally do not feel safe in the classroom, and teachers must relearn how to teach the students represented in the classroom today. If students of color do not feel safe in a classroom, how do they feel in an acting studio?

In *Teaching to Transgress*, hooks touches most deeply on ideas that could change the educational system. She proposes "engaged pedagogy" as a means of transforming curriculum so that it "does not reflect biases or reinforce systems of domination" and allows students and teachers to take risks that make the classroom a site of resistance.[11] What better site for "engaged pedagogy" than in the theatre classroom and on the university stage? Theatre pedagogy and performance are avenues to raising the consciousness and improving the skills and self-esteem of at-risk students and students of color on the stage in the audience.

Research has shown that successful students bring with them the cultural capital needed to succeed in higher education. At-risk students and students of color often do not have the cultural capital to succeed. They do not have the background, appropriate high school curriculum, cultural opportunities, or parental support and expectations that their upper- and middle-class counterparts have. Theatre programs could be useful purveyors of cultural capital through outreach projects to K–12 students. By involving themselves in the university's goals of increasing diversity and preparing at-risk students and students of color for college, theatre programs could position themselves for greater visibility and become indispensable to the life of the campus and the larger community.

In an article in *The Chronicle Higher of Education*, James Duderstadt, President Emeritus of the University of Michigan, proposed that universities need new models as they undergo these amazing transformations. He suggests that we consider becoming "A Diverse University, where we use our growing ethic, cultural, economic, and geographic diversity to encourage a range of approaches and opinions." He describes the "Diverse University" as one that will

> . . . serve a society of growing diversity—ethnic, racial, cultural, economic, and geographical—and that new reality will only continue to intensify. Although our colleges and universities have taken steps to better reflect such diversity on their campuses, we might imagine a bolder model. The diverse university would draw its intellectual strength and character from the rich diversity of humankind, and provide an environment in which people respect and tolerate diversity in living, working, and learning together as scholars and teachers.[12]

For universities to thrive today, we must be open to a multiplicity of approaches and opinions. At the same time, we must recognize that an institution of higher education is first and foremost a "uni"-versity, not a "di"-versity. Our challenge will be to weave together the dual objectives of unity and diversity in a way that best serves our mission and society.[13]

NOTES

1. The Alliance for Equity in Higher Education reported that "The proportion of the total U.S. population comprised of people of color (including African Americans, Asian Americans, American Indians, and Hispanics) is expected to grow from 28% in the year 2000 to 36% in 2020 and 47% in 2050.". The Alliance for Equity in Higher Education is a policy-based coalition comprised of the American Indian Higher Education Consortium (AIHEC), the Hispanic Association of Colleges and Universities (HACU), and the National Association for Equal Opportunity in Higher Education (NAFEO). *The Alliance for Equity in Higher Education*, http://www.msi-alliance.org/ (accessed May 15, 2006).
2. "In July 2004, 34% of the Hispanic population was under the age of 18 (National Population Estimate, U.S. Bureau of the Census, 2005: http://www.census.gov/popest/national/asrh/NC-EST2004/NC-EST2004-04-HISP.xls)" "Facts on Hispanic Higher Education," *Hispanic Association of Colleges and Universities*, http://www.hacu.net/hacu/Data,_Statistics,_and Research1_EN.asp?SnID=70494933.
3. I served the Association for Theatre in Higher Education in a number of roles beginning in 1987 as the first Forum Chair. I continued my service with two terms as Vice President for Conferences, a term as Secretary and as President-elect, President, and Past President completing my term on the board in 2001.
4. The Latin American Educational Foundation states on its website: with Hispanics comprising the fastest growing minority population in the nation, and the workforce requiring more education than ever before, something must be done to increase the number of Hispanics who complete degrees in higher education, lest more Hispanics end up in poverty. Today, access to Higher Education is critically important in order "to advance the economic and social status of Hispanics the Hispanic community," as demonstrated by the following statistics:

    • In the year 2050, Hispanics will be the second largest racial/ethnic group in the United States.
    • College enrollment for Hispanics between 18–24 rose slightly from 13% in the mid-70s to just 16% by the mid-90s.
    • During the same period, the percentage of Hispanic low-income high school students enrolled in college fell from 50% to 35%.
    • As of 1996, only 9% of the Hispanic population held a university degree.

    (Statistics from the Aspen Institute, Hispanic Association of Colleges and Universities, U.S. Department of the Census) (*Education Commission of the States) The Alliance for Equity in Higher Education*, http://www.msi-alliance.org (accessed May 15, 2006).

5. This is not the only time I have been involved in diversifying theatre education. The dissolution of the American Theatre Association and the subsequent founding of multiple organizations divided the membership in ways that homogenized the smaller associations. I served the Association for Theatre in Higher Education (ATHE) in a number of roles from 1987 to 2001, including President-elect. Already in 1987, the first ATHE board of governors discussed how to maintain the diversity of the membership, including the major groups from the former associations such as Women and Theatre, Black Theatre Network and the Asian Theatre focus groups. However, due to the Black Theatre Network's desire to maintain a membership beyond higher education, it left ATHE within the second year, although it maintained some of the membership through the development of the Black Theatre Association.

   In 1996, the board sought unsuccessfully to plan a joint conference in New York with the Black Theatre Network, but timing was off for such collaboration. In 1999–2001, the ATHE president's agenda encouraged exploration of the issue of diversity through plenary conference sessions and the development of a new Latina/o focus group. It was in 2003, when ATHE president-elect Marvin Sims was also the president of the Black Theatre Network, that reciprocal conference agreements were achieved. ATHE continues to seek strategies to diversify the membership and programming.

6. Michael W. Apple, *Official Knowledge: Democratic Education in a Conservative Age*, 2nd ed. (New York: Routledge, 2000), 175.

7. Paulo Freire, *Teachers as Cultural Workers: Letters to Those who Dare Teach*, trans. Donaldo Macedo, Dale Koike, and Alexandre Oliveira (Boulder, CO: Westview, 1998), xiii.

8. bell hooks, *Teaching to Transgress: Education as the Practice of Freedom* (New York: Routledge, 1994), 7.

9. Ibid., 46.

10. Ibid., 174.

11. Ibid., 21.

12. James J. Duderstadt, "A Choice of Transformations for the 21st Century University," *The Chronicle of Higher Education*, February 4, 2000, sec. B-6.

13. Ibid, sec. B-6.

7 The Wild, Wild East
Report on the Politics of American Actor Training Overseas

Lissa Tyler Renaud

SOME PERSPECTIVES ON GLOBALIZING AMERICAN ACTOR TRAINING

Internationally, the theme continues to be globalization, frequently sub-suming the vital issues of world poverty, the environment, technology, and peace and security. For those who benefit from it, globalization means the opening up of information, a sharing of ideas—and the exchange of cultural lives that has become possible through the Internet and easier travel. For those whose lives are by and large impoverished by globalization, the word suggests that the core of our shared moorings is now American jeans, McDonald's arches, and drug networking. In the field of entertainment, globalization on the one hand continues to broaden our interaction with ever more diverse kinds of theatre and theatre training, and on the other hand binds the world together with many of America's most visible and least admirable cultural products. In the theatre, many hope globalization will synthesize disparate cultures into a kind of theatre performance that transcends language and cultural barriers; others fight against this force that imposes the cultural norms of the more powerful on the less powerful, and predict a terrible sameness in our creative work once it is cut off from its cultural sources.

As an American acting teacher,[1] it has been instructive for me to teach in countries where mainstream American actor training is irrelevant, cas-tigated, or at best, viewed with skepticism. From outside the country, one is struck anew that America, which is three times the size of India, is also only half the size of Russia and a third the size of Africa—i.e., smaller. And the world is less charmed by America's theatre than one would think growing up in it. For example, since 2000, the World Social Forum has organized large protests against American humanities funding agencies such as the Ford Foundation, arguing that they serve as fronts for cor-porations that pour funds into underdeveloped countries, compromising the infrastructures of the countries they claim to be helping.[2] This became personal for me in 2005 when I received a Ford Foundation grant to teach Aesthetics and Theatre in New Delhi, and protests there delayed the formal grant offer so long that it became impractical to accept it. Also in 2005, UNESCO adopted a resolution in Paris "on the Protection and Promotion of the Diversity of Cultural Expressions,"[3] which was widely understood to be protecting the rest of the world from being colonized and plundered by American cultural interests and squashed by its influences. Again, this matter was close to me since, from 2004 until 2008, I lived in Asia[4] and professionally trained Korean, Vietnamese, Indian, Taiwanese, and Singaporean actors and directors of all levels, for periods lasting from two days to two years, with a range of mostly Western approaches to theatre practice.

All around Asia, I found that the response to American theatre training was inextricable from national and personal attitudes towards us politically, and I was there long enough to witness shifts in cultural attitudes occurring directly in response to political shifts. I saw, for example, actor training approaches falling in and out of favor with the change of a nation's president. Indeed, American actor training within America itself has had its political dimension from the outset. Like the eighteenth-century touring actors who either flaunted or hid their British identities once the colonial war for independence began, fledgling nineteenth-century training emphasized or de-emphasized its European model.[5] In the 1920s, American actor training came up against Russian training just as U.S.–Russian relations were about to enter decades of political tension. Louis Scheeder illuminates the role actor training played in "transform[ing] Russian theatrical practice into a symbol of American freedom and nationalism and elevat[ing] American acting into an international art form"[6]:

> Under Strasberg's guidance, Method acting became "a marker of cultural value to shore up the identity and purpose of the [American] national culture" during the Cold War. Strasberg took Stanislavsky's theories . . . and transformed them into "a sign of patriotism rather than communism." . . . Strasberg likewise engineered a complicated maneuver whereby he posited that New York, if not the Studio itself, was the center of the postwar theatrical landscape . . . As the Truman Doctrine proclaimed American dominance over former European spheres of influence, the Method overshadowed European styles of performance.[7]

This passage points to a related political reality, which is that Communist China embraced Stanislavsky precisely because of its friendship with Communist Russia. That is, while America was transforming Stanislavsky's theories to "shore up" U.S. nationalism, China was doing the opposite—using Stanislavsky's own work to corroborate Communist ideals. Scholar Sy Ren Quah writes:

> In 1953, Stanislavsky's system was officially canonized during a forum organized by the National Association of Drama Workers. It was pronounced that the system accords with the "performance science of

materialistic dialectics" and is the "performance theory of realism." After that, Soviet specialists of Stanislavsky's system of directing and acting were invited to deliver speeches, conduct workshops, and assist in the staging of performances. Books by and on Stanislavsky were also in line for publication. The escalation of the reception of Stanislavsky was the result of amity between China and the Soviet Union . . . [8]

As a result, while American Method may have at one time, as Louis Scheeder put it, "overshadowed European styles of performance" somewhere, it has been of little interest in China, which prides itself on knowing Stanislavsky's work more directly from the master himself than Europe— and especially America—does. The many theatre people I lived and worked with in Asia certainly took it for granted that the Chinese understanding of Stanislavsky was superior to the Western. We can hear this perspective expressed in the context of Xu Xiaozhong's work.[9] Xu, a prominent director and honorary president of Beijing's Central Academy of Drama, was one of the first Chinese directors trained in Russia as part of the Communist project; the new People's Republic of China, proclaimed in 1949, sent Xu to the Lunacharsky Institute of Theatrical Art from 1955 to 1960[10]:

Xu may be regarded as exemplary of the [Communist Party's] concept of the nature and purpose of theatre. Xu had and continues to have a strong commitment to the founding ideals of the People's Republic of China, which can be taken as informing his life-long commitment to Stanislavskianism in the theatre. (Stanislavski as studied in Russia and China in the 1950s is not the same cultural quantity as the Stanislavski method as promulgated in America by Richard Boleslavski and his disciples.) The translator of Russian drama and scholar of Russian theatre, Tong Daoming, has claimed: "The former USSR and China must be the only two countries among those that have strong traditions in drama, to have carried out Stanislavski's method comprehensively."[11]

A 1990 trip to Moscow gave me an experience of the mutual interest and feeling of natural kinship between the theatres of Russia and Asia overall. When I received a visit from members of an independent theatre company in Moscow, the actors quickly moved our extended conversation from polite questions about U.S. theatre training to focus almost entirely on the theatre I had seen while working in Japan from 1979 to 1981. Coincidentally, it was in that same time period that political events in South Korea unfolded which not only turned the South Koreans' cultural interests towards Russia, its Republics, and Europe as a whole, but also turned them emphatically away from the United States.

Contemporary South Korea is haunted by the events of May 1980, when protests against the new Korean military government erupted in a 10-day massacre of civilians—many of them students—in the southern city of

Kwangju. Still today, Kwangju is the subtext of much theatre and other cultural work. The number of deaths in the uprising has been estimated at 200 by the government, and at 2,000 by other witnesses. During the escalation of tensions, the South Koreans widely believed the United States was poised to intervene on the protestors' behalf, and were dumbfounded when no help came to prevent or stop the killing. Dr. Kim Yun-Cheol wrote a sobering explanation of how this betrayal played out in South Korean actor training:

> Anti-American sentiment soared after the Kwangju massacre. Although there were many other factors that turned Korean students to Europe for their theatre education and training, this episode of political aloofness on the part of the American government was a crucial one. The fantasies the Korean people had about the U.S. died—their illusions about its commitment to justice and democracy. From that time on, more Korean students chose Russia and other European countries for their education and training in theatre arts and studies, rather then the U.S., which up to that time had been by far "the" favored country for such studies.
>
> Another important reason for this new trend was that the Koreans began to be introduced to more European theatre performances. They discovered that American theatre was not the only Western theatre, and that European expressions of reality were more "true-to-life" than those of their American counterparts. Consequently, today Korean universities recruit both Korean and non-Korean theatre educators more from Europe than from America.[12]

One could see this shift precisely reflected in the School of Drama where Dr. Kim and I taught in Korea: in the acting department, along with longtime, U.S.-trained Korean teachers, there were also pivotal Korean teachers who had been trained in Spain and France, and the newest faculty acting teacher had trained in Russia. At the end of my two-year visiting professorship, the position that had been held by Americans for the ten years the school had been open, was re-configured for one year to accommodate hiring from countries such as Mongolia and Greece, and was then phased out.

On a daily basis the anti-Americanism born of the Kwangju disaster was offset by good feelings left over from our Korean War alliance—but I also faced a newer Korean anti-Americanism that surfaced before my eyes, and in my classrooms. During my stay in Japan, there had been subtle but ever-present reminders that America and Japan had been enemies in World War II; in my first year in Korea, though, I was continually struck by how different it felt to be where the Korean War had left most Koreans feeling warmly towards Americans. At work, there was a general but palpable sense that students and colleagues personally knew, or knew of, someone who had been aided by an American soldier in the war years. My acting students were well-disposed towards having an American teacher, and my first meeting with them felt more like a reunion than an introduction. But they were also somewhat more timid and overly-respectful than one might hope for in an acting class.

Two things happened during my stay, from 2004 to 2006, so that the end was different from the beginning. First, in the popular press, Koreans began to question, with gathering intensity, the motives of the U.S. in fighting Communist aggression on Korean soil from 1950 to 1953. With this in the news, my students in the classroom got braver about asking me to explain things I said, and more expressive in their acting, as if they were released from having to feel grateful, and could now get down to the business of art. Second, when rumors of North Korean nuclear activity began to fly in 2005 and 2006, South Korea's responses centered on concessions and aid. America's hostile stance and talk of sanctions were widely seen to be boorish, and to work against the delicate balances that North and South Korea, Japan, China, and Russia maintain without American interference. With American approval less and less sought after in the national news, my students became visibly feistier during our lessons; they looked less for my approval, and approached the material more independently, freely, and creatively.[13]

Learning to negotiate the sensitivities of each country—even as they changed in different parts of the country and population—became a crucial skill to have as an American training actors and directors overseas. In Asia, where I spent most of my overseas teaching time, countries with volatile histories live close together and, as when paying calls to families that have complicated relationships, it behooves a visitor to tread lightly. As a teacher dealing with dramatic texts for the actor and director, it takes practice to avoid sensitive areas. Sometimes it is not possible to avoid them, especially since each faculty colleague and each student will also have his own concerns. Even the most simplified look at how the countries are intertwined alerts us that choosing classroom materials is not going to be a simple matter: India, Hong Kong, and Singapore were colonized by the British, so work with Shakespeare texts, for example, has the potential of being fraught with political considerations; Singapore, Korea, China, and Taiwan have all been occupied by the Japanese, so work with the Japanese Kabuki and Noh, which are at least familiar to many Westerners, are problematic, or at least involve responses with dimensions sure to surprise outsiders; Japan was occupied by the U.S. and other allied forces (some say the U.S. military in Okinawa constitutes an ongoing occupation) and remains at odds with Russia over ownership of Sakhalin Island and islands nearby, so the entire Western canon—which tends to claim Eastern European works as its own in cultural matters—is sometimes resented and often ignored. Add to these complexities all their intricate relations with the many countries nearby, with countries in other parts of the world (as one example, Taiwan has been occupied by the Dutch and the French at different times), and the internal relations the governments have with their indigenous populations, some of whose members may be in your classroom. Readers who have traveled widely, or who pore over the international pages of the newspaper, will surely recognize at least some of these dynamics; in the arts, editors of international essay collections, curators of international art shows, and selection committees for international theatre festivals all confront these issues as a matter of course. But it is a still-emerging consequence of globalization that these politics and national histories play such an active role in the concrete realities of an American offering sustained training for actors overseas.

AMERICAN ACTOR TRAINING AS SEEN FROM OVERSEAS

One serious obstacle for an American who is training actors overseas is the way students in foreign countries see America in general and American actors in particular. My discussion here focuses on the more developed countries of Asia, but it is easy to provide examples from almost anywhere in the world. On television, newscasters routinely read reports on the U.S. with barely-relevant violent photographs displayed behind their heads: soldiers with machine guns for no apparent reason; drug dealers in handcuffs; police with piles of recovered weapons.[14] U.S. gangs, cults, protests, prisons, slums, obesity—all are featured in the media, and rival warped U.S. media portrayals of their own countries. For example, Americans are used to hearing stories on banned Chinese toys; Asians are just as used to hearing about bans on U.S. rice, beef, pharmaceuticals, baby formula, and more—bans which tend to be underreported for U.S. citizens, but which are synonymous with "America" in an Asian theatre student's mind.[15]

Without any real-life context to mitigate these impressions, for students who are in training, the broader American entertainment industry seems only to corroborate them. Inexplicably, young American women, who sing on television uncovered like the poorest prostitutes in the world, are actually millionaires; young men showing their underwear and rapping strings of profanity are wearing diamonds.[16] U.S. pop idols with drug problems are embraced by the public, who support the performers as they go in and out of rehab by buying their music and magazines with stories on their progress. This last has particular impact, since young people around Asia have seen the official Japanese response to a rock band member's drug arrest: their albums were pulled from music store shelves, their T.V. theme songs for *anime*—popular animated versions of graphic novels—were quickly replaced with another group's music; the troubled band member disappeared from the group.[17]

Asian theatre students know "American actors" *per se* not from theatre or film, but largely from the advertisements that feature movie stars. Full spreads in magazines and enormous pictures on the sides of buses and on animated billboards show American actors selling watches, perfume, food, cars, and the like: oversized, heavily-airbrushed images of Ben Affleck, Jennifer Aniston, Tom Cruise, Leonardo DiCaprio, Jodie Foster, Nicole Kidman, Arnold Schwarzenegger, John Travolta, and many others hover over public spaces of every description.[18] Hilary Kramer reports:

> [Harrison] Ford and his fellow A-listers Brad Pitt, Meg Ryan and Demi Moore have all worked [in Japan] as highly paid celebrity endorsers for an array of foreign products ... Most Americans are completely unaware that their movie stars also moonlight as high-paid product pitchmen [and] go to great lengths to prevent their foreign commercial spots from ever being shown in the U.S. ... [S]imilar to corporate marketing titans, Hollywood stars and their agents are conscious of localizing their brands to suit foreign tastes; [t]hose tastes tend to portray stars in images that might make American moviegoers cringe ... What may be surprising is that despite antagonism toward America and its politics, American brands—both products and celebrity endorsers—continue to translate well in foreign markets.[19]

Movie houses, too, show American movies of the "action" and "slasher" varieties (not least because the dialogue can go without translation); in the absence of good American films and with limited chances to see our live theatre, it isn't easy for the overseas theatre student to imagine "American actor training" from these movies alone. I can't forget a narrow hallway in an underground train station, where the entire wall on my left—floor to ceiling—was covered with an enlarged movie poster of Harrison Ford pointing a gun vaguely in the direction of a small boy, while the entire wall on my right showed a movie poster of Catherine Zeta-Jones, with truly enormous breasts poised to emerge from her period costume. I have never understood more forcibly both the associations the rest of the world has with America—our repellent use of male violence for entertainment, and our unashamed use of the female body for commercial titillation—and the overseas acting student's confusion about American acting.

Acting students in Asia are, naturally, curious about acting students in America. In conservatories, universities, and institutes, they themselves typically train in curricula that require studies in both the traditional and Western arts. This means they move between study modes throughout the day: they will have classes for traditional dances and various forms of vocal performance, which have both defined teacher–student relationships and the expectation of lengthy study; they will also study with Asian teachers who are having various degrees of success adapting their Western training to Asian culture, and these will still have established teacher–student relationships, but less clarity about length of study. During training, their closest contact with their acting student counterparts in America will be through studying with their American teachers—and here they will be on unfamiliar ground, unsure of what the relationship should be or what the studies entail.

English-speaking teachers are likely to be short-term visitors in any case, brought to teach a specific "method" or "technique" the students may recognize from their reading. In this way, the students see the teachers in much the same commercial terms they see the movie actors: they are celebrities of the foreign teaching world, packaged with catch phrases and marketed with strategies, teaching a consumable product. Without any societal context, the students are hard-pressed to glean whether their American teacher might be "famous," or how, unlike their traditional arts, Western acting skills can be passed on in a fixed, brief time period. I felt it as a compliment when my B.F.A. and M.F.A. students started asking about the lineage of my work—the names and careers of my teachers and my teachers' teachers, back as far as I could go. To me, it meant they thought of me in terms closer to their own traditional teachers—not as an "American acting teacher" but simply as their teacher, who was giving them skills they could use to strengthen the theatres of their own nations, or of any other.

THE POLITICS OF AMERICAN THEATRE
TRAINING AS SEEN IN THE CLASSROOM

When I was invited to move my teaching from the U.S. to Asia in 2004, I had both academic and professional familiarity with the arguments surrounding globalization and cultural colonialism. Nevertheless, I was unprepared for the extent to which these matters intruded on the daily, practical work of teaching and directing theatre.

I knew before I went that classes with scene study would look different on many levels. Between 1979 and 1981, I became attached to an independent theatre group in Osaka, Japan, and was invited to watch and direct rehearsals, presumably from an American training perspective. I remember the tangle of issues that arose with these lively, dedicated actors while working even briefly on *Uncle Vanya*'s Act II scene between Astrov and Sonya. These "tangles" included whether the actors wanted to behave like Japanese or Russian people, whether an older man would allow a younger woman to sit in his presence, why the actress' Sonya talked in baby talk, why Sonya stopped poor Astrov from having his drink, whether Astrov had seen a ghost when he mentioned his patient's death and, unavoidably, whether their translations of Stanislavsky's writings from the Chinese were better than ours in English.[20] And these inquiries were preceded by a warm-up regimen of a distinctly military ilk, replete with actors in company uniforms and the group's director shouting commands.

Nevertheless, this prior experience notwithstanding, attitudinal surprises abounded during my recent years visiting American actor training upon Asia. At many institutions I taught in, the wildly gifted acting students believed doing well would reflect honor on their countries. It was as if every class were a day at the Olympics, for which each sportsman does what he does for his team and, ultimately, for his country. For the most part, the students were ferocious in their focus, and voracious for information in a way that made even the most intense American acting classroom, lacking overriding concerns, seem pale. In Korea, this made it especially poignant that the military loomed over so much of the students' lives: sustained work on a specific performance skill was interrupted when a student left for, or returned from, his required military duty; in response to yet another of North Korea's threats, occasionally the commuter trains were commandeered to move tanks; SWAT teams in full riot gear appeared in the popular theatre district; a military exercise was carried out around the university, with lovely young men in army fatigues standing around tanks with machine guns poised. I had unwittingly timed a 1980 visit to Seoul so that I arrived during a military coup, and had seen soldiers then, too, with what seemed like those same machine guns, held at the same angle.

Overall, to the extent that acting is an expression of culture, any dependence in this culture on American training concepts such as "acting truthfully" or "filling the space" or "public and private behavior" or "seeking conflict" was bound to cause confusion. The cultural equivalents were murky and the students' preoccupations were elsewhere. One contingent of B.F.A. students was adamant that nasal vocal resonance is only for white people because the bridges of their noses are high rather than flat; one student did a final exam in speech melody that featured a sound score for moving his bowels—performed with his female classmates looking on fondly, the way a mother sometimes smiles over her baby's dirty diaper. As a whole, all the theatre people I worked with appeared to be models of liberal open-mindedness, and seemed to share with me cultural coordinates that would allow American-inspired training to make a useful contribution to their theatres. So I was thrown for a loop when a student design show at a school in Korea displayed cartoons featuring Hitler, when a brilliant and gentle Indian director told me that Hitler "wasn't all black," and when a stylish, well-stocked arts bookstore in Taiwan featured blank notebooks with pictures of Hitler on the cover. A thoughtful, perceptive theatre critic visiting East Asia from non-Arab Iran told me placidly that all Arabs are cockroaches and should be stepped on. I knew it would take me a long time to understand the forces that shaped the perspectives suggested by all this—and in the meantime, studio exercises related to "action" or to text analysis often followed some astonishing trajectory.

While many an earnest U.S. theatre teacher may bring his or her favorite "acting exercises" or "intercultural theatre" workshop to Asia, the Elephant in the Room is the matter of translation, both oral and written. This is a difficult subject to broach in the moment, because Asians are often extremely sensitive about having studied English in school but still not being able to communicate in it (just as Americans so often find their "school French" useless in France), and even the suggestion that a translator is needed may embarrass them. Foreign visitors to Asia are not expected to speak the Asian languages, whereas Asian visitors to American institutions, as well as hosts in non-English-speaking countries around the world, are nearly always expected to speak English. In Asia, a colleague's job may depend on his reputation as an English speaker, so it is no small matter if a natively English-speaking visitor visibly does not understand a word he says.

Since knowledge of spoken English is a matter of national pride in Asia, students and others who don't understand a visitor's English are often highly practiced at concealing the fact, and get their cues from elsewhere as to what to do—as anyone does who spends time in the company of people whose language they don't share. In theatre training, the result is that short-term visitors without translators often leave Asia never knowing that their workshop students, or members of their lecture audiences who were smiling and nodding encouragingly, were mainly in the dark. In worse cases, foreign visitors to Asia do know when their students or other audiences can't understand them, but proceed exactly as planned anyway, since the grant money has been received, or trips already otherwise paid for. In the case of workshops, I have seen what amounted to active collusion between foreign visitors and native speakers, both knowing that communication was not being achieved and coming to a silent agreement not to acknowledge it; it is to the students' benefit to be able to claim that they "attended" a workshop given by a foreign instructor, and to the instructor's benefit to have "taught" in a foreign country. Photos are taken, videos are shot and carefully edited, and enthusiastic follow-up reports are written on both sides. This is not to say that valuable, even life-changing, cultural exchange cannot or does not take place—but that cross-cultural projects will become richer when such distasteful opportunism is no longer able to thrive.[21]

Oral translators (also called interpreters) who are assigned to long- and short-term visitors are also human—meaning they won't want to interrupt you to say there is no translation for the words or concepts you are using, or that you've just offended someone, or vice versa. After some weeks of translating for one of my skeletal alignment classes without warning or preparation, one perky young lady told me, in charming arpeggios of giggles, that she had made up much of what she told my class, having had no clue what I was talking about; another conscientious translator confessed to having translated all my lessons on the individual cervical vertebrae using the word "neck," not wanting to alienate the students with formal medical terminology. Miscommunications such as these may seem innocuous at the time but can have real consequences for the students. In other cases, my in-class translators rendered something I said into their own languages, whereupon what seemed to me to be a neutral remark was met by the students with inexplicable outrage or hilarity; an excellent translator was understandably reluctant to translate for me a racist pun a student had made about the name of a classmate from an Asian country less developed than his own.[22]

The challenges surrounding the matter of translation are also significant in working with dramatic texts. In countries such as Korea or Taiwan, at different times I decided that my educational purpose was better served by working with texts from my students' culture, or from mine. Why was I teaching them their own dramatic literature? Why were they learning to perform Western plays? Why had they studied my language in school? Why hadn't I studied their language growing up? Could I now study their language for a few months, and then teach them dramatic literature in their own language? If I had studied their literature longer than they, did they still understand it better than I for having grown up in their culture? In the case of a Western text, did they have to understand it the same way I did, or was their own cultural perspective on it valid even if it would be unrecognizable to a Western audience member? Should our spatial senses jibe? These questions multiplied exponentially as we went deeper into the work.[23]

The theatre texts available in English had sometimes been selected for translation into an Asian language only because they seemed relatively easy rather than for any merit; a text originally in an Asian language might have been translated by being divided up among trepidatious graduate students with a range of English abilities who all did their best with their assigned sections and then stuck all the sections back together without having a native speaker check them, whether from lack of access or from shyness. If you are an American professor, the excellent people who hired you may themselves have published Asian-language translations of English-language theatre texts that contain fatal errors which, out of politeness, you can nevertheless not correct for your students' benefit. Because they are more accessible, minor English texts have often received more weight in the curriculum than is their due, and it is awkward either to risk embarrassing one's hosts by putting the text in correct perspective, or to seem to agree about the value of the texts. Many foreign English majors understand Steinbeck to be the pinnacle of English prose and—just as the huge gaps in English translations of foreign literatures skew our cultural views—have never heard the name of James Joyce, for example. Also related to the subject of texts, copyright laws are still handily disregarded in many Asian countries, so that your lecture or workshop may be transcribed, translated very approximately, and then published within days without crediting you—and you are unlikely ever to know.

To contain these problems, the texts for cross-cultural theatre projects tend to rely on limited vocabularies and simple grammatical structures, and to avoid altogether language that is idiomatic, poetic, or rare. The texts exclude historical, literary or topical references, and culture-specific humor. Bypassing the translation problems that accompany language-based plays, many projects attempt to create a performance style that averages out, or otherwise combines, a selection of disparate cultures,[24] and emphasizes movement, dance, rhythmic sound, projections, and music from indeterminate sources.[25] Conventional theatrical blocking is replaced by displays of choreographed martial arts, and dialogue is exchanged for chanting, overtone singing, and other non-linguistic vocal scores. While every sort of performance may have the potential to appeal to audiences and to enrich the history of the theatre, an important part of the theatre over the centuries has been text-based acting, and actor training is responsible for enabling actors to handle complex language and ideas.[26]

I asked my Ph.D. theory students and my M.F.A. and B.F.A. acting and directing students overseas to consider the futures they hoped for their national theatres, in light of these questions:

> What can theatre be in the global age? The "global age" means that people of different languages and cultures come into increased contact. How will they communicate?
>
> Historically, the theatre has already proposed various solutions to this problem. Pantomime, with its international appeal, has of course been with us for centuries. Some early Modernists, too, proposed a "language-less theatre" of nonsense, and poetry made up only of sounds. Closer to our time, we have seen the growth of physical theatre, visual theatre, performance art, and a return to re-enactment of rituals. While all of these may be striking, dynamic, challenging and moving, none of these is able to provide audiences with the deep play of ideas so characteristic of classical dramas in many parts of the world.
>
> So we must ask ourselves: Is the Theatre of Ideas doomed in this new world? Will we make our language and arguments superficial so we can be easily translated? What will happen to language-based thought in our increasingly visual world?[27]

Those readers here who have had, as I have, talented oral and written translators experienced in handling technical and poetic language as well as inter-personal relations, know that they—and the administrators committed to hiring them—are heroes of the inter-cultural actor training classroom and rehearsal hall. Overseas, the usefulness of all but the most short-term or superficial American actor training depends on them.

CONCLUSION

If American actor training is going to stay relevant to world theatre, American acting teachers abroad will need to be knowledgeable about matters far beyond the methods they teach. Along with the concerns raised previously, my current thinking gravitates towards the following questions and reflections:

How can we create a culture around teaching internationally that integrates the teacher's artistic and diplomatic roles? What assistance can informal networks offer? What mentoring or other resources can professional organizations provide, both at home and abroad, to orient U.S. theatre workers and teachers about the larger considerations inherent in doing creative work in a foreign country? Has the time come for universities to be responsible for producing graduate theatre students cultivated in matters of national cultural policy and cultural colonialism? It may seem obvious that an acting teacher's or director's work will be richer if it has a clear context, and yet so many work abroad without it.

Related to this, I hope we will make a conscious effort to combat the perception overseas that Americans are parochial and insensitive in cultural matters. Jane Alexander had to confront some of America's cultural missteps when she headed our National Endowment for the Arts in the 1990s. Both the Endowment and the State Department have pitifully small budgets for international programs, and that alone signals U.S. disinterest in other nations. Alexander wrote:

> I was taken to task more than once by the ambassadors or cultural ministers of other nations who rightly claimed that they imported . . . some theatre from the United States to their countries but we did not invite their artists in return. [Many artists] have had significant careers in Europe, Japan and elsewhere because of the government largesse of those countries, but the United States is not at all generous in return invitations. I am ashamed that the United States of America has no abiding interest in cultural exchange. Too many members of Congress don't even have a passport. They choose to believe that the United States is superior to all other countries and that we have nothing to learn from any of them.[28]

How are we to train actors overseas in a way that honors the political issues embedded in the teaching project, without getting waylaid by them? Are there countries where this would simply be impossible? Do poverty or war make foreign training impossible—or essential? Is it enough for teachers to make it an initial part of their classes to talk about cultural matters? In my experiences, it has been important to consider with my students the adjustments we would be making for the translator. Beyond these, the task of the overseas classroom mainly overlaps with that of an American one: to focus on the goals of training—that is, on the inquiry into the art and skills of acting. In my classrooms, our work is always blocked more by political correctness than by politics, and more by training jargon than by training. My students and I are always united when our common purpose is to make live theatre informed by past and current history, and grounded in practical skills.

Finally, teaching acting overseas brings new dimensions to the question: What is the place of a critical vocabulary in an artist's work life? The field of theatre has examples to show what happens when critical jargon controls a work, and when work is created to realize critical concepts. But these are abuses of criticism, and I have to think there are uses of criticism especially meaningful in the context of overseas theatre teaching and directing. Where there are aesthetic issues that revolve around racial and cultural sensitivities, artists have a heightened obligation to be able to articulate their positions along a critical spectrum. Whether it is Western theatre featuring Asian martial arts, or Asian theatre featuring Shakespeare's plays, it is no longer enough simply to say: It's interesting to me, or, We liked it that way. I propose that familiarizing acting students with even the basic concerns of theatre criticism—that is, integrating criticism into practical American actor training—can provide foreign and U.S. actors with a shared context, and a responsible set of communication tools, for making theatre on the world's stage.

Complex cultural matters will continue to become an ever more intrinsic subtext of worldwide theatre. American actor training needs to adapt to a global world that does not share its aesthetics or priorities. In our time, choosing an approach to acting—at home or abroad—is not a matter of preference, but of cultural politics.

NOTES

1. Not everyone would find my actor training "American." Mainstream training in America is typically associated with, for example, American Method, Spolin-inspired improvisation, or the work of foreigners such as Grotowski and Suzuki. My teaching, on the other hand, comes from my own broad training, experience, and interests. Over time, it has been called classical, avant-garde, interdisciplinary, historically-informed, and project-based. In any case, my approach changes with my students' needs. My teaching only became "American" actor training when I was an American training actors abroad.
2. For more on the World Social Forum and its India chapter, see "WSF Mumbai 2004 and the NGO phenomenon in India," Part II of "The World Social Forum and the Struggle against 'Globalisation,'" in *Economics and Politics of the World Social Forum*, No. 35 (September 2003), http://www.rupe-india.org/35/wsfmumbai.html.
3. For more, see "Convention on the Protection and Promotion of the Diversity of Cultural Expressions 2005," Paris (October 20, 2005), http://portal.unesco.org/en/ev.php-URL_ID=31038&URL_DO=DO_TOPIC&URL_SECTION=201.html.
4. Throughout this article, I refer to my living and teaching "in Asia." In discourse on Asia in many disciplines, each country is listed among "the more developed countries of Asia" or "the less developed countries of Asia." This article describes my experience teaching mostly, but not exclusively, in the more developed countries of Asia, where a few students in my classes were also from the less developed countries of Asia.

5. Arthur Bartow, ed., introduction to *Training of the American Actor* (New York: Theatre Communications Group, 2006), xvi–xx.

6. Louis Scheeder, "Strasberg's Method and the Ascendancy of American Acting." Ibid., 3.

7. Ibid., 6.

8. Sy Ren Quah, "Searching for Alternative Aesthetics" in *Gao Xingjian and Transcultural Chinese Theatre* (Honolulu, Hawaii: University of Hawaii Press, 2004), 191 ff. 1.

9. Asian names are in customary order throughout the article: family name first.

10. In thinking about communication between the Chinese and Eastern European theatres, it is interesting to note that Grotowski was also at the Lunacharsky Institute from 1955 to 1956, and visited China in 1962. See Theatre Profiles on the culture.pl site for Polish Culture, published online by Instytut Adama Mickiewicza, http://www.culture.pl/en/culture/artykuly/os_grotowski_jerzy.

11. See the "Shakespeare in Asia" website by the English Department at Stanford University, California: http://sia.stanford.edu/china/FILES/XU/XUINTRO/XUINTR2.HTM.

12. Received in a March 4, 2008 e-mail from Kim Yun-Cheol to the author, continuing a conversation begun in 2005. Dr. Kim is a professor in the School of Drama at the Korean National University of the Arts, where I was Visiting Professor from 2004 to 2006. He is editor of *The Korean Theatre Journal*, President of the International Association of Theatre Critics, and the author of nine books.

13. For in-depth investigation of these shifts, please see David I. Steinberg, ed., *Korean Attitudes toward the United States: Changing Dynamics* (Armonk, NY: M.E. Sharpe, 2005).

14. The impression young people have overseas that violence is the norm for Americans is exacerbated by the jokey names the U.S. uses for its military activities in the Middle East. Some examples: Operation Planet X, Operation Desert Scorpion, Operation All American Tiger, Operation Aloha, and Operation Centaur Rodeo all sound disturbingly like video games or comics. See more at http://www.globalsecurity.org/military/ops/iraq_ongoing_mil_ops.htm.

15. Such stories are widely circulated in Asia. See Geoffrey Lean, *The Independent* (27 August 2006), http://www.organicconsumers.org/articles/article_1844.cfm: "Japan immediately banned all US long-grain rice imports, whether or not accompanied by certification." See also Marla Cone, "U.S. Rules Allow the Sale of Products Others Ban," *Los Angeles Times* (October 8, 2006), online at http://www.commondreams.org/headlines06/1008–01.htm: "Some [U.S.] toys, nail polishes and other beauty products are made with plastic softeners and solvents called phthalates that the EU has banned as reproductive toxins. Several of U.S. agriculture's most popular herbicides and insecticides, including atrazine, endosulfan and aldicarb, are illegal or restricted to emergency uses in other countries. And a few electronic items, including Palm's Treo 650 smart phone and Apple's iSight camera, were pulled off shelves in Europe this summer because of lead components but are still sold here [in the U.S.]." See also Mark Stevenson, "World's Biggest Importers Ban U.S. Beef," Newsday.com (December 24, 2003), http://www.newsday.com/news/health/wire/sns-ap-mad-cow-world,0,2346980.story: " . . . Mexico, Japan and South Korea closed their borders to U.S. beef. The three largest importers of U.S. beef were among more than a dozen countries that halted imports—the source of billions of dollars of sales for U.S. cattlemen."

16. Actor Danny Hoch gives an accurate picture of the corrosive violence and profanity that America markets abroad, and the impressionable overseas youth populations that consume them. In his one-man show entitled *Jails, Hospitals & Hip-Hop*, one of Hoch's characters, Emcee Enuff, comes to terms with the money he's made outside the United States rapping graphic lines such as "Break a bitch pussy, bust a nigga brain": "I'm grateful to all the French people and the Japanese people, Italians, Swedish [and Indonesian] people that bought those records." Hoch's character describes the turning point he reached on a Japan tour that ended in a breakdown: "I'm standin' there in front of fifty thousand Japanese kids. I start singin' "Murder Every Day," right? They were singin' it with me! On some karaoke-type shit. They knew every word to that song. Every word! They was breakdancin' out there and everything. I said, this is some powerful shit . . . And one morning I just woke up shakin' in a cold sweat, all fucked up and depressed, and . . . rich." (The full text is in the July/August 1998 issue of *American Theatre Magazine*, pp. 29–44.) Many an overseas theatre student who struggles to make a simple sentence in English can recite, word-perfect, long sequences of rap lyrics on the most appalling aspects of U.S. ghetto life.

17. One of many accounts of this news story on the sensational Japanese band, L'Arc-En-Ciel ["The Rainbow"], can be found at http://larc-punk.blogspot.com/. A Japanese pop culture site posts this regarding the drug arrest: "I know that he's now regretted his mistakes . . . I'm a bit . . . irritated at the record company officials for making such a big deal out of such a small thing. Countless rock stars in America are caught with drugs and continue to have careers as long as they make an effort to rehabilitate (or at least try to pretend)." See http://www.furinkan.com/tomobiki/wagaku/artists/laruku.htm. I am grateful to Kiril Bolotnikov for this point.

18. *Time* magazine was already noting the relationship between movies and advertising as early as 1925: "The virtual control of foreign markets by U.S. cinema producers is bearing rich fruit in constantly increasing exports of U.S.-made films . . . U.S. films are said to be the most valuable advertising for U.S. goods that exist, particularly in South America. Makers of clothing in this country are said to be profiting heavily by the demand for their goods created by U.S. motion pictures exhibiting in South America and the Orient." See http://www.time.com/time/magazine/article/0,9171,728553,00.html.

19. Hilary Kramer, "Brand New Hollywood Star Power," FOXNews.com (Tuesday, August 26, 2003), file:///c:/Documents%20and%20Settings/hjkramer/My%20Documents/. Also see Christine Champagne, "Selling Out is Now In," *Adweek* (Feb. 6, 2006): "It also seems there isn't nearly as much work for American stars in Japan as there once was . . . 'In recent years, the Hollywood and U.S. celebrity has been challenged more by other celebrities,' says Jonathan Cranin, McCann's worldwide creative director, adding that Japan is relying more heavily on homegrown talent, as well as China and Korea, these days." At http://micechat.com/forums/entertainment-lounge/19978-big-stars-big-ad-bucks-adweek-february-6-2006-a.html.

20. Sharon Marie Carnicke tells a thought-provoking story about working across cultures with differing understandings of Stanislavsky's teachings; here, director Sam Tsikhotsky from the Moscow Art Theatre was directing a workshop production of Chekhov's *The Seagull* at the Actors Studio in New York: "While they began work assuming that because they were all grounded in Stanislavsky they shared the same values, they soon learned that this assumption was faulty." See Sharon Marie Carnicke, "Lee Strasberg's

Paradox of the Actor" in Alan Lovell and Peter Krämer, eds., *Screen Acting* (New York: Routledge, 1999), 82.

21. To gain more perspectives on issues that can arise in cross-cultural projects, it is useful to read about international theatre festivals. For example, international theatre scholar and profound cultural analyst, Dragan Klaic, writes: "Festival programming formulae show much crass opportunism (focus every year on another country in order to profit from the promotional drive of the respective government) and a tendency to creep into a highly specialized niche or float in a vague multidisciplinary framework. Real interdisciplinary density and conceptual coherence are quite rare. New media and digital creative platforms make use of festivals, as does a growing range of intellectual and social causes: literature, philosophy and science festivals; feminist, gay, exile, émigré festivals; urban and rural festivals; thematic festivals (e.g. 'The Body')." Dragan Klaic, "Festival," in Lexicon, *Performance Research*, 4, 11, 2006 (June 2007), 54–55. Online at http://www.efa-aef.eu/newpublic/upload/efadoc/11/D%20Klaic%20festivals%20Perf%20Research%202006.doc?-session=s:42F9438C0ed8804EA7mMq41CED11. Also see Clive Barker's penetrating article on international theatre exchanges: "To some extent the mutual expressions of appreciation [at festivals] become incestuous, and back-slapping replaces any other form of exchange." Here he describes watching a Papua New Guinea jungle performance in an Edinburgh church: "[It] was to experience a sense of numbed culture shock ... There was no shared context which would allow any meeting or meaningful exchange. In general, what works best in festivals or on prestige tours is either what is very close to the home-grown production style or some exotic beauty which can be appreciated visually, with little or no regard given to its content or cultural significance." At a symposium in Morocco: "I found myself leading a seminar on G.B. Shaw's *Pygmalion* for a class of thirty university students, only two of whom had ever seen any form of theatre which would be recognized as such in Europe." Clive Barker, "Intercultural Penetration and Exchange" in Patrice Pavis, ed., *The Intercultural Performance Reader* (London and New York: Routledge, 1996), 249–251.

22. I would like to thank the extraordinary translators who understood my thinking in one language and gave it words in another, making the language-bridge across which my life's work traveled to my students, from 2004 on. It is these full-time translators who made possible the sustained, complex, humor-filled, passionate and true communication in our classrooms: in Korea, Yoo Lim, M.F.A., director, writer and teacher who spent her early years in the U.S.; in Taiwan, Lin Yu-Chen, Ph.D. (A.B.D.), theatre scholar and performer, with education in the U.K. Crucial translation also came from Chiang Wei-Hua, M.A. Fine Arts, actress, dancer and teacher, with education in the U.S. For sensitive shorter-term translation for classes, workshops, interviews, deep thanks to: Chandradasan (Cochin City in Kerala, India), Tanabe Hiroyuki (Osaka, Japan), Yao Hai-Shin (Taipei, Taiwan). Vladimir Bolotnikov was the translator during the 1990 trip to Moscow. For an account of my experiences working through oral interpreters in the theatre, see Lissa Tyler Renaud, "The Voice Translator's Voice," in *The Moving Voice: The Integration of Voice and Movement Studies* issue of the Voice and Speech Review, ed. Rena Cook (San Diego, CA: University Readers Publisher), July 2009.

23. There is an expansive literature that methodically examines many issues touched on and implied by these questions. For powerful reading on cultural colonialism and intercultural theatre, see Rustom Bharucha, *The Politics of*

Cultural Practice: Thinking Through Theatre in an Age of Globalization (Hanover and London: Wesleyan University Press, 2000) and the essays collected by Pavis in *The Intercultural Performance Reader.*

24. For a systematic overview of theories and terminology related to intercultural theatre, see Patrice Pavis, introduction to "Towards a Theory of Interculturalism in Theatre?" in *The Intercultural Performance Reader* cited above, 1–21.

25. Indian director Chandradasan speaks to this "averaging out" of cultures that is endemic to international theatre projects: "The projects encouraged by [foreign] funds are mostly productions featuring fake physicality, characterized by a lot of wasted human effort, and with movement bordering on gymnastics and circus. Much of this activity holds only academic interest." See Chandradasan's chapter, *The Politics of Western Pedagogy in the Theatre of India*, in this volume. This is related to the problem of making theatre where the theatre-makers are cut off from subtle or idiomatic use of their respective languages.

26. For a deeper look into issues of translation for the theatre, see David Johnston, ed., *Stages of Translation* (Bath, England: Absolute Classics, 1996), and the Theatre and Translation issue of *Theatre Journal* (Baltimore, MD: Johns Hopkins University Press, October 2007).

27. Text from my program notes for "Scenes Without Speech: A Theatre for the Global Age," an evening of fourteen "language-less" scenes and short plays I collected from classical, new, Eastern and Western plays, directed by my M.F.A. Directing Group in the School of Theatre, Taipei National University of the Arts, Taiwan (June 2007).

28. See Jane Alexander's *Command Performance: An Actress in the Theatre of Politics* (Cambridge, MA: Da Capo Press, 2000), 125.

Part II

8 Beyond Race and Gender
Reframing Diversity in Actor-Training Programs

David Eulus Wiles

Diversity is both a buzzword and a byword in American higher education. As applied over the last four decades, it has helped to transform our
society in ways that are recognizable and, for all of the controversies surrounding the issue, in ways that are, in my opinion, profoundly good. The
colleges and universities that have pursued diversity have recognized and
taken seriously their role as transformative institutions. Coincidentally, it
is also primarily since the 1960s that college and university theatre departments have, in their BA, BFA, and MFA training programs, transformed
the training of theatre artists and administrators in ways that have had a
significant impact on both the quantity and quality of professional theatre
in the United States. In doing so, theatre departments have often been in
the vanguard when it comes to promoting and creating diversity in their
student populations and downstream, in the profession. Up to a point.

It is my contention that theatre programs that are dedicated in a significant way to training actors and that select their students from a pool of
applicants (as opposed to teaching anyone who is free to declare a theatre
major at the undergraduate level) have understood their commitment to
diversity in terms of race, ethnicity, nationality, and sexual orientation,
while at the same time continuing to use and validate the norms of the commercial world of theatre, film, and television when it comes to ways actors
are "supposed" to look and present themselves.

Actor-training programs that purport to train students for professional
careers tend generally to follow professional norms in choosing whom to
train based on the various categories of acting "types," such as ingénues,
juvenile leads, leading women, leading men, character actors, and so on.
This tendency can lead programs to favor one gender over another in decid-
ing what ratio of men and women to accept, and it can lead to a significant
anomaly in the admittance of students to colleges and universities: the consideration of potential students' physical appearance and style of personal
presentation as a major, even decisive, criterion for selection.

But should this be so? Should certain departments in colleges and universities, which on the whole are dedicated to innovation—the production, integration, and dissemination of knowledge, and the questioning

of orthodoxies—ever consider the physical appearance of an otherwise qualified student and include it in their criteria for admission? Should students, once admitted, be encouraged to alter their physical appearance or self-presentation (by losing or gaining weight, altering their speech, or having plastic surgery, for example) in order to meet the expectations of the postgraduate professional world? Should some potential students, those with physical abnormalities that significantly mark their appearance as something other than "mainstream," be excluded altogether? Should programs assign classroom work or cast plays based on industry standards, thereby reinforcing those standards even as colleagues in other disciplines criticize those standards and produce studies that demonstrate their destructive nature?

My thesis is based on the assumption that the primary purpose of training actors in colleges and universities should be consistent with the purposes of higher education generally: that offering an education within a particular discipline presupposes the importance of the discipline and of its study, but does not presuppose what students who receive an education focused in that discipline will do in their working lives. No one who wants to major in literature or creative writing has to promise to become a writer, critic, or teacher. No one has to promise to practice law to get into law school. But the emphasis placed on the marketability of a potential acting student's appearance—an emphasis that is, while not universal, common in selective actor-training programs—in effect exacts an implicit promise from potential students that they pursue a career as professional actors, and that they pursue their careers in markets that value physical appearance as much or more than skill. Ironically, training programs and teachers exact this tacit promise while knowing the likelihood that the students they train will spend their working lives as professional actors is incredibly small.

My view is that training in the arts, in theatre, and more specifically in acting, is intrinsically valuable to those students who successfully pursue such training and to the culture in which they live, regardless of the professional paths they eventually take. That training should be available to anyone who wants to pursue it and who meets those criteria for study, which are not dependent on appearance. That training should be available to students whose identity (as transgendered, for one example) or mode of self-presentation ("butch," "redneck," "street," "queen") is viewed either negatively or one-dimensionally in the professional marketplace. There is no justifiable reason in my view that actors shouldn't look like the society they perform in and represent, in all of its diversity. And there is no defensible excuse for colleges and universities to pursue or settle for less diversity, in the broadest sense of that term, in their actor-training programs than they do in any other discipline.

This chapter is grounded in my experience as a graduate acting student, a professional actor, and a teacher of acting at the graduate and undergraduate level over the last three decades. I don't claim to have definitive answers to the questions I raise but hope instead to pose what I think are a set of commonly unexamined questions rooted in an underlying set of assumptions about the purpose of acting training at the undergraduate and graduate level. I will discuss some widely followed practices for casting actors in the professional world that affect the selection of actors for training programs, and the cultural messages those practices send and perpetuate. I will describe the decision-making process as I have experienced it from different perspectives when it comes to selecting students for study, structuring acting classes, and casting plays. I will examine the degree to which those practices are so common as to go unquestioned even in the arena of higher education where we might be expected to find orthodoxies challenged. I will conclude with a discussion of models and strategies for change for those who may wish to examine their own practices, and who may expect resistance to those changes.

Two decades ago, I lived in New York while I pursued a career in acting. One of my many "survival" jobs involved working part-time as a paralegal at a prominent law firm that stood at the center of the fast-paced world of corporate mergers and takeovers. This firm operated on a twenty-four hour basis, Thanksgiving, Christmas, and New Year's included. There were over two hundred part-time paralegals and proofreaders, along with word processors, telephone receptionists, copy machine operators, and the like. Many of those who worked part-time were, like me, actors. Others worked in the full range of the arts and humanities as practitioners, aspirants, and students.

I worked at this firm during the time the television series *L.A. Law* was on the air. The law firm represented in that series wasn't much like the firm that employed me. It was smaller and had a wider range of legal practices that allowed for its multiple story lines, and the lawyers on TV did not appear to work one hundred-hour weeks. Most of all, they looked fabulous. They looked of course like what they were, actors; chosen for their visual appeal as much as their acting skills; chosen to make watching the program as attractive and pleasurable an experience as possible; chosen to bring the largest possible audience to the program and to the messages of its advertisers. That is, after all, commercial television's purpose.

There were, however, variations on the type. One lead actor was bald, and we were left to understand that he was also a sexless stuffed shirt. Another actor was short and middle-aged. His relationship with a taller and more conventionally attractive woman was considered unlikely (even a source of comedy) because of his appearance. There was a character actor, a bit heavy and in conventional terms plain if not unattractive, who played an employee with mild retardation who was also sexless. There was a secretary played by an actress whose looks lacked the sexual firepower of the women lawyers on the show, all of whom were involved at various points in romantic story lines. When a story line emerged in which her character had a relationship with her womanizing and attractive boss, the story revolved around the idea that men who looked like him did not become involved with women who looked like her.

On balance, the degree to which characters on this show had personal lives that contained a sexual component was determined by the degree to which those characters were played by actors cast for their sexual desirability to a broad audience. Sexually attractive characters were always in or between relationships. Less attractive characters had their looks accounted for in the story line when and if they became involved, whether with each other, or with one of the "pretty" people.

It is disingenuous, of course, to compare real workplaces to the fictional ones on TV. But it was nonetheless striking to work in a firm that employed over five hundred lawyers and several dozen actors and to notice how much the actor/paralegal/proofreaders look liked actors and how much the lawyers . . . didn't. Among the lawyers and among the actors in our real lives, physical appearance offered no clue as to the nature of our characters as human beings, our competence in our jobs, nor success or a lack of it in our romantic lives. And one could not have predicted who among the firm's attorneys, full-time staff, and part-timers were not actors simply by looking at them.

One could have known a great deal, however, about the professional prospects of those of us who were actors—talent, training, and business acumen aside—by noting how we looked. Many of us had already trained formally at the undergraduate and/or graduate level. Others aspired to and would go on to some of the top graduate conservatories in the country. But while there were those among us who would go on to play lawyers (or in some cases, become lawyers), we collectively looked nothing like those who were. We didn't because the range of looks among the lawyers at the law firm was, while not as broad as the range of looks among the population of New York City at large, much broader than the range of looks among the actors. The actors could almost all be broken down by the categories found in the *Players' Guide*, in which many of our pictures appeared. It mattered little that there were those among us who had trained at some of the top colleges and universities in the country, places where life-changing areas of new knowledge were being opened up in the physical sciences, where groundbreaking research was being done in psychology, and where old orthodoxies in the humanities were being overturned as new information was unearthed and new theories of analysis and interpretation were created and fought over. We had all come from actor-training programs that prided themselves on their "professionalism" and modeled almost everything they did, from the way they selected actors, to the ways they trained them, on models imported from professional theatre, television, and film—from "Show Business!"

In some ways this isn't surprising. Human beings were creating theatre long before theatre became a topic of study in the academy, and actors were (and are) trained in apprenticeships and by teachers in professional studios long before the rise of BA, BFA, and MFA degree programs. Indeed most of the theories and techniques that dominate modern acting training in colleges and universities were devised in working theatres and professional studios as they developed their particular aesthetic visions and discovered ways of working that enabled them to realize their creative goals.

There have also been innovations in approaches to actor training that have originated in higher education since the rise and proliferation of academic actor-training programs. People who shift back and forth between professional and academic practice, or engage in both, have devised some. Other innovations have arisen from the application of knowledge from other disciplines (psychology and physiology, for example), and the application of pedagogical theories that come from educational research. So while college and university training programs in acting began by adopting techniques from the profession, they have for some time now contributed new techniques and new knowledge that flow the other way and inform the profession. It is in the selection of students for training, and the training of students (including the self-selected students who populate most BA programs, take undergrad acting classes, and appear in campus productions), that a deeply problematic set of practices concerned with physical appearance and self-presentation—imported into the academy from the profession—have taken root and continue to dominate decision making.

Imagine that a school is considering the possibility of starting an actor-training program. When asked by administrators for a detailed look at how the program will select its students, the faculty says that decisions will be based primarily on the quality of student auditions. If asked whether or not those auditions will be "blind," as they are for some instrumental music programs, the administrators are of course told that actor auditions cannot be blind because acting involves physical, not merely vocal, performance.

When asked what qualities the program will look for in the students it selects, imagine the faculty members describing the qualities that they think constitute a "talent" for acting. They also include those abilities that make someone a suitable student beyond the issue of talent, an aptitude for the intellectual demands the program makes, for example, and the likelihood that a potential student has the maturity and psychological flexibility necessary for such an intimate and emotionally challenging thing as actor training.

Somewhere along the way, they mention the qualities that make it likely a student will succeed professionally. Asked what those are, the faculty is likely to mention physical appearance in some way or other and to do so without regarding that category as anything other than obvious and not at all problematic. They tell the administrators that since they will be preparing their students to compete in what is perhaps the most competitive job market there is, they must select for training students who have some chance of professional success. They note that the industry places a very high value on physical appearance and self-presentation, and that it emphasizes these things far more in the case of women than in that of men.

When asked whether they will adhere to any and all legal provisions regarding discrimination, they answer in the affirmative and are surprised when the administrators wonder how they can do so considering the range of things that laws against discrimination make it illegal for them to consider? How can they, for example, justify taking more men than women as some programs have and do? When the faculty points out that the classical canon contains many more roles for men than women and that many classically oriented programs have traditionally accepted more male than female actors, the administrators point out that traditionally more men play college sports than women but Title IX must be enforced all the same. When the faculty is asked about foreign and minority students and volunteer that foreign accents or culturally specific English accents may pose a problem, they are told that the institution's commitment to diversity and perhaps to civil rights law must override those concerns.

Then there is the issue of students with disabilities. The faculty will in all likelihood point to the fact that what they want to establish is a professional or preprofessional training program, and that they should no more be expected to accept students who can't meet some of the demands for professional success than any other program should. That might of course lead to the most uncomfortable conversation of all, the one in which the faculty is asked to justify the expenditure of scarce resources to build and run a program that prepares its graduates for a profession in which the unemployment rate is, they hear, 90%. If you are one of the faculty members involved, you think but don't say, "wrong, it's ninety-five." And if you're lucky, the meeting ends without a final decision on your funding. If you're not so lucky, you may be asked why your institution should risk violating its own standards on diversity, and risk violating local, state, and federal laws so that every now and then a successful graduate shines a bit of national light on the department and the school by appearing in a television series, feature film, or Broadway play.

It's possible that the most vexing series of questions faced by a department faculty proposing an actor-training program would come from colleagues in other departments who might want to know how preparing actors for a profession that doesn't seem to need or want them serves the institution's educational mission. The legal profession may need university law schools to educate attorneys and medicine needs doctors. The humanities need scholars, education needs teachers, industry and basic research need engineers and scientists, and the society as a whole needs educated citizens who can read, write, think, and communicate effectively. But why does the entertainment industry need college- and university-trained actors as opposed to those who come to them from stand-alone conservatories, professional studios, and private teachers?

I would suggest that the only defensible justification for an acting training program that is consistent with the various missions of higher education is that actors are artists and that the study of the arts and the training of artists are as important to the culture and to the academy as the study of the rest of the humanities. But if that is the justification put forth, then the selection of students for study should be intellectually and ethically consistent with the criteria used by every other discipline on campus.

Shortly after I started my first teaching job, a colleague enthusiastically mentioned having seen a former graduate acting student on a national television commercial. At that point in my teaching and professional career I thought, "sure, okay," but wouldn't it be better if the student had appeared on a TV series, or in a Broadway play? I believed then that the professional success our students might have performing in "legitimate" venues justified teaching acting on a college campus but that making a big deal about a commercial was, in a sense, trivializing our mission. I did not realize at the time that there were administrators in my institution and no doubt faculty members as well, who wondered why the school was spending money on a graduate program at all, a program that, for the most part brought in students from out of state who, after graduation, left the state to enter a profession that few of them would ever thrive in and most would eventually leave. Why, in other words, was public money that might support the education of students who would contribute to the cultural and economic development of the state and region going to prepare other students for an uncertain life in the entertainment industry?

When, after the "dot-com" bust, the state experienced budget shortfalls and the university went through a period of belt tightening, the need to defend our budget became real. It was at that point we realized that, like it or not, we could not defend the portion of our budget that went to our MFA programs in acting, directing, and design by saying that it was important for the nation's cultural life that we do what Yale, NYU, and the many other graduate professional training programs ranked above ours were doing.

When we decided that we had better look at what we were doing for the state, two things happened. First, we began to value something that we had always known: a significant number of our MFA graduates had in fact never left the state. They were teaching in secondary schools in a field—theatre—that the state education department had declared a "critical need." They were teaching at other colleges and universities in the state. They were staffing and/or performing in some of the small professional theatres in various parts of the state as well. Some had entered other professions but served on theatre boards, or simply gave money to the arts, including to our program.

These were students who had formerly been criticized for not having the talent or the ambition to strike out for Chicago, New York, or LA, or had done so and returned. They included people who were regarded as talented

but who instead had "settled" for the relative safety and stability of corporate and family life. They included people who were, for a variety of physical reasons, simply not "castable" in the rough-and-tumble of professional
life because they didn't fit easily into the range of commercial types that
theatre, television, and film find acceptable.

We had recruited some of them for our program because they were willing to enroll while our more commercial-looking "first choices" went elsewhere. Once we had begun to train them, we worried about their looks
and wondered where they would fit in professionally or if they ever would.
(The students we had worried about were, more often than not women, for
whom the range of acceptable "looks" is of course much narrower.) But
in a fight for scarce resources, the graduate students who had stayed or
returned to the state became our reason for being. They became the shin-
ing examples of why the public funds we spent on stipends, tuition forgive-
ness, internships, and professional level production values were being spent
wisely and well.

Later we began to host high school drama competitions on our campus, sometimes featuring productions directed by our former students,
and to offer workshops in schools, as well as in classes taught by some of
our graduates. We made it known that we welcomed high school students
from the state into our BA program (we discovered that many high school
drama teachers in the state had been telling their students not to attend
our school because our graduate program made it certain that they would
never get to act in main stage productions), and provided opportunities
for them to participate in substantial ways in our production program
alongside the working professionals on our faculty and the professional
guests we brought in. We increased the number of undergraduate majors
in our program in part as a result of these efforts, among them students
who sometimes reminded us that we'd first met them when they performed
on one of our stages in a competition, or when we had come to their high
schools to teach workshops. Our service to the cultural and educational
life of our state moved from background to foreground and we spoke of
our graduate program as a central part of that service. We did so because
in lean times the abstract concepts those of us in the arts often use to
defend our share of the resources need to be spoken of in terms of their
undeniably practical value, so that those providing the funds understand
the effects on the ground of what they're paying for. Nonetheless, during
my time there we never quite came around to the conclusion that the work
we were doing in our graduate program did not need validation from the
entertainment industry. While we understood that the theatre we produced had immediate local value as art to those who made it and saw it,
and while we understood that many of our graduates would become educators and artistic leaders in the state, we reserved our deepest praise for,
and took our deepest pride in, the few who made it to the national stage.
And we continued to make our first offers to those who "looked" like

they could. We never came around to recruiting and admitting students on a "looks-blind" basis.

It is not enough to rest an argument for "looks-blind" criteria solely on the grounds that students may contribute to the local and regional cultures where they are trained, or to which they move or return after training. Among the principle ways that colleges and universities contribute to the larger society and that individual disciplines contribute to their fields, are the ways by which status quos are challenged, innovative approaches to old problems are developed, and new knowledge is born. While innovations in the pedagogy of acting training (and other areas of the performing arts) and new creative methods have come from the academy (along with new critical theories), actor-training programs have, in my experience, done little if anything to reexamine, much less challenge, the appearance standards established and maintained by the industry.

Those of us who train actors on college campuses work with colleagues in other disciplines who study the deleterious effects of commercialized standards of physical appearance on the identities and self-perceptions of, among other people, our students. Some of the students who take their classes come to our productions and see reinforced on our stages the standards they've studied and critiqued. Some of their students are our students who take our classes and/or audition for plays and are "typed" sometimes even in the scenes they are assigned in class and cast or not cast in productions because they do or don't "look the part." The words "she doesn't look like a Juliet" should never be spoken as if they are self-evidently true by anyone claiming to be intellectually astute enough to teach college, but they are spoken in theatre departments including the ones I've worked in and far too often they've been spoken by me. And I had a colleague say once that he tried to give the role that carried the author's message to an attractive actor on the theory that the audience would be more likely to accept it.

It is reasonable to suppose that all of us who create theatre believe in its power to affect the lives of those who make it and witness it. If we believe in theatre's power then we must also be aware of the power of the intentional and unintentional messages we send in choosing whom to train, and whom to present to our audiences. When we cast our students according to industry stereotypes, we say a great deal to our audiences and our students about who we believe is good or evil and who deserves or does not deserve love, trust, respect, or compassion. Industry casting norms involve "pointing" us using the visual cues (including casting) evident towards certain ways of seeing. We know that music, lighting, design, and staging in theatre—aided by cinematography in television and film—are designed (usually) to move us towards certain interpretive conclusions. We know that this is true of casting as well. But I have never encountered a theoretical critique of student selection and casting practices that addressed the impact of those practices on campus audiences and the department's own students. While I've certainly heard colleagues lament, sometimes bitterly, the absurd standards the mass media has for what constitutes acceptable physical appearance, particularly for women, those laments have the quality of complaints about the weather; there is nothing to be done, that's just the way things are.

What is to be done? There are several factors to consider since the student–actors we train come to us from a wide variety of sources. Up to this point in my career, undergraduate students have self-selected for the BA programs I've taught in, at least initially. They've chosen to take acting classes and have registered for them. They've been theatre majors sometimes, but more often not. My approach to teaching emphasizes the communication, concentration, and observational and physical tools that actors need so that those students whose exposure to acting ends at acting class get something to transfer to other areas of their lives where the ability to present themselves and communicate publicly (to "perform") is important.

The graduate students I worked with when I taught in a professional training program were selected in nationwide auditions or from among students who specifically sought out that program. They were (for the most part) intending to pursue professional careers, and the majority intended to locate themselves in the markets that gave them the best chance to make a living after graduation. How might training and casting in nonselective BA programs be improved by ignoring or aggressively challenging the entertainment industry's stereotyping standards? And how might selective actor-training programs engage the issues I have raised?

For a long time, I have assigned and cast the scenes that the students in my classes perform. I assign plays and scenes because I focus on text analysis in all the levels I teach, and it helps if I am familiar with the plays and scenes that students are working on. I have also found myself exposing at least some of my students to the first plays they have ever read, and I want to use works that meet my standards for quality and authorial, dramaturgical, and linguistic diversity. I cast the scenes because it avoids the depressing and pedagogically damaging scramble that I've seen and been subjected to in acting classes where everyone wants to work with certain people and no one wants to work with others.

Until recently I cast the scenes according to which scenes might be fun, interesting, or emotionally resonant for particular students. I also paid attention to "type." In a Shakespeare class I might choose the most attractive-looking students for Romeo and Juliet. In a condescending fit of "generosity" I might have cast the student least likely to play either role so that he or she could be seen as "beautiful," in my class at least. In such cases my good intentions were no better than casting to type since my casting strategy was sometimes seen through and remarked on by the students involved and sometimes by their classmates.

In the last couple of years I've left it to my students to choose their own roles within a scene if I have partnered two women or two men. Sometimes they cast themselves to type. The more attractive of the two women (in their opinion, not mine) plays Juliet for example, the other the Nurse.

The "tougher" looking man plays Lee in Shepard's *True West*. Sometimes they will cast themselves against type, and say as much when I ask them how they chose their roles. At other times, it is other factors unrelated (at least consciously) to physical appearance that determine which roles they choose—a feeling about the different dilemmas the characters face perhaps, or personal experiences that the play recalls, or the words a character speaks.

Lately, in an effort to avoid even unconscious typecasting, by my students or by myself, I've asked my students about their interests, academic and otherwise, and attempted to partner them based on their shared interests in scenes from plays that hinge on those interests in some way (an English major and a premed student in Edson's *Wit* is one example). This is the best approach I've found so far to avoid taking physical appearance into account in my acting classes.

The problem is different when it comes to casting plays. In the nonselective BA programs I've taught in, the actors who audition self-select to do so. Even here, typing enters in because some students will only audition for the roles they themselves think they'll be cast for, based on the models they have internalized from mass media, from secondary school, or from the plays they have already been cast in or seen. I've encountered students from my classes who I hoped would audition for a production but who had already decided that they would never be cast because they didn't fit the mold for any of the roles or, in some cases, didn't believe that anyone who looked like them would ever be cast in any role. I've recommended to colleagues student–actors who were talented but were not cast because their physical appearance was thought to be either entirely unsuitable or too difficult to alter sufficiently with costume and makeup.

Were we simply to rule out physical appearance as a selection criterion when it comes to recruiting, accepting, and casting students at the college and university level, some things would change, but I question how many and how much. Students who are interested in acting often "know the score" long before they come to us for training. They know what they look like. They often believe they know what others think of their looks, and where they stand in the pecking order. If they have mistaken notions of how others will generally judge them, those notions tend to run to the negative (by which I mean they perceive themselves further from the media standard than they actually are). They often have all but unshakable personal attitudes towards their appearance, and those attitudes are likely to run to the negative as well. This seems to be especially true for women.

In my opinion, were we to rule out physical appearance as a selection criterion in recruiting, accepting, and casting students, our choices would be fairer and much more like the choices our colleagues in other departments make when choosing which students to educate. We would be less likely to send unintended messages and less likely to reinforce commercial stereotypes. We would implicitly critique, resist, and undermine that stereotyping. But in this essentially passive model, where we do nothing to change the pool of possible students, our resistance will go only as far as self-selection by our students will allow. If we genuinely want to examine, critique, resist, and overturn the problematic assumptions that govern the profession of acting within the academy, and perhaps challenge them outside of it, we will have to do it affirmatively.

I once studied with an acting teacher who said that everything the audience sees and hears onstage is part of the play, and is therefore part of the story the play tells the audience. Working from that perspective, casting is storytelling. Who is worthy of love? Who is virtuous, malevolent, ambitious, tyrannical, violent, dishonest, honorable, sluttish, vengeful, or vain? Whom should we root for, root against, laugh with, or laugh at? Typecasting in the classic sense has an answer to all of these questions, so much so that it is sometimes a surprise to see an actor one has always seen play villains, play a hero or a love interest.

In daily life of course, looks give no clue to character. Someone with the looks of a "leading man" can be a serial killer. A short and heavyset man or woman can be a genius and a leader. And anyone can be the object and recipient of love. When we select students who fit commercial models of types, or when we cast them that way even in nonselective BA programs, we reinforce the fantasies of commercial fiction and undercut what we know about the real world and realism in drama. In reinforcing fictional conventions, we fail to use theatre as a means of attempting to carry on an honest conversation about our culture.

An affirmative attempt to avoid or subvert commercial stereotypes requires that we examine our selection of students and our casting choices with an eye towards challenging the expectations of students and audiences, and present them with stories in which the storytellers look much more like them in all their variety. There is no reason not to cast the actor whose looks we normally associate with low comedy as Hamlet, assuming he (or she—yet another issue) has the ability to play the role. There is no reason not to cast the woman who might more typically play the Nurse in *Romeo and Juliet* as Juliet, as I have recently done, particularly if her verse speaking is among the best in the company.

This kind of approach should be undertaken consciously with respect to the range of diversity it is possible to find on a college campus. There are no constraints contained in the text of Chekhov's *The Three Sisters*, for example, that forbid casting one of the sisters with an actor who is genuinely wheelchair bound or whose movement has been altered from the norm since birth or by injury. There is no reason at all why the woman who is over six feet tall and/or by conventional standards overweight can't play Rosalind in *As You Like It* and several reasons why she should. And there are no valid reasons for not selecting and training students who fit these and a wide range of other descriptions, apart from our insistence that we are trying to train all of our students for a profession that we know lacks employment for most of them regardless of talent or looks.

There is, I would suggest, a greater benefit that might accrue to college and university programs that adopted such an approach to selecting students for training, and actively pursued a greater diversity of appearance in casting. We might join the conversations already taking place in other departments on our campuses about cultural stereotyping and its nature, roots, and consequences. We have a great deal of experience with the stereotyping of appearance and a great deal to say about it from our experience as professionals, practitioners, and analysts of dramatic literature. We might find ourselves looked on as participants in a larger cultural and academic conversation and looked on less as on outpost of the entertainment industry occupying valuable space and using precious resources only to provide amusement and an outlet for student creativity.

Using this more diverse approach might also provoke conversation among the student body about something more than the merits of a given production or its subject matter. Injecting something new would add subject matter and deepen the level of seriousness with which the students who are not majors, but who make up the bulk of our audiences, take our work. And to those who might suggest that it undermines the text of those canonical works that praise the beauty of their heroines, it's worth remembering that those heroines were played in ancient Greece and Renaissance England by men.

Secondary school drama departments are commonly led by teachers who have had at minimum, a long-term interest in drama, and in many cases have had formal undergraduate or graduate level training. These teachers are in a position to challenge assumptions within their programs and perhaps to affect the assumptions of students outside of drama programs about what an "actor" looks like, about what actors are suitable for which roles, and most importantly whether or not a student should pursue further training and experience in college.

College theatre programs can influence teachers (and future teachers) of secondary drama through the use of affirmatively diverse approaches to training and casting. This influence can be extended through bringing secondary school students to campus for productions, drama camps, and campus visits during the recruiting process. It may be taken further by demonstrating new approaches to diversifying physical appearance and moving away from commercial models in courses offered to secondary teachers as part of their continuing education and in workshops within secondary schools.

I do not necessarily believe that changing the way we select students for training and cast students in roles will have any impact on commercial culture, driven as it is by a profit motive that requires more attention to be paid to fantasy in every aspect of cultural production than to offering a genuine reflection of the world we live in. But we can change the cultures of the artistic environments over which we have control and influence.

I believe that we should select artists to train based on their aptitude, as students in other disciplines are selected. I believe that we should affirmatively select people who reflect diversity in all of its aspects without regard to commercial viability. Those who are commercially viable will find their way. We have the opportunity to challenge and perhaps change notions of what constitutes appropriate appearance onstage by creating theatre for the local campus and off-campus communities that reflect their diversity. We can become far more conscious of the messages we send regarding human value by how we select students for training and by how we cast our productions. We can cast against "type" as well as to type and train actors to act, not simply to play the roles that we predict the industry will cast them in should they successfully pursue professional careers. We need to accept (at last) that the industry cannot absorb everyone we train no matter how well we train them, and with this in mind, we need instead to train artists for the value that training has to the culture, to the academy, and most importantly to the artists themselves and those whose lives they will affect.

9 "Typed" for What?

Mary Cutler

In her 1992 essay, "Liberating the Young Actor: Feminist Pedagogy and Performance," Rhonda Blair warns performance teachers:

> [P]erforming a role is a kind of "training for life," a rehearsal and patterning of a way of being in the world. It guides a young woman [and anyone] in developing a sense of what her [his] choices for living are. Theatrical roles are constructions which make assertions about the way the world is, and more often than not, they re-inscribe the dominant culture . . . [1]

These constructions of gender that we assign to our students for performance are the core concern of this chapter.

Gender constitution, according to gender theorist Judith Butler, is a complex phenomenon. According to Butler, "the acts by which gender is constituted bear similarities to performative acts within theatrical contexts."[2] Butler's theories figure even more significantly in Blair's work with Butler's assertion that "the gendered body acts its part in a culturally restricted corporeal space and enacts interpretations within the confines of already existing directives."[3] Both Butler and Blair concur that gender constitution occurs in a restrictive and confining cultural context. Additionally, Butler's writings are aligned with Blair's in that Butler believes: "gender identity is a performative accomplishment compelled by social sanction and taboo,"[4] and "the body is always an embodying of possibilities both conditioned and circumscribed by historical convention."[5] In addition, Butler asserts that gender identity is influenced by "social sanction and taboo."[6] These concepts resonate with Blair's caution that theatrical roles may "re-inscribe the dominant culture."[7] In other words, Blair's perspective is grounded in established gender theory.

Elsewhere in her essay, Blair argues ambitiously for the responsibilities of acting teachers:

> Performance students are inherently engaged in a process of self-realization, and this should be inseparable from their theatre work. If our

processes of training young people for the theatre remains separate from our fostering of their development as increasingly autonomous and socially responsible beings, their theatre work risks remaining shallow and somehow opaque or masked, derivative of others' ideas and values, and mimicking models which may have outlived their purpose.[8]

Blair's "shallow . . . and mimicking models"[9] can be linked to Butler's theory of the "illusion of gender essentialism."[10] Both theorists aspire to a gender constitution, more unique and individual than that "circumscribed by historical convention."[11] The gender models Blair describes are those that we have come to call "types."

U.S. actor training frequently "types" young performers for specified roles (e.g., ingénue, leading man, character woman). We teach young directors to do the same when we model casting of actors whose appearance would not challenge audience expectation, meaning actors who could appear to be biologically related, or actors who might pose as a conventional-looking couple, or actors of appropriate ethnicities for specific ethnic narratives—in other words, actors who are "the *right* type." This very "typing" system is organized by the dominant culture's standards, and, is, of course, connected to the "male gaze," predominant even in our training schools.

Sue Ellen Case, an early theorist of feminist theatre studies, explains how the "male gaze" (a notion introduced by feminist film theorist Laura Mulvey) operates within "the theatrical gaze."[12] Case considers how a "Juliet" may be cast under this system: the character's casting "usually conforms to certain standards of beauty found in the present-day culture. These standards control her costuming and make-up in foregrounding her beauty for the audience."[13] Case goes on to assert: "Similarly, the common practice of casting blonde women in the roles of ingénues, and dark women in secondary and vamp roles, is not based on the demands of the text, but betrays cultural attitudes about the relative innocence, purity and desirability of certain racial features."[14] Case's theories of representation can be applied to lesbians and gay men as well, since such "patriarchal prejudices" control all views of gender.[15]

To resist these restrictive practices, it is professors trained in dramatic criticism and in teaching performance who seem best poised to challenge typecasting. Not only have we observed students' highly inspiring work in performances contrary to their "type," but we have also frequently comforted and sympathized with student–actors with distinctive physical characteristics or pronounced markers of (non-white) ethnicity who remain uncast due to "justifiable" typecasting. We risk such ongoing destructive consequences, if type trumps talent.

To bring this issue into better focus, two performance venues within the educational theatre demonstrate the risks of "typing": educationally-oriented auditions and main stage production selections. The specific auditions treated in this chapter are the American College Theatre Festival's (ACTF) Irene Ryan

Acting Competitions. In the United States, ACTF's "Irene Ryans" have become the gold standard in academic theatre proficiency for students and professors; the "Ryans" hold widespread recognition in academe, and their prominence in the ACTF structure distinguishes those who win as "good" actors and their institutions as "good" programs. Indeed, talented young actors perform effectively in this forum, but the range of audition material selected for the "Ryans" and the typing of students are potentially troubling.

My ire regarding "the Ryans" came to a boil in the mid 1990s as I watched—through my feminist lens—a semifinal round of a Ryan competition. In that particular year, the competition featured an impressive array of talented young women using audition material that consistently featured powerless, sexually obsessed caricatures of women—enough to make me question whether their professors had ever heard of feminism. Additionally, that particular year, casting directors from daytime soap operas, a genre renowned for its reification of the male gaze, were selected to adjudicate the Ryan competition. In the years since then, the selection of such adjudicators has not occurred again, and I credit more progressive regional ACTF administrators. However, the audition material selected continues to be problematic, especially when we as professors take the easy route and advise eager-to-win auditioners to select from the genres that won the previous year, as opposed to more complex material. As their coaches, should we not see that educational auditions are just that—educational—rather than conforming to market standards? Through our privileging of such stereotypical gender constructions, we risk the consequences for our students that Blair and Butler describe.

Additionally, main stage productions at universities are taking on an increasingly commercial air. Many collegiate theatres seem to be playing to the box office, while private schools curry favor with their boards and donors, with main stage selections geared to combat decreasing funding. Feminist theorist Jill Dolan criticizes this practice: "Rather than employing a pedagogical model of theatre production and practice, they adopt the market strategies of the industry they seek to emulate."[16] Our current economic picture is, perhaps, to blame for our less adventurous repertoire, as we select safer main stage material—accompanied by stereotypes in gender—to obtain or retain what little revenue is available. Additionally, in meager times, the academic "quality control police" make us compete for what little funding there is—a phenomenon Jill Dolan, in her *Geographies of Learning*, reads as political. Dolan, along with the National Association of Schools of Theatre, finds that the intense scrutiny of academic budgets, accompanied by departmental paperwork to prove "quality" programming, seems to be a strategy developed by politically conservative academics to curtail progressive liberal arts education and gender studies, with the arts being prime targets of such a strategy.

Instead, Dolan urges academics to adopt Robin D.G. Kelley's theory of liberal arts education in which Kelley asserts that our academies "have been the sites of historic movements for social change precisely because the ostensible function of the university is to interrogate knowledge, society, and history."[17] Educational theatre provides an exceptionally rich laboratory for such critical interrogations. We should question the "quality" gurus, and maintain the university as Kelley inspires, keeping our main stage as a laboratory for social critique in which we train young artists.

To train artists for the theatre, Blair suggests four goals to enhance creativity in students' portrayals of gender. Below, I elaborate on these goals as they play out in my current teaching and as I would encourage others to work with them. Blair asks performance teachers:

1) "[T]o liberate actors from stereotypical limitations in approaching roles, particularly in relation to gender and sexuality, thereby freeing women and men" (including lesbians, gay men, and trans performers).[18] As stated earlier, acting teachers and directors need to select characters not limited to stereotypes; we must encourage young directors to work similarly and interpret gender roles in less stereotypical ways. Blair's work, scaffolded by Butler's theories, challenges acting teachers and directors on selection/interpretations of texts and characterization. Our selections of texts, as well as our work with performative gender acts, needs to be expanded. Blair even suggests gender-separate rehearsals, but I would redefine such rehearsals as ones in which actors could discuss/rehearse/experiment with a variety of gender interpretations. Such investigations would allow a cast "to get past certain power issues, self-consciousness about body image/sexuality, etc.," and thus allow a student to "move through fears and resistances (often unconscious) which can limit the freedom of her [his] work."[19]

2) "[T]o provide actors with a critical frame in evaluating the material with which they're working and the structure within which they're working."[20] This rubric is made even more important within the framework of Butler's theories. In all performance and academic classes, young actors and directors need to be encouraged to experiment with gender constructions within canon favorites and newer forms; students' increased confidence in their critical faculties and their creativities will encourage them to give priority to expressing these new meanings to their audiences. Toward this goal, Dolan strongly urges academics to separate from the marketplace and promises of stardom. She suggests that we, instead, position our institutions more as political/social agents of change by developing artists, not actors who merely fit outmoded stereotypes.[21]

3) "[T]o make room for actors who typically find limited or no space on our stages."[22] This objective is long overdue. All of us have been among the ranks of the uncast and have experiences with the uncastable—in other words, talented but restricted or disabled students not given a chance; skilled actors of color playing only minor characters; gay men and lesbians not cast as love interests; actors of size only cast as sidekicks; hordes of young women not cast because of the canon's prominent interest in men. How can we call our institutions sites of higher learning if we seek no higher goals than our students' suitability for market standards? Blair's final urging will serve as my conclusion:

4) "[T]o aid our students in developing a directness, immediacy, vulnerability, and joy in their work, based upon a secure knowledge of who they are (rather than upon someone else's sense of who they ought to be)."[23] We will best convey the importance of Blair's values if we promote them not only within the safety of our classrooms and studios, but also—perhaps especially—in the shows we stage for public audiences and when students venture into national auditions and their first professional endeavors.

Blair's pedagogy, discussed herein, might well assist in the elimination of typing in the academy, but the crucial players are performance teachers. We must investigate, and thus encourage students to question, those well-worn "models which may have outlived their purpose"[24] and which reify "the illusion of gender essentialism."[25] The hands holding the keys to transformation are our own.

NOTES

1. Rhonda Blair, "Liberating the Young Actor: Feminist Pedagogy and Performance," *Theatre Topics* 2 (1992), 16.
2. Judith Butler, "Performative Acts and Gender Constitution: An Essay in Phenomenology and Feminist Theory," *Theatre Journal*, 40 (1988), 521.
3. Ibid., 526.
4. Ibid., 520.
5. Ibid., 521.
6. Ibid., 520.
7. Blair, 16.
8. Ibid., 13.
9. Ibid., 13.
10. Butler, 528.
11. Ibid., 521.
12. Sue-Ellen Case, *Feminism and Theatre* (New York: Routledge, 1988), 118.
13. Ibid., 117.
14. Ibid., 117.
15. Ibid., 117.
16. Jill Dolan, *Geographies of Learning* (Middletown, CT: Wesleyan University Press, 2001), 51.
17. Robin D.G. Kelley, *Yo' Mama's Disfunktional!* (Boston: Beacon Press, 1997), 139.
18. Blair, 16.
19. Ibid., 21.
20. Ibid., 16.
21. Dolan, 47–55.
22. Blair, 16.
23. Ibid., 16.
24. Ibid., 13.
25. Butler, 528. See also American Theatre in Higher Education, "ATHE Outcomes Assessment Guidelines for Theatre Programs in Higher Education," (Downer's Grove, IL: American Theatre for Higher Education, 1990) and Council of Arts Accrediting Associations, *Achievement and Quality: Higher Education in the Arts* (Reston, VA: March 2007).

10 "They accused me of bein' a homosexual"

Playing Kerry Cook in *The Exonerated*

Derek Mudd

> *Human life is so subtle, so complex and multi-faceted, that it needs an incomparably large number of new, still undiscovered 'isms' to express it fully.*
>
> Konstantin Stanislavsky

A few weeks into my first college theatre class, the instructor made a statement that I found shocking. She said, "Actors shouldn't be too smart." My best friend Jessica (now a theatre historian) and I exchanged glances of amazement. While I do believe that in the moment of performing the focus must be on doing, I also believe that the process of preparing for and researching a role should involve a certain amount of rigor and study. Unfortunately, my experiences in two separate MFA acting programs reveal a devaluing of both the intellectual life of the actor and his or her personal convictions. Instructors in certain programs feel that they are preparing the student–actor for a career in which they will work at the whim of producers and directors who are the real creative forces in the theatre. This conviction sometimes plays out in domination and even abuse.

In the meantime, new play development and theatre collectives require an entirely different kind of actor. Playwrights and directors seek out talent to assist in the creation of original works, a process which requires the dramaturgical experience of actors within a role. Companies throughout the country are experimenting with new paradigms for creating plays that defy the old system of actor subservience and involve the actor as collaborator.

My preparation and rehearsal process working on the role of Kerry Max Cook in a 2006 production of *The Exonerated* may serve as a way to reflect on how power relationships play out between instructors and students in a traditional professional training program. As mentioned previously, I attended two different MFA acting programs, first at a large Midwestern university directly after graduating from college (I quit this program after three semesters), and second at a large Southern university ten years after the first. In the years between, I worked steadily in the theatre while supplementing my career with odd jobs. In 1998, after leaving the first program, I moved to Austin, Texas, and felt at home in the theatre community I found there. My first show in Austin was with Austin Script Works, a local playwriting organization that also produced their members' work. I loved the collaborative nature of working on new plays, and the group dramaturgy involved. Having spent my time before Austin performing in musicals and children's theatre, I decided that I would focus on new and experimental work. The productions I worked on in Austin were all marked by a sense of equal involvement by members of the artistic team. In the development of new work, the playwright and director looked to the dramaturgy of the actor to assist in the development of the play. Additionally, my continuing training in Viewpoints and Suzuki techniques with the Rude Mechanicals, a homegrown Austin theatre collective, developed my creativity and openness as an actor.

I decided to return to graduate school for many reasons. First, my partner was finishing a master's degree and wished to pursue a PhD. This meant that we would most likely be leaving Austin for a few years. Second, I had been asked to take on larger responsibilities in a number of productions in the capacity of vocal or movement coach and even director. I felt that a degree would solidify my skills and increase my marketability as a coach and director. Lastly, I was interested in teaching acting on the college level. Since an MFA is required to teach acting, voice, and movement at universities, I assumed that an MFA program would provide the pedagogy I needed as a university instructor.

My experience within my second program impressed upon me that these were not the correct reasons for going to graduate school. The programs I encountered on my search for a school all claimed that their intent was to train actors, not teachers. In the end I chose a university associated with an Equity theatre and a newly hired professor who had worked with both Tadashi Suzuki and Anne Bogart. These were the elements that drew me to the program, although I felt I needed to keep my aspirations hidden in order to succeed.

I was flattered to be cast in *The Exonerated*, the first production I was eligible for at my new university's Equity theatre. I wanted to use my work on the play to explore the techniques that I had been trained in during my first semester of acting classes. Because, at that time, there was no text required for these classes, it is difficult to say exactly from what school of thought the instruction was derived, but I would characterize it as a mix of Stanislavski, Meisner, and various psycho-physical approaches to acting. Specifically, my first year focused on realistic acting within twentieth-century American and British plays. In class we developed scores for the scenes using objectives, actions, and intentions. Each day we would present scenes to be evaluated by the instructor and performed again. I had assumed that MFA training would include reading the major works of theatre practitioners. Indeed, my request to do so independently over the summer (my reading list included Stanislavski, Meisner, Hagen, Chaikin, M. Chekhov, and Bogart) was denied on the grounds that nothing could be learned from reading these books. I assumed that we would be learning other techniques in subsequent semesters that I would be able to experiment with in production in the same manner. Unfortunately, these same techniques intended for realistic, contemporary plays were to be applied to everything from Chekhov to Shakespeare, Ibsen to the Greeks. Sometimes I was successful in making the techniques work for the role. Other times I was not. I don't know whether my problems with playing the role of Kerry Max Cook—which I will discuss later—were based in my own misunderstandings about the techniques associated with realism, or if there is something inherently flawed about the techniques themselves, or if the wholesale application of these methods advocated by various teachers and coaches (regardless of genre) is at fault.

My personal understanding of performance is much more flexible than that which training in realism allows. Many who advocate this style of theatre place it above all others—as the ultimate achievement in performance. My point of view, in contrast, is perhaps best expressed by Phillip B. Zarrilli in the introduction to the first section of *Acting (Re)considered:*

> We can celebrate the freedom of not having to find a "universal" language once and for all. Rather we can spend our energy on the continuing challenge of searching for languages of acting which best allow one to actualize a particular paradigm of performance in a particular context for a particular purpose.[1]

I strongly believe that every show, every production, requires the actor to approach his work organically, using the techniques that best serve that particular piece.

These revelations were to come later, however. My focus at the time was to develop a character using the training I was receiving. As instructed, I began my work on *The Exonerated* by looking at what Kerry Max Cook says about himself in the show, what others say about him, and what he says about others. Since Cook is not a fictional character, I also conducted outside research. I found several websites devoted to Cook. His case—his wrongful murder conviction, years on death row, and activism after his release—was featured in both newspapers and television programs. As a self-identified gay man, my interest was piqued by an interview in which Cook said, "I don't know if I was bisexual or just partially bisexual, . . . I had relationships with girls as well as guys."[2] Although Cook as a character makes no mention of this in the show, I felt that to play him truthfully, information regarding his sexuality was relevant to my performance. I began experimenting with ways to apply this information onstage.

To understand Cook, I should briefly put the role into the context of the play. The text of *The Exonerated* is culled from transcripts of interviews with living persons exonerated from death row, as well as of legal proceedings. The play focuses on six particular exonerees who tell their stories directly to the audience. These "characters" do not interact with each other, although they are onstage for the duration of the show, along with four other performers who take on multiple roles throughout. As Cook reveals in his first monologue, he was found guilty of raping and killing Linda Jo Edwards in 1977. The police found Edwards brutally murdered in the apartment complex where she and Cook were neighbors. Her sexual organs had been mutilated by the killer. This led a local psychologist to profile the murderer as a homosexual who hated women. While explaining the events leading up to his incarceration, Cook, in the play, mentions that he was "working in a gay bar at the time."[3] Cook's place of employment and the fact that he identified as a bisexual man made him the prime suspect in the case.

In my course work at the time, we had not experimented with direct address. In that first year of class, we had only worked with scene partners (both real and imaginary, as in the case of monologues) always assuming the presence of a fourth wall. So that I could better experiment with the new tools I was learning in class, I thought of the audience as my scene partner and set out to establish a clear understanding of who they might be—how to characterize them within realistic terms established by the scene. I imagined that my character, Cook, was seated on a couch, speaking with authors Erik Jensen and Jessica Blank about his case. From what I knew, this wasn't necessarily the way the interviews were conducted, but it was close: their discussions were informal.

The production was performed in an arena configuration, with the actors turning to face different sections of the audience at different times. I discovered that the scenario I had created (Cook, Jensen, and Blank on the couch) did not work. I knew from my research that Kerry now toured the country giving lectures on the American justice system and his experiences on death row. When I tried to use this as my imaginary situation in rehearsal, I found that it significantly changed the dynamic. In the vein of realism, I had to ask myself, wouldn't there be a huge difference between what Kerry would choose to say in his own living room and what he would choose to say to an audience of over a hundred strangers?

With a more concrete and dynamic sense of my scene partners, I moved forward with my work. Now that I knew who my scene partners were (the actual audience), I could begin to focus my intentions toward them. As I did, I noticed that, taken out of context, the lines that Kerry speaks could be read as homophobic. During his second monologue, Cook gives the details of his legal proceedings:

> KERRY: They had a lead that the victim's boyfriend, Professor Whitfield, had done the murder. But they didn't go after him; they went after

me. They said that the crime was done by a homosexual, maniacal murderer who hated women. The prosecution accused me of being a homosexual—before the jury . . . [4]

The scene shifts to a courtroom as Kerry's defense objects to "the defendant's alleged homosexuality" being brought into the case. The judge overrules and the prosecutor concludes his speech:

KERRY'S PROSECUTOR: So let's let all the freaks and perverts and murderous homosexuals of the world know what we do with them in a court of justice. That we take their lives. [5]

Because Cook never says he was sexually confused at the time in the play, I was worried that people in the audience might not realize that he was queer, or worse, would feel he was condemning queers. For my own sake, I needed to somehow convey Cook's queerness to the audience, but wasn't sure how to accomplish this using only the given circumstances of the scene, as established by the playwrights and the director.

While I don't think I was necessarily conscious of it then, looking back, I can see that I had begun to create distance between the character and myself. In attempting to do service to the character, I had started thinking about Cook not so much in realistic terms, but rather as a mask. I feel my approach was successful in rehearsal. I received positive feedback from the director and my fellow actors. Indeed, more than a week before the show was to open I was told, "Don't change a thing!" by the director. Despite this note, I found myself called for a special rehearsal.

One weekend, while the rest of the cast was off, I was called to an individual rehearsal that included the director, the vocal coach, and an invited acting coach who, at that time, served as a member of the undergraduate acting faculty. We met in the theatre lobby and started at the beginning of the show, working through all of my monologues. The director and vocal coach sat in chairs around me to convey the feel of the arena space. They were mostly quiet during the rehearsal as the acting coach worked with me, dissecting each scene line by line. According to the acting coach, my characterization and dialect were inhibiting my "intentions."

We eventually came to the line about being accused of homosexuality. I began the monologue and was interrupted. The professor asked something to the effect of, "Why do you say that, that way? What are you trying to do?" I tried to explain my intention of making the audience see how ridiculous the accusation was, when the acting coach interrupted me again.

She said, "By accusing you of being a homosexual they cut your balls off. They emasculated you."

I began to explain again, "Well, I think Kerry . . . "

"Please say I," she requested.

I went on, "Well I think I . . . I was bisexual at the time of my arrest . . . so—"

She proceeded to tell me that I couldn't play that onstage, that that was my "invisible work," and that what I needed to do was show how "I" had been emasculated by the prosecution when they accused "me" of being a homosexual.

I felt as if I was being asked to ignore what I knew about Cook and the arc of his story. The acting coach had not been present for our dramaturgical work on the show; why should I allow myself to be swayed by her opinions? I had done my homework, and had come to the conclusion that Cook says they accused him of being a homosexual not because he is ashamed, or emasculated, but to properly set up the fact that once he was incarcerated, his fellow prisoners punished him for being publicly labeled queer. The papers had reported it, and by the time Cook arrived in prison, everyone knew. In Cook's fourth monologue he describes being gang raped. The rapists carved the words "good pussy" (or "p-u-s-s-y," as Cook says in the show) on his backside, which created a cycle of more rape. Although he doesn't talk about it in the play, this abuse lead to Cook's actual emasculation of himself by cutting off his penis, but I suppose this knowledge of the character is just part of my invisible work.

As the afternoon proceeded, the acting coach became increasingly abusive, to the extent that I asked for a break to cool my rising temper. My request was denied on the basis that I needed to "work through it." Eventually I folded, having been emasculated, so to speak, and tried to play the role as I was coached. When next I saw the vocal coach who witnessed all of this she told me that she felt most of it was inappropriate and wanted to defend me, but didn't feel that it was her place to do so.

The final blow to my portrayal of this important line came the last week of rehearsal. After a long session of restaging the show, some new blocking was added. I was in the habit of writing my notes on post-its and sticking them in my script. The post-it that still lives in my script next to this scene says:

Punch "The prosecution accused me of being a homosexual—
    BEFORE THE JURY"
Pick up chair
Bring to center
Bang it down

A light and sound cue followed as the prosecutor rose to begin his speech. I sat in the chair with my head down listening to him speak. Because the audience was forced to read the line as a dreadful accusation, I as a gay man performing the role, felt raped and emasculated.

For me the incident of coaching in the theatre lobby felt familiar. In a different theatre lobby in my previous graduate program, I had experienced a similar situation. When I was to play a character with a clubfoot in a particular production, our faculty movement instructor was called in to coach me. After the cast, crew, and director had left, the coach proceeded to rework my monologue for several hours. Despite his brief contact with the script he felt it was his duty to "save the show," as he stated. When he felt I had presented a performance that was to his liking he said, "I need to see this sort of work in class, or you are going to get it, and you know how mean I can be." Although I was already considering leaving the MFA program at that time, this encounter prompted me to offer my resignation the next day. When we resumed rehearsals, and I presented the scene as I had been coached, the director said to scrap it all and go back to the way I had been performing the role.

In both situations I felt powerless. I felt that it was my place, as the dutiful actor, to simply accept abuse as a part of the artistic process. I have witnessed both undergraduate and graduate acting students at several universities receive treatment worse than my experiences. Personal attacks on intelligence and appearance seem to be a favored technique for producing results. In my professional work outside of university training programs I have never experienced this kind of abuse (nor did it occur at my undergraduate program). I suppose that there are theatres in the professional domain where abuse is accepted as just part of the field. One of my mentors once said, "I have been hit and abused by the best. It always hurts, and it's always wrong." From research in the field of communication studies, I know that verbal aggression is destructive of interpersonal relationships.[6] How are we to maintain working relationships with each other under such conditions?

While my situation in *The Exonerated* coaching session included verbal abuse, I also feel that it betrays a certain homophobia at work, as well as a devaluing of the political convictions of the actor. It is one thing to play a character who is homophobic in a play, it is quite another to be complicit in portraying a living human being as holding values which he may or may not hold. I was trying to walk a fine line of ethical representation of a living person onstage given what I knew about him. The prevalent attitudes that I have encountered in actor-training programs teach the actors that they must put their convictions aside in favor of employment. A friend of mine, an African American actress in an MFA program, declined a role as a maid in a show (the third time in a year that she had been cast as a maid). She was sick of playing demeaning roles. The department warned her that she was breaking her contract and defended their position with claims that in the real world one doesn't have the luxury of choice.

I wish that I had been able to stand up for myself in the situation with *The Exonerated* in the same manner as my friend, but unfortunately I felt that I could do nothing. The power dynamics at work were not in my favor. I was a student in my first year, working on my first show with an Equity theatre alongside faculty and staff with whom I needed to establish a good relationship to ensure my continued success in the program.

I cannot say that these sorts of experiences are endemic of all programs. However, I fear that these examples of abuse are quite common and sanctioned by some as acceptable practices. My experiences have set me on my current path. Rather than returning to the field, I have chosen to pursue a PhD in performance studies. This has afforded me the opportunity not only to study the performance techniques that I had imagined I would study in my MFA, but also allowed me to contact good pedagogical practices that I will be able to employ when I teach. I continue to work in the theatre and develop original performances with collaborators both at my university and in the broader community. It is my hope that as a teacher I will empower student–actors to value themselves as contributors to a vibrant field that prides itself on artistic collaboration.

NOTES

1. Phillip Zarrilli, Introduction, *Acting (Re)considered: A Theoretical and Practical Guide*, ed. Phillip Zarrilli, (New York: Routledge, 2002), 16.
2. Mark Donald, "Innocence Lost; Prosecutors Lied and Cheated to Put Kerry Max Cook on Death Row for 17 Years . . . ," *Dallas Observer*, July 15, 1999, Features (http://www.lexisnexis.com/us/Inacademic; accessed July 29, 2006).
3. Jessica Blank and Erik Jensen, *The Exonerated* (New York: Faber and Faber, 2003), 13.
4. Blank, 41.
5. Blank, 42.
6. D. A. Infante, "Teaching Students to Understand and Control Verbal Aggression," *Communication Education* 44 (1995): 51–63.

11 Identity Politics and the Training of Latino Actors

Micha Espinosa and
Antonio Ocampo-Guzman

> *The more knowledge we gain from that which makes us cultur-*
> *ally diverse, the more we will be able to appreciate what unifies us*
> *throught the mixing and mutual exchanges of our culture.*
>
> Elizabeth Lozano[1]

INTRODUCTION

Latinos are the fastest-growing minority in the United States and are beginning to have a significant impact on large sections of its society and culture,
including theatre, film, and television.[2] There are numerous Latino theatre
companies and festivals across the nation, as well as a thriving generation
of Latino writers producing compelling work. These companies and festivals tend to attract actors mostly from their surrounding communities—
actors who are filled with generosity and energy, but who have little of
the substantial training in voice, movement, and acting needed to achieve
true excellence and sustain a professional career. At the same time, very
few actor-training programs are able or willing to understand the complex
navigation of identity—an integral part of the Latino experience in the U.S.
As a result, these programs measure their Latino students against rigid,
old-fashioned and unexamined Eurocentric values.

According to the United States Census Bureau, there are 44.3 million
Latinos in the United States, 14.8% of the total population of 299 million. Between 2000 and 2006, Latinos accounted for one half the nation's
growth, and Latinos growth rate (24.3%) was three times the growth rate
of the total population (6.1%). The Pew Hispanic Center, an organization
that is part of The Pew Charitable Trust, and whose major focus is the
examination of the rapid growth of Latinos in the U.S., reports that, "the
Latino population, already the nation's largest minority group, will triple
in size and will account for most of the nation's population growth from
2005 through 2050. Hispanics will make up 29% of the U.S. population in
2050, compared with 14% in 2005."[3] Because of this booming population,

Latinos are also significantly affecting the political and financial landscape, as evidenced in the 2008 presidential campaign. Both parties actively courted the Latino vote, and many a nightly news segment was dedicated to Latino voters and their issues.

This is such a historic time for Latinos in the U.S. that in the fields of politics, culture, and education, it behooves the country at large to understand the Latino experience more fully. Furthermore, where the goal is an equitable and thriving theatre community, it is essential, in both the academic and the professional arenas, to examine the full impact of this experience, and to better serve the growing number of young Latinos seeking professional actor training.

Broadly speaking, there are three main challenges to be met when training Latino actors. First, there is the fluid relationship that most Latinos have with language, having been exposed to both Spanish and English in varied degrees and disparate circumstances. Secondly, there is the complex relationship most Latinos have to the physical body, having been given contradictory messages about sensuality and expression by religious ideology and/or cultural beliefs, as well as by the media. And thirdly, Latino actors face many difficulties finding work in an industry that frequently holds them hostage to phenotype, relegating them to the playing of stereotypes, disregarding their fullest artistic potential.

We have been studying these predicaments since 2004 in order to better understand and contextualize them, and have been developing workshops to offer solutions to the most pressing issues.[4] Contributing to the discussion about the politics of actor training, this chapter presents our current insights into these challenges, while offering suggestions to training programs on how to meet them. Our hope is that training programs will then be able to enhance the quality of the training, as well as advance the development of the artistic and cultural identities of their Latino students, and in so doing, might be better able to help them establish successful and rewarding professional careers.

RELATIONSHIP TO LANGUAGE

Professional actor-training programs in the U.S. offer instruction exclusively in English. There is a wide spectrum of ways Latinos in the U.S. relate to English, depending on each individual's relationship with the foundational Spanish. This spectrum encompasses both the experience of being monolingual and the experience of being fully bilingual—that is, able to generate thoughts and communicate in written and spoken word in both languages. More often than not, these gradations of bilingualism are intricately related to each individual's experience of immigration and assimilation. For example, recent immigrants may have acquired English as a second language in their country of origin, or even in the U.S. through

English as a second language programs, but immigrants may limit their use of English to spheres outside of the family unit. Likewise, children of immigrants, born in the U.S., might use English exclusively in all interactions. They might never have acquired Spanish; they may also have lost their Spanish either by choice in order to assimilate, or by force—being denied the right to speak in Spanish. A common scenario for younger generations, especially for young Latinos in college, is for Spanish to be the dominant language at home, while English dominates their social and school spheres. For many Latinos of the younger generation, the ability to use Spanish or English with precision—let alone eloquence—may be deeply compromised as they give precedence to a very fluid form of bilingualism, commonly known as *Spanglish*.

This fluid relationship to language in the Latino culture is usually manifested in rather flexible speech sounds, where vowels and consonants do not consistently fit the same clear standard of pronunciation found in monolingual speakers. The sounds of our voices, our dialects and our accents have a significant impact on our sense of belonging and identity. As much as we take pride in hearing our own dialect used in a respectful manner by others, we are deeply insulted when the dialect is derided. Thus, we learn how to disguise or reveal our identity in our speech. Dr. Lisa García Bedolla from the University of California, Irvine, writes:

> English is the dominant and preferred language in the United States, and as a result language minorities have been encouraged by state institutions to adopt English as quickly as possible. In the Latino community, this was accomplished through Americanization programs, English immersion in school and other methods to ensure that Latino children use English as their primary language. I argue that this has given the Spanish language a negative attribution, one that has created a paradoxical relationship between Latinos and the Spanish language. Spanish remains a source of ethnic pride and solidarity, but is also seen as an obstacle to socioeconomic and social mobility. As a result, the Latinos in this sample are engaging in what we call *selective dissociation*—the selective distancing of themselves from the sectors of the community that they see as to blame for this negative attribution: those community members that are Spanish monolingual. This process has a negative effect on community cohesion.[5]

A Latino may very well be fully bilingual and yet speak English with an accent. Or a Latino may be fully monolingual in English, and still speak English with a recognizable Latino dialect developed from these complex experiences regarding language. In professional training programs, where English is the dominant language of instruction and artistic expression, Latino students are typically required to standardize their speech sounds. With this standardization practice, programs may inadvertently shut down an inherent part of the individual's identity, and diminish their students. With a conscientious understanding of this problem, programs can support a fundamental part of the artist's identity.

We might suppose that training programs are still operating under the "myths" described by Dr. Diana Ríos from the University of Connecticut, who writes that "one of the myths of the American melting pot suggests that losing one's mother tongue 'makes more room' for English. Another myth offers the illusion that learning how to be 'American' by Euro-American standards is the golden key to opportunity in this country."[6]

Although there is much conversation about diversity at both the Association for Theatre in Higher Education (ATHE) and the Voice and Speech Trainers Association (VASTA)—where there is also serious concern about the inherent oppressiveness of Standard American Speech—these standards are still being upheld by theatre companies, as well as by critics and audiences. Surely in the context of professional training in the art of theatre, out of respect for the complexities underlying Latino speech, alternatives to these standards must and can be found.

Any actor's voice needs to accomplish three basic goals: the voice must be heard, it must be understood, and it must meet with efficiency and health any demand made on it. As such, it is of great value for an actor to learn how speech sounds are generated and how to shift them in order to achieve maximum intelligibility and the widest spectrum of possible characterizations. Some Latino actors, however, have faced the predicament of not having their speech reflect what is expected of their phenotype (i.e., speaking too articulately for a stereotypical character). At the same time, they may not speak articulately enough for the classical theatre. The profession cannot have as its goal simply the teaching of standardized speech as a way of eliminating regionalisms. Rather, it needs to offer a student–actor a creative way to manipulate speech sounds according to the artistic needs of the job at hand, from speaking classical texts to maximizing or minimizing original speech sounds. Increasingly, there are other such methods of voice and speech training, such as the Detail Model developed by Dudley Knight, and the "phonetic pillows" developed by Louis Colaianni, which teach the actor how to shift speech sounds in the construction of characters, as a creative endeavor.[7] These creative speech-training methods are especially useful given the recent increase of Spanish-only jobs in the Latino entertainment industry.

RELATIONSHIP TO THE BODY

Latinos have a complex relation to their bodies and self-image, as confirmed by the substantial amount of recent scholarship.[8] The basic conundrum is that many Latino actors find themselves straddling two worlds: the values of their original culture, which reveres tradition, family, and religion, contrasted with the media-constructed U.S. Latino craze, which projects and celebrates a generic sensuality or eroticism. Even if one fits the model, these projections make it difficult to establish a healthy self-image.

In her book, *Hijas Americanas*, Rosie Molinary explores the many stereotypes and the quest for identity:

> The average woman of ethnicity is different from what's celebrated on television, in magazines, and in life. But, often, in Latina culture, these differences are exacerbated by the fact that the families' input offers such a distant point of view—one that's often at odds with the larger culture. Thus, as Latinas, we can be caught in between two standards of beauty—not feeling beautiful in either culture, or feeling beautiful in one but not the other. No matter where we stand, we're on the precipice of judgment, with one set of values that informs our lives shaped by American pop culture and another set shaped by our families' culture and traditions.[9]

It is important to say, of course, that feelings of self-esteem and minority identity are not exclusive to the Latino experience. But it is also true that there are complexities unique to this population in light of how geographically close Latin America is to the U.S. If nothing else, this proximity itself has the effect of exaggerating some of the Latino culture's own inherent racism and social-class discrimination: the lighter the skin, the taller the body, the closer the person is to the European genetic pool and to the upper classes. Those whose features are more indigenous are usually considered less attractive, as well as socially inferior. In the realm of acting, the roles available to such as these include the fat, lazy, drunk with a sombrero; the gang lord/street-wise drug dealers; and buffoons or maids who speak in broken English.

Aspiring Latino actors are forced to navigate their cultural-racial identity every time they are confronted with these stereotypes in the media. In her *Culture and Difference*, Antonia Darder writes: "The media, with its highly centralized and almost monolithic structure, provides an essential link between the ruling ideology of the dominant culture and the society at large. In a society such as the United States where most of the people do not have any direct access to nor power over the bulk decisions that affect their lives, the media play a powerful legitimating role in the social production of mass consensus."[10]

In the media, Latinos are perceived as having a communal, cultural sensuality. Though obviously a stereotype, the highly-visible Latino role models found all over in U.S. media reinforce this image of sensuality. For women, it is the "seductress": Shakira, Jennifer López, Penélope Cruz, Salma Hayek, Eva Longoria, Rosario Dawson. For men, it is the "Latin lover": Antonio Banderas, Ricardo Montalbán, Ricky Martin. These images of primarily white to olive-skinned, thin, and scantily-clad actors and actresses send clear messages to young aspiring Latino actors: If you want to work and succeed in the U.S. entertainment industry, you need to be lighter-skinned and fit into the mainstream ideals of what is beautiful and sexy.

Coya Paz, Associate Artistic Director of Teatro Luna, a Chicago-based, all-female theatre company devoted to new work, discusses how their show, *The Maria Chronicles*, came about: "When we first started Teatro Luna we got together as Latina women. What does Latina mean? We all come from different backgrounds. One of the things we have in common is a shared stereotype. Casting agents would say, 'you're not Latina enough' or 'be spicier!' For our third show we wanted to show how the media constructs Latina women to fit the stereotypes that people want to see and how we, as actresses, have to deal with it."[11]

In Molinary's survey, respondents expressed frustrations about stereotyping that focus on Latina sexuality—for example, on having larger buttocks and breasts, and on being fantastic lovers.[12] If one looks at the leading Latino actresses of today, one sees that these women indeed meet the media's stereotype of the beautiful woman. The roles offered to them are often those of eroticized characters whose beauty is part of the story line. Latino actors are often confronted with this inescapable commercial ideal—with the need to "be sexy"—which is so often in direct conflict with the messages of a family-centered, strict upbringing.

It would be a gross generalization to state that all Latinos are Catholic and practicing; Latinos participate in a multitude of religious and faith-based organizations, and there is growing scholarship on Latino identity and religion (cf. De la Torre, Espinosa and Wilson). However, in a national survey by the Hispanic Churches in American Public Life that sought to examine the impact of religion on politics and civic engagement, it found that 70% of Latinos are Catholic and 23% are Protestant or "other Christian."[13] Father Allan Figueroa Deck, in his article "The Latino Catholic Ethos: Ancient History of Future Promise?" discusses how Latinos carry their roots in faith:

> At the heart of Latino cultures, in whatever national forms they take and even among diverse social classes and generations, are an exuberant orientation toward and fascination with religion. The Latino sense of community, which is at the heart of Latino identity, is nurtured by a deep religious orientation that, as we have seen, escapes the bounds of institutional Catholicism and all other religious institutions as well. Turned outward to the challenges of life in the United States and in the world this sense of transcendence may be the source of a new identity, that of the *mestizo*, a word that captures the essence of our Latino culture.[14]

The cultural identity conflict associated with strict religious upbringing is especially prevalent in college-aged Latinas, who contend with the phenomenon of *marianismo*, the traditional set of values derived from the Catholic Church. Marianismo includes describing Latinas as sacrificing, virginal, dutiful and following in the image of the Virgin Mary. "Latinas are taught to put their families' needs before their own, to feel guilty about sexual pleasure, to feel guilty about expressing their needs, and to live at home until marriage."[15] For Latinas with *marianista* values, the internal social/cultural conflicts when trying to break into the media-driven industry are many.

Equally confining and confusing are the directives that young Latino men receive to be a "macho"—a man in control, an authority figure, a patriarch. On one hand, aspiring Latino actors are exposed to prevailing images of the suave and handsome-yet-detached Latin lover, images that not only exploit notions of male beauty, but also combine them with the stereotype of the *macho*. This creates the perplexing message that in order to be a successful actor, one must be tall, sensual, debonair, while at the same time emotionally detached. On the other hand, these aspiring actors may look at the other end of the spectrum, where Latino actors who do not fit the generalized standard of beauty are relegated to the playing of thugs, criminals, and lowlifes. Regardless, both ends of the spectrum trap Latino actors in insidious stereotypes.

The navigation of these cultural expectations and the acculturation process can lead to psychological distress: low self-esteem, submissive or passive-aggressive behavior, anxiety, and/or depression. Professional training programs will be richer for developing an awareness of the thorny issues of identity development their Latino students might be experiencing. Programs should be able to identify the students in need, and to serve them as a referral agent.

PROFESSIONAL OUTLOOK AND CASTING

As professional actor trainers, we must ask ourselves and the programs we work in: Are we training young people (a) to be fully expressive artists with a clearly defined identity, (b) to have voices and bodies that give them access to their emotional lives, and (c) to have vocal and physical skills that efficiently serve them as vehicles for their fullest self-expression? Alternatively, are we training actors merely to get work in the entertainment industry? This, of course, is a complicated question, and one that has no clear answer.

What is clear, however, from our teaching and research, is that Latino student–actors entering the profession are not fully aware of the challenges and possible restrictions their phenotype will afford them, and that their training programs have not given them enough opportunities to explore their identities or to expand their casting possibilities. With the goal of fully preparing Latino actors to succeed in as many arenas as possible, professional training programs, directors, and casting agents will benefit from examining and understanding first what it means to be a Latino.

As it stands, most professional theatre programs train actors to seek work in theatre and in the film and TV industries—but what kind of success do young Latino actors see their peers achieving? Even taking into account popular TV programs such as *Dora the Explorer, Go, Diego, Go, The George Lopez Show,* and *Ugly Betty,* positive portrayals of Latinos in film and television remain the exception rather than the rule, and very few Latino actors thrive in the mainstream regional theatre. Given the tremendous number of ethnicities in the Latino culture, some Latino actors are able to portray characters from other ethnic backgrounds. And of course, many Latino actors find work in the Latino theatre companies and festival across the country, but are seldom able to make a living through their art in such companies.

Victoria, an actress from New York, responded to Molinary's survey: "When a Latina looks Latina, has black hair and brown skin that go along with a more typical look, she is portrayed as the girl with the baby, or the crack-head, whore, prostitute. But, if she looks more European, or already looks like an already famous Latina, then she is allowed to pull off other roles and can be more legit."[16]

The following comments, taken from students in Micha Espinosa's article, *Insight into the Challenges Latino Students Face,*[17] give us an opportunity to reflect:

> I remember last semester I auditioned for a play and the director actually came up to me. She said, "Oh, you did really well on your audition but the only problem was—." Then she pulled down my hair. "I can't use this." Like cause my hair was so dark or that that gave away my ethnicity. I could put make-up on or a wig; I could have manipulated it but she couldn't see past that. It's really frustrating that people aren't more open-minded.

Another student continues:

> The thing that was really wild for me was in college doing all that stuff, getting out of college, and one of my first auditions was at X. I got my first big show at Y and I was a bellhop with no lines. That, to me, was one of the most devastating things I had ever done. It made me feel like a piece of shit, because it made me feel like I couldn't do what these people were. I couldn't do what I was trained to do and other people were doing it, and they were getting a chance, and they were getting better at it. The more they kept doing it, the better they got, and the less opportunity I had, the less I cared.

In an interview with Michelle Adam, Professor Moisés Salinas, of Central Connecticut University, warns:

Contrary to what many believe, stereotypes and prejudices have not disappeared from society; they are merely more subtle than 40 years ago and continue to negatively impact minorities and more marginalized groups within education and in our society at large. Stereotypes can have a very powerful effect on the person who ends up thinking, "I am like this . . . " We also know that stereotypes affect education as a whole. A behavior of stereotyping often demonstrated in the classroom—and documented through studies and research—is that of teachers' low expectations of minority students. Society tends to have certain expectations, which policy decisions are based on. Not only does stereotyping impact policies, it affects the way in which those being stereotyped view themselves.[18]

Latinos who seek work in the ever-growing Spanish-only field face a number of challenges as well, with the Latino entertainment market rife with unacknowledged identity politics. Although age and nationality are supposed to be given equal opportunity, Cubans in fact tend to hire Cubans, Mexicans are favored because of their generic accent, and Puerto Ricans, Dominicans, and Argentines have difficulty finding work because of their identifiable accents. *Spanglish*, rarely heard on the networks, is considered polluted, and is generally used for comedic purposes only. Univision and Telemundo, the major producing studios for the Latino entertainment market, prefer actors to speak in an upper-middle-class Mexican accent rather than Caribbean or South American Spanish, presumably thinking they will be able to market their shows to a wider audience. Bilingual vocal coaches in Miami, New York, and Los Angeles are beginning to work with clients from a broad range of Spanish-speaking countries, who speak in very different regional accents of Spanish, and who are seeking the equivalent of Standard American Speech in Spanish. This trend, and its role in fragmenting communities, has deeper implications that need examination. In the meantime, since there are as yet no training programs in Spanish in the U.S., the industry continues to look to conventional standards of training. This overall situation in the Spanish-only acting market leads us to reinforce our suggestion that actors be taught how to alter their speech sounds in a creative, rather than prescriptive, way. Simply put, it will open more opportunities for work while at the same time respecting the individual's identity.

CONCLUSION: WHAT TRAINING PROGRAMS CAN DO

We are advocating that professional theatre training programs accept the challenges of intercultural communication. The dynamics of multi-cultural teaching and learning pose challenges that actor-training programs have, by and large, failed to take on. However, cultural misunderstandings are a continuous challenge of contemporary society and therefore, for a rounded education, must be discussed and explored in our training studios. Too many of our students continue to be dominated by another cultural group, and to function with a sense of culture shock; too many of our courses continue to have content that represents a limited perspective. As trainers, we have the power to empower or to silence.

In essence, we are advocating that professional theatre programs strive to reflect the current makeup of our society, embrace the true meaning of living in a multi-cultural age, and commit to enhancing learning while affirming and creating cultural identity. Professional training programs must aid in the cultural understanding of their students by stretching their own boundaries and generating new approaches and knowledge. Programs need to examine what is truly required for students to succeed in this day and age when people who have been marginalized are changing our society, changing our discussions, and changing our language. We are a society in flux, and theatre across this country is by and large stuck in the past, holding tightly to its fixed point, afraid of its identity changing. Antonia Darder writes:

> Bi-culturalism entails an ongoing process of identity recovery, construction, and reconstruction driven by collective efforts of subordinate cultural groups to build community solidarity, engage tensions surrounding nationality differences, revitalize the boundaries of subordinate cultures, and redefine the meaning of cultural identity within the current social context. Further, this phenomenon is influenced by persistent efforts of those who have been marginalized to establish a sense of place from which to struggle against the relations of dominance.[19]

Professional training programs routinely produce mainly European or white U.S. playwrights, offering students little if any connection to multi-cultural theatre, or to the bi-culturalism Darder speaks of. On behalf of their Latino student–actors, we advocate that professional training programs expose them to Latino playwrights, giving them the chance to experience the rich heritage of classic and contemporary Latin American and Spanish theatre, both in classroom settings and in mainstage productions. Additionally, any chance to create in both of their languages has the potential to open new doors to their creativity, and to their abilities to listen and speak intelligibly without a standardized speech.

Likewise, professional training programs must examine their own prejudices when it comes to accepting Latino students into their programs and how these young actors are cast throughout their training careers. Of particular importance is how the program responds to the body-image conundrum discussed above: Are their choices supporting the establishment of healthy self-esteem and realistic future casting possibilities?

Professional training programs must also provide positive role models for these Latino student–actors among their faculty members and, for interested students, establish mentoring and apprenticeship programs with

Latino theatre companies and festivals. Undergraduate programs should give special attention to encouraging the most promising Latino students to pursue graduate work, where the training will continue to enrich them, as well as our nation's cultural life. During our bi-lingual/bi-cultural collaborations, we have found Latino student–actors hungry for an outlet, for a chance to express, for a person in the training milieu who understands their specific trials.

Training program representatives may also benefit from participating in forums at ATHE and VASTA, where discussions on cross-cultural communication and the challenges therein are held among professionals nationwide.

Ultimately, the most significant and positive impact that training programs can have may be in fostering among their faculties, staff, and student body, a clear understanding of the politics of identity. All parties to the training should know that students may choose different terms to define their identity, and that these need to be respected; they should all be encouraged to appreciate the history of bilingualism; they all need to know the issues pertaining to the Latino individual's speech sounds and their willingness and ability to shift them, as well as the navigation of their relationship to their body and body image, and a clear understanding of the professional possibilities and challenges. As a result, programs will be better prepared to train flexible and competent actors who are at the same time fully aware of their cultural identities, and able to find work in as many areas as possible.

Perhaps these words of Stuart Hall, the visionary race theorist at Birmingham University, can offer inspiration:

> There is no way, it seems to me, in which people of the world can act, can speak, can create, can come from the margins and talk, can begin to reflect on their own experience unless they come from some place, they come from some history, they inherit certain cultural traditions . . . You have to position yourself somewhere in order to say anything at all . . . The relation that peoples of the world now have to their own past is, of course, part of the discovery of their own ethnicity. They need to honor the hidden histories from which they come. They need to understand and re-value the traditions and inheritances of cultural expression and creativity. And in that sense, the past is not only a position from which to speak, but it is also an absolutely necessary resource in what one has to say.[20]

NOTES

1. Elizabeth Lozano, "The Cultural Experience of Space and Body: A Reading of Latin American and Anglo-American Comportment in Public," *Our Voices: Essays in Culture, Ethnicity and Communication* (Los Angeles: Roxbury Publications, 1997), 109.

2. The terms "Latino" and "Latina" are socially constructed, market-driven terms that consolidate numerous national and cultural identities. Throughout this chapter we will use these terms, fully aware of the multitude of languages, cultures, and traditions that the terms encompass.

3. Pew Hispanic Center, "U.S. Populations Projections: 2005–2050," at *http:// pewhispanic.org/reports/report.php?ReportID=85.*

4. In 2006, we offered our first bilingual theatre workshop in Phoenix, AZ, sponsored by Teatro Bravo; in 2007, we presented at the VASTA Conference in Denver. Also in 2007, we were named to the inaugural VASTA Fellows Program, for which we will offer workshops and symposia on bilingual theatre training.

5. Lisa García Bedolla, "The Identity Paradox: Latino Language, Politics and Selective Dissociation," *Latino Studies 1, no. 2.* (2003), 266.

6. Diana Ríos, "Mexican-American Cultural Experiences with Mass-Mediated Communication," *Our Voices: Essays in Culture, Ethnicity and Communication* (Los Angeles: Roxbury Publications, 1997), 109.

7. More information on "The Detail Method" is found in the article, "Standard Speech: The Ongoing Debate" in *Vocal Vision* (New York: Applause Books, 1997). Professor Knight, in collaboration with Professor Phil Thompson, offers workshops throughout the United States. See http://drama.arts.uci.edu/faculty/ thompson.html. Louis Colaianni published *The Joy of Phonetics and Accents* with Gale Nelson (New York: Drama Books Publishers, 1994). Colaianni also teaches workshops frequently in the U.S. See www.louiscolaianni.com.

8. Some of that scholarship includes the following: Rosa Maria Gil and Carmen Inoa Vasquez, *The Maria Paradox; How Latinas Can Merge Old Word Traditions with New World Self- Esteem* (New York: G.P. Putnam's Sons, 1996) and Bernadette Marie Calafell, *Latina/o Communication Studies; Theorizing Performance* (New York: Peter Lang Publishing, 2007).

9. Rosie Molinary, *Hijas Americas: Beauty, body, image, and growing up Latina* (Emeryville, CA: Seal Press, 2007), 181.

10. Antonia Darder, *Culture and Difference: Critical Perspectives on the Bicultural Experience in the United States* (Westport, CT: Bergin & Garvey, 1995), 10.

11. Patricia Stallings, *Teatro Luna Defies Stereotypes* (October 13, 2004). See http://www.tcpulse.com/2004/10/13/ac/mariachronicles/.

12. Molinary, *Hijas Americas: Beauty, body, image, and growing up Latina,* 185.

13. Gaston Espinosa, et al., "Hispanic Churches in American Public Life: Summary of Findings," *Institute for Latino Studies at University of Notre Dame* 2003.2, ed. 2 (2004).

14. Father Allan Deck, "The Latino Catholic Ethos: Ancient History or Future Promise?" *Journal of Hispanic/Latino Theology* (2002), 19.

15. Melissa Rivera-Marano, "The Creation of the Latina Values Scale" (PhD diss., Rutgers—The State University of New Jersey, 2000), 2209.

16. Molinary, *Hijas Americas: Beauty, body, image, and growing up Latina,* 165.

17. Micha Espinosa, "Insights into the Challenges Latino Students Face while Training in Theatre," *The Voice and Speech Review: Shakespeare Around the Globe* (Cincinnati, OH: VASTA, 2005), 133.

18. Michelle Adams, "Equality Requires Embracing Differences," *The Hispanic Outlook in Higher Education* 14, no.12 (2004) 17.

19. Darder, *Culture and Difference: Critical Perspectives on the Bicultural Experience in the United States,* 3.

20. Stuart Hall, "Ethnicity: Identity and Difference," *Radical America,* Fall, 1989, 18.

12 Keeping It Real
Without Selling Out
Toward Confronting and Triumphing Over Racially-Specific Barriers in American Acting Training

Venus Opal Reese

> *. . . to come wit you/ i hadta bring everythin*
> *the dance & the terror*
> *the dead musicians & the hope*
> *& those scars i had hidden wit smiles & good fuckin*
> *lay open*[1]

Ntozake Shange

Ron Eyerman, in his book *Cultural Trauma: Slavery and the Formation of African American Identity,* regards trauma not as an institution or experience, but as a collective memory that serves as the basis for identity formation of a people. He writes, "There is a difference between trauma as it affects individuals and as a cultural process. As a cultural process, trauma is mediated through various forms of representation and linked to the reformation of collective identity and the reworking of collective memory."[2] Eyerman's "collective memory" is more a function of language than cognitive psychology, in that he examines how each generation of African Americans goes through its own process naming and renaming American slavery. This renaming, this reconstituting of self at the communal level, is not a monolithic experience; there are many Americans of African ancestry who may have never known a day of hardship in their life; some do not know about the history of slavery in North America. This reconstituting of self has to do with the representation of experience encountered generationally and historically by a person of African ancestry—simply by virtue of skin color and the historical site that skin color represents. In other words, cultural trauma is not the institution of or experience of slavery, but rather the collective stories we tell and reconstitute generationally about slavery and its impacts. This (re)membering of cultural trauma is immortalized in plays.

Playwrights who write about historical traumatic incidents—whether the Holocaust, Apartheid, the Trail of Tears, Transatlantic Slavery, exploitation of Chicano farm workers, or Japanese labor camps—and the residue of those historical events, call for a distinct approach to performing their works. "Embodiment" is a performance style/approach called for by racially conscious African American playwriting, and the training that best serves said style.

Embodying a racialized history is based on the wounds, strategies, rage, and distortions that are indicative of a history of traumas. Embodiment is not about emptying out; it is about the courage to take on all that is not said. This taking on, as if one were putting on a coat and letting it distort/impact you, is not a fabricated "inner life" or "method acting." The courage to embody the past provides, for the audience member, her or his courage and catharsis. The courage of the actor to feel historical cultural traumas as well as the technique to remain emotionally distant is written into certain texts and requires a different approach than traditional Western acting methods. If we consider trauma not as a function of the institution of or a direct personal experience of slavery but, as Eyerman suggests, as a cultural process that reforms, reshapes, rearticulates a represented collective identity, then embodiment becomes the actor's tool for both representing and reshaping collective identity and collective memory for both the performer and the audience.

Embodying history, specifically a racialized history, is very distinct from acting in the twentieth-century European tradition. *An Actor Prepares* instructs the student to let go of the self and all that constitutes it in service of the opportunity, the space to craft an internal life for the character; to create a whole world of subtext that informs how the performer speaks, moves, pauses, and breathes, distinct from that performer's own identity. The American Method, in contrast, instructs the student to act from experience, to pull from one's individual past, senses, and endeavors. These two antithetical approaches—and many of the approaches to actor training in the U.S. that mix, match, or rebel against these two—are identity based at the level of individual. Embodiment is rooted in history, a history of traumas no less, at the level of community. Embodiment has very little to do with an individual's personal experience; it has to do with how a history, told through cultural memory, reformation, and representation, impacts a community in which the individual is directly linked to the collective.

The work of many of America's most major playwrights of African ancestry requires and elicits specific approaches: Ntozake Shange, George C. Wolfe, and Suzan-Lori Parks write embodiment into their texts through sentence structure, punctuation, stage direction, grammar, and syntax. The works of Glenda Dickerson, Will Power, Sara Jones, Rick Herby, Carlyle Brown, and Robert O'Hara all call for embodiment, and this call is written as a remembering, a reimagining of history that requires what W.E.B. De Bois, in *The Souls of Black Folk*, called a double-consciousness. This double-consciousness is often written as signifying, irony, satire, and camp in the actual text. Often it is misunderstood or ignored, or attempts are made to force the actor to use Western norms to access these works. What Robert O'Hara, Suzan-Lori Parks, and I (as both a playwright and performer) are making visible through theatre is a history of traumas that have impact and tangibility today. The actor of African ancestry must be trained to confront and deconstruct that history at the level of both community and individual in order to fully realize dramatic texts. Operating "on top of," instead of *using* that history, lends itself to hollow performances that are plastic, splintered, and forced.

KEEPING REAL VS. SELLING OUT

The foundations of American actor training are Stanislavski, Meyerhold, and the Method. Brecht, Grotowski, the Viewpoints, and other approaches serve as alternatives to the dominant model of training circulated and disseminated in our colleges, universities, and conservatories. If one is of African ancestry (which I am), and has been trained at universities (which I have), one is keenly aware of how the historical racial concepts, views, values, paradigms, and paradoxes that make up what it means to be American, permeate actor training. What is more, acting techniques are then paired with dramatic texts that have the tendency to further leave the actor of African ancestry with yet another space in which "blackness" becomes servitude, violence, or God-like sainthood—racialized. Because of the history of Trans-Atlantic Slavery, "blackness" is automatically positioned as wrong, less, subservient.

There is the propensity to feel inadequate as a black American actor-in-training. The black actor's training (as well as the desire to prove one's worth and experience a sense of accomplishment) can leave the actor with the strong impression that one must erase all racial markers, signs, and signifiers, in order to be marketable. My argument is not unique to actors of African ancestry. The same argument can be, and has been, made for all sorts of historically marginalized performers. My point here is to draw attention to both the external and internal disavowal performers of African ancestry may undertake. That is, in order to make a living wage and experience a sense of accomplishment some sort of erasure is needed. An actor of African ancestry may embrace transformations in diction, speech, body weight, hair, posture, style of dress, passion, and the like, in order to be more "marketable" (read: white)—beginning in graduate school or actor-training programs. Or the actor of African ancestry, generally, must be willing to be cast as the maid, thug, ho, or Uncle Tom. Indeed, *Uncle Tom's Cabin* coined many of the types that people of African ancestry can occupy in public spheres. Today, coons, mammies, jezebels, and bucks still saturate TV, film, cyberspace, and the theatre.

Times have progressed, indeed, and more "blacks" are being seen and circulated. However, what goes unnoticed is that while we have more "blacks" in theatre and film, they are more of the same sort of "blacks" that have been circulated and disseminated since *Uncle Tom's Cabin* and Transatlantic Minstrelsy. Realism is still the dominant form of acting training in America; what people believe is real about "black people" is what roles are written, what plays get produced throughout the U.S., and what is taught in schools. For example, August Wilson's canon of plays that chronicle the experience of Americans of African ancestry for each decade of the twentieth century reinscribe a heterosexual, patriarchal, essentialist notion of the "black" experience in the twentieth century. His work includes every stereotype that has been circulated since *Uncle Tom's Cabin* (Bo Willie in *The Piano Lesson* reads like a traditional coon, Levy in *Ma Rainey's Black Bottom* is a raging buck, Ma Rainey in *Ma Rainey's Black Bottom* is mammy to both her all-male band and the white producers nursing at her symbolic titty in the form of the Blues, and on and on.) His work is produced all over the world. In contrast, Rhodessa Jones' *Big Butt Girls and Hard-Headed Women*, which addresses incarcerated women of all hues, or Robert O'Hara's *Insurrection: Holding History*, which addresses sexuality and slavery, are not widely circulated, taught, or produced. August Wilson is an extraordinary playwright, but there are others who point to a different "black" experience that has not always been championed. My intention with this article is to offer an approach that is useful for actors who find themselves playing stereotypical roles that stand in for the "real"—whether the playwright is black or not—and to offer insight for teachers who may be teaching historically marginalized students who are committed to "keeping it real" without selling out.

EMBODIMENT DEFINED

My notion of embodiment is the intersection of personal history with collective memory. Historically, people of African ancestry have adapted to survive in a world that systematically reinscribed servitude, social death, and erasure.[3] This adapting for the sake of survival was a reaction both appropriate and necessary. Embodiment is not about adaptation however—it is about deconstruction. In order to take something apart, one must have a comprehensive understanding and the wherewithal (or patience) to take it apart and execute it. Once something is taken apart, it loses its charge—it can be reconfigured to the specifications of the deconstructionist.[4] When one can deconstruct a stereotype and reconfigure it to serve one's intention—with full knowledge that an observer tends to read the stereotype in a traditional historical sense—one has one's finger on the lever and dials of the social-geographical psyche of what it means to be American.

It is only when one can deconstruct the historical stereotypes, the historical roles, and the historical spaces people of African ancestry may occupy in public spheres (i.e., mammy, buck, sambo, Uncle Tom, topsy, coon, jezebel, Aunt Sarah, tragic mulatto, etc.) that one can embody them. The ability to take them apart frees one from the rage, hatred, hurt, and dishonor affiliated with these historical signifiers. When one is free to put on mammy or take off sambo, one has access to ways of bringing the history of hurt, pain, betrayal, sacrifice, love, and disgust to *any* role created—purposefully, powerfully, authentically. One has permission, internally, to bring forth all of the racial slights, violations, and traumas that are simultaneously historical and personal.

Embodiment is not acting at all—it is the courage to relive publicly the breaks in belonging that constitute self at the level of community. Said another way, embodiment is the act of historicized enactments distilled, crystallized, and refined to the point that the human condition is nakedly and unapologetically exposed. Embodiment is immediate and urgent; there is no "build up." Every hurt and betrayal, every do-wop diddy—from Bo Diddley to P. Diddy—every bowed head and raised fist that constitutes "blackness" is simmering just beneath the surface, waiting for permission to manifest itself. This simmering, this heat, is written into many of the texts of American playwrights of African ancestry. Sometimes it is in the words—more often than not it is in the form.

The strong language of these playwrights serves as the vehicle by which embodiment can be identified by the reader and employed by the actor.[5] I am not suggesting that every American playwright of African ancestry incorporates profanity in their writing—although many of them, from August Wilson to Leoi Jones, have curse words in their plays. I am also not taking the position that all American playwrights of African ancestry *only* write about negative situations that result from the history of slavery in North America. The playwrights I discuss here are playwrights who do, intentionally, address the historical impact of the lived experience of that history through the folk experience of everyday people in a language that reflects that particular experience—swearing, violence, violation, and all.

These playwrights craft their words very deliberately, specifically when dealing with a history of traumas. The opportunity here is for both the reader and the actor to confront and deconstruct their own reactions and fears.[6] I refer the reader to the line in *Angels in America*, Act II, Scene IV, when Louis says to the man in the park: "I want you to fuck me, hurt me, make me bleed." It is clear to me that the playwright is evoking an experience and a history within American gay culture that, if edited out, would undermine the intent and power of his work. The language of a history of traumas is immediate, urgent, vivid, and visceral. The examples that follow demonstrate how embodiment is written into the text as both content and form.

FIRST SAMPLE OF EMBODIMENT

Venus Opal Reese, *Redemption: A Collision of Memory and History in Four Breaths*[7]

The first sample is an abbreviated scene from my own play/performance text, a piece about the crevices and cracks where racialized identities are born and die. In this scene, the immediacy of the language is indicative of the roles embodying a history of traumas that are being acted out across time. What is more, the language employed is comprised of a series of signs and signifiers rooted in the impact of the history of slavery in regard to the power dynamic between the male and the female genders, which in context, become racialized. This scene demonstrates through the text and staging a series of physical violations that require an immediacy and urgency in order for the bodies embodying this history to survive the moment re-lived on multiple levels: physically, familially, and emotionally.

The form or structure of the scene is just as telling as the language. When the performers step out of character to check on each other, only to *put on* a different version of the same role, the performers become the embodiment of the stereotypes deconstructed. The performers are freed from reacting to the stigma associated with the stereotype of "black pimp" and "black drug addict" while simultaneously calling on the historical and personal positionality, experience, and/or knowledge of these types to manipulate them in service of the audience. The performers have to do the requisite work in order to relate to these roles as roles and not reiterations of themselves. They have to take apart the stereotypes and confront viscerally the stigmas in which they are routinely positioned. The access to embodiment is courage and authenticity. At the end of this chapter, I include a few exercises that support performers in accessing the courage and authenticity for embodiment.

Restitution

> (DARK FEMALE EMBODIMENT is in the bathroom sitting on the edge of the tub. Isaac Hayes' "By the Time I get to Phoenix" plays audibly in the background. It's the 1970s. Her arms are heavily tracked with needle scars. It is important to find the humor in this monologue.)

DARK FEMALE EMBODIMENT
I use to be pretty. I remember someone telling me that, I think.

(DARK FEMALE EMBODIMENT starts smacking her lips and stretching her tongue out, and turns to the audience.)

Hey, you want me?

(Seductively.)

You want me? Nobody ever wanted me. They just wanted what I could give them or what they could take out on me.

(DARK FEMALE EMBODIMENT rolls a joint and takes a hit. She looks around the bathroom.)

I've been here all my life and I never said a word.

(DARK FEMALE EMBODIMENT picks up needle and prepares heroin in bong. She ties a belt around her arm, pulls belt with her teeth. Music comes up. Enter BLACK MALE EMBODIMENT. She sees him. She then picks up needle and touches her face, making the decision.)

BLACK MALE EMBODIMENT

. . . That's right bitch, say my name.

DARK FEMALE EMBODIMENT
Brother man . . .

(She kisses him in the mouth.)
(Kiss.)
I'm pretty for you.

(She stabs the needle into neck and pushes the dope into his veins. His eyes pop wide open and his hand goes around her neck. He squeezes. Lights fade. Music comes up loud, then abruptly stops. Working lights come up on stage, both EMBODIMENTS step out of character, check on each other and BLACK MALE EMBODIMENT exits, s.l. while DARK FEMALE EMBODIMENT changes on stage for plantation/1970s scene.)

SECOND SAMPLE OF EMBODIMENT

Suzan-Lori Parks, *In the Blood* [8]

Hester, a homeless woman with five children, is being admonished by the world. She is regarded as slut, hussy, stupid, and worthless. She is the quintessential jezebel gone bad. Suzan brilliantly modernized this historical type by superimposing welfare mother onto the jezebel. The notion that there is "BAD NEWS IN HER BLOOD" positions her plight as a genetic one: "Once a triflin' ho nigger, always a triflin' ho nigger." Or, said in Black Vernacular English, she got it from her momma (which implies that she got it from her mother, and she got it from her mother, and on and on backward—slavery was passed down through the maternal line).

The language of the prologue is immediate and urgent. While it is informative it is more an embodiment of all of the racial unspoken opinions American society generally holds regarding black women, unwed pregnancy, and homelessness.

The all caps, lack of punctuation, and use of sentence fragments requires that the performer let go of "acting" in order to create the requisite urgency for the audience to be in the world of this play. Realism will not work here, embodiment will—embodiment of those opinions, judgments, assessments of black women with multiple children who do not work and who float in the American air like invisible smog. It takes a level of courage, authenticity, and deconstruction at the level of self to perform these unspoken judgments with the full vehemence of a KKK member while maintaining the awareness of wearing the mask.

> PROLOGUE
> *All clustered together.*
>
> All
> THERE SHE IS!
> WHO DOES SHE THINK
> SHE IS
> THE NERVE OF SOME PEOPLE HAVE
> SHOULDN'T HAVE IT YOU CANT AFFORD IT
> AND YOU KNOW SHE CANT
> SHE DON'T GOT NO SKILLS
> CEPT ONE
> CANT READ CANT WRITE
> SHE MARRIED?
> WHAT DO YOU THINK?
> SHE OUTGHTA BE MARRIED
> THAT'S WHY THINGS ARE BAD LIKE THEY ARE
> CAUSE OF

GIRLS LIKE THAT
THAT EVER HAPPEN TO ME YOU WOULDN'T SEE ME
HAVING IT
YOU WOULDN'T SEE THAT HAPPENING TO ME
WHO THE HELL SHE THINK SHE IS
AND NOW WE GOT TO PAY FOR IT
THE NERVE
SOME PEOPLE HAVE
BAD LUCK
SHE OUGHTA GET MARRIED
TO WHO?
THIS IS HER FIFTH
FIFTH?
SHE GOT FIVE OF THEM
FIVE BRATS
AND NOT ONE OF THEM GOT A DADDY
PAH!
  They spit.
  . . .
All
All
All

SHE KNOWS SHES A NO COUNT
SHIFTLESS
HOPELESS
BAD NEWS
BURDEN TO SOCIETY
HUSSY
SLUT
PAH!
They spit.

THIRD SAMPLE OF EMBODIMENT

**Robert O'Hara, *Insurrection: Holding
History,* Section II, Plantation**[9]

Ron, a contemporary gay graduate student, has traveled back in time with
his 189-year-old grandfather to a plantation in South Hampton, right before
Nat Turner's insurrection. Ron employs multiple performative devices—
everything from camp to musical numbers—to excavate the intersection of
race, class, and sexuality during North American slavery. Ron takes all of
the historical stereotypes of "black" Americans and using wit, humor, and
melodrama, he adds another marginal type to our canon: Faggot/queen.

Ron employs many of the tropes we have come to recognize as "black gay man" in his text. He writes sarcasm, wit, humor, irreverence, camp, sexual innuendoes, sensitivity, charm, and sheer audacity into his texts as tools for embodying a history of (homo)sexuality within the "black" canon of stereotypes that has been virtually ignored. His use of language and form allows the performer, as well as the audience, to step out of the prescribed roles allotted historically, such that a different history gets told. Faggot says and does all the things we think we would say and do if we were on a plantation with our contemporary mindset. He is degraded and put in his place for having the nerve to stand up as a "black" man. It is not an accident that OVA SEEA JONES spits in Faggot's face, not for being a "faggot," but for defending a "black" woman against the violence of a "white" man.

OVA SEEA JONES: *(Deep.)* ANSWER ME NIGGRA TAKE TIME OUTTA MY BUSY SCHEDULE ON SIX FARMS TA—

IZZIE MAE:—TA BEAT THE SHIT OUTTA MY BLACK TRIF-LIN' STUPID SHIFTLESS NO-COUNT LAZY NIGGA ASS SUH.

(IZZIE MAE IS NOW STRIPPED NAKED.)

OVA SEEA JONES: That's right.

BUCK NAKED!

BUCK NAKED: Yes suh boss?

OVA SEEA JONES: Tie her ta that whippin' Post Buck.

BUCK NAKED: Yes suh boss.

OVA SEEA JONES: Tie Her Tight.

BUCK NAKED: Yes suh boss.

OVA SEEA JONES: And her legs too.

BUCK NAKED: And her legs too.

OVA SEEA JONES: TIGHT.

BUCK NAKED: Yes suh boss.

(BUCK NAKED ties IZZIE MAE.

TIGHT.

OVA SEEA JONES LIFTS WHIP.)

T.J *(Low)*: Nuthin 'Bout Nuthin.

(Over Seea Jones Lashes IZZI MAE once.

STRONG.

She screams.

He RAISES Whip Again.)

Nuthin 'Bout—

RON: MUTHAFUCKA HAVE YOU LOST YO' FUCKIN' MIND!?!

(DEAD SILENCE.)

OVA SEEA JONES: nigga what's yo' name?

RON: . . . Faggot.

OVA SEEA JONES: Faggot what did you just say to me?

RON: I said MUTHAFUCKA—

(*OVA SEEA JONES spits in Ron's face.*)
OVA SEEA JONES: How did you find out I was Fuckin' yo' Mutha boy?

All three of the embodiment examples—Reese, Parks, and O'Hara—demonstrate the reliance on a shared cultural identity, deconstructed and inverted racially specific stereotypes, and the use of form to convey a sensibility indicative of attempts to capture "blackness" in the text. Each example uses tropes that are readily recognizable to American audiences, and yet the use of the tropes circumvents the historical meaning associated with those tropes. Embodiment allows for a reimagining, a remaking, and a remembering of self at the level of community for both the performer and the audience.

But how? How does one begin to access and employ the positionality and history of trauma that comes with being historically marginalized? What exercises move one toward embodiment?

EXERCISES

Here are three sets of notebook and role-playing exercises I use to access embodiment for myself, both as a performer and as a director. I have also included some exercises and resources teachers can use. As I stated earlier, access to embodiment requires courage and authenticity. These exercises can be done alone, in a group, and/or with a partner. Actors from any racial background can use these exercises. People who have historically been marginalized may have a richer well from which to draw, but the exercises can be a useful tool for any actor.

WRITING A WRONG

- Write down a time when you experienced racism personally or witnessed it. Write down how it made you feel, what you made it mean about yourself, the other person involved, and the world. Say everything you need to say about it. Leave nothing out. You do not have to be fair or politically correct. Write it all down. Notice the emotions that arise for you in writing this down.
- Read the story to your partner. You partner's job is simply to get what it is like for you. Keep reading your story until you experience being heard and having a sense of freedom. Switch.
- Now write the same story from the perspective of the racist. Write what you were feeling about the incident, what you made it mean about yourself, the other person involved, and the world. Say everything you need to say about it. Leave nothing out. You do not have to be fair or

politically correct. Write it all down. Notice the emotions that arise for you in writing this down.
- Read the story to your partner. You partner's job is simply to get what it is like for you. Keep reading your story until it you experience being heard and having a sense of freedom. Switch.

ACTING OUT/MIRROR WORK

- Select five stereotypes that really upset you. Write down the characteristics affiliated with the type as actions (i.e., blonde hair = bimbo = act ditzy, etc.). Then grant yourself the permission to act out the stereotype until it becomes a role that you can put on or take off without reacting. Do this work in the mirror until you are free.

RACIAL AUTHENTICTY

- Write down each reference to race, stereotypes, and discrimination mentioned in the media, conversations, and in your immediate environment within a one-hour timeframe. Just make a little note about what happened and what you made the incident mean. Start to distinguish "what happened" from "what you made it mean."
- Create other valid meanings of instances of racists' acts—from Jim Crow to the Holocaust. Create a comic interpretation, a tragic interpretation, a sitcom interpretation, etc.
- Ask yourself the questions: How do I participate in my own degradation? What do I need? What am I pretending about me about race? What is that hiding? What is the impact of this pretense on myself, in my life, and in the world? What is the payoff? What do I get out of it? What does it cost me? What can I create that inspires me?
- Feel free to write down the answers to these questions or to express them with a partner or in a group. Please remember you are not looking for a "right" answer—you are saying what you have never articulated before and letting yourself experience the impact of a life of racial pretense. And if you have already done this work, great—now do it again, more profoundly than before.

Considering that many students have not had the opportunity to participate in these sorts of inquiries, writing (as opposed to improvisation) creates a safe place to begin. I find that just giving the students the space to say what they did not realize they had to say about race allows for a level of creativity and community in the classroom that is both inspiring and intimate. Creative writing within actor training allows actors to begin to understand what it takes for playwrights to write, and it also gives them the opportunity to know themselves as the author, not simply a vessel. Some students discover that they are actually playwrights or directors; others realize they are not interested in writing, but have gained an honest sense of how to tell a story. All of the students leave the exercises having had the experience of being known and of discovery.

As at teacher, it is extremely important to recognize and have compassion for the fact that students, and perhaps teachers themselves, have limited, constrained, and historical ways of talking about and viewing race. In a rapidly globalizing world—with the issue of race being the current that flows through every aspect of American life, and with the social changes that come with a president who self-identifies as black—what's wanted and needed is new language and new ways to talk about race. These exercises give access to a new realm of speaking and listening regarding race. Sometimes you have to be willing to listen to the students' stories to hear where they are "coming from" instead of what they are saying. I had one such teacher, Jeanine Thompson at Ohio State University, who listened to everything I could not say and literally gave me space, safety, and then language so that I could create my own voice from my lived experience, as well as from the training she and my other teachers were providing. People only speak in safe spaces. Feel free to do the exercises yourself before doing them with the students, so that you are teaching from an informed place. You may be surprised to discover rage and trauma regarding race in your own experience that may be defining or limiting your pedagogy.

I must address the appropriateness of dealing with matters of rage and trauma in an acting class. I am not advocating that a student expose traumatic personal experiences (i.e., rape, incest, abuse, etc.). I am advocating the space and the safety to confront, on a piece of paper, racial incidents that may not have been articulated or simply expressed or heard. One of the biggest challenges for teachers who are teaching students who have been historically marginalized is fear. Teachers are, sometimes, afraid to address the obvious in a class because they do not want to offend a student or they are afraid of the reaction of the student. Teachers have racial memory, too—it goes both ways. What I do, and what I recommend teachers do, is create a space where race and all sorts of difference can be safely and openly discussed in a discussion format. One way I do this is by showing my students a film called *Race: The Power of An Illusion*. This is an extraordinary resource to evoke a conversation about race as a social phenomenon instead of a personal affront. There are three one-hour videos in the series along with a comprehensive PBS website for teachers that includes questions, exercises, and web resources concerning race.[10] I use this resource regularly with my students.

I have also developed, in a university setting, a series of courses concerning race: "Performing Race," "Constructing Race," and "Transforming Race," in which I teach my students to begin to consider race a function of language and of the stories we tell, instead of a biological fact. This sort of relationship to race creates space to have conversations or do exercises that otherwise could become charged with tension. One assignment I give beginning acting students is to select a scene that they would generally not be cast for in commercial theatre. I encourage them to go to the extreme: a straight, white, non-disabled male selects a scene in which he is a lesbian, Hispanic, disabled person. Students have to do the exercise over one week's time, then come back to present the scene and discuss what it was like for them, what they learned, and how could they be truthful in the role. While many students of color have played roles historically assigned to white actors like Hedda Gabler or Biff Loman, white students or even students who identify as heterosexual have not had to confront and deconstruct the many self-identified assumptions that come with privilege. What is more, even if a student of color performed a role that was written for a character of European ancestry, many times the student has not recognized that he or she is applying stereotypes of whiteness that can now be deconstructed.

My intention with the various exercises is to give permission, space, and safety for students to use what they already have with them: their talents and their histories in the service of their passion. Embodiment both makes use of and validates what the actor of African ancestry, or any other historically marginalized actor-in-training, brings to the classroom.

NOTES

1. Ntozake Shange, *For Colored Girls Who Have Considered Suicide When the Rainbow Is Enuf* (New York: Scribner Poetry, 1997), 41. This text demonstrates the point of this chapter, capturing also the intent of its title, "Keeping It Real Without Selling Out." *For Colored Girls . . .* was the first work by a black (female) playwright in the history of the Americas to be nominated for Tony, Grammy, and Emmy awards. Shange was speaking in a vernacular that was all about "keeping it real," and was doing so without compromising her voice. Her writing points to the central argument of the essay: African American playwrights who evoke the lived experience of many African American students who do not see themselves reflected in the language or the form of traditional Western plays. These students often feel that, in order to "make it," they must erase, ignore, or otherwise compromise their lived experience. Traditional Western actor training tends to reject, minimize, or be frightened by the rich complexities of building on a history of traumas. This chapter is designed as a catalyst such that the histories of traumas written by American playwrights of African ancestry become an opportunity for both the students and the teachers who teach them.
2. Ron Eyerman, *Cultural Trauma: Slavery and the Formation of African American Identity* (Cambridge, UK: Cambridge University Press, 2002), 1.
3. Orlando Paterson's text, *Slavery and Social Death* (Cambridge, MA: Harvard University Press, 2007), deals brilliantly with the notion of slaves as nonbeings and the destruction of natal roots throughout the world.
4. It can be argued that this is what Bertolt Brecht was attempting with various alienation devices.

5. There may be teachers who are concerned that just the reading of these plays in a classroom setting or even reading this chapter is, in a way, encouraging students to use profanity in class. I simply encourage these teachers to ask themselves whether the question also arises when teaching David Mamet's work, for example, and in the same way?

6. If the curse words in these texts make people uncomfortable, this discomfort points to and mirrors the experience that many graduate students feel when they encounter a form they don't understand or that is unfamiliar to them. It may be off-putting for them to memorize Ibsen or to read "Woyzeck," but we do not as a result remove them from the "classics." Some students of color, too, may very well be offended by profanity; they, too, may link cursing to poor, ghetto society. In response, I teach all my students to honor the words of the playwright while giving them the tools to deconstruct any tension that she or he may experience when there is profanity in a text.

7. Venus Opal Reese, *Redemption: A Collision of History and Memory in Four Breaths*, unpublished play text. The play was produced at Stanford University in California (Dir. Reese), and has received featured staged readings at the National Black Theatre Festival, the Bay Area Playwrights Festival, and the La MaMa Umbria International, in Spoleto, Italy.

8. Suzan-Lori Parks, "In the Blood," in *The Fire This Time: African American Plays for the 21st Century*, ed. Harry J. Elam, Jr. and Robert Alexander (New York: Theatre Communications Group, 2002), 9–10.

9. Robert O'Hara, "Insurrection: Holding History," *The Fire This Time, ibid.*, 291.

10. California News Reel, "Race: the Power of An Illusion," produced by Larry Adelman, 2003, http://www.pbs.org/race/000_General/000_00-Home.htm.

13 Disability and Access
A Manifesto for Actor Training

Victoria Ann Lewis

(The first character is called "Open the Door," who begins after knocking.)
OPEN-THE-DOOR:
Open the Door, and let me in
A merry Act I will begin,
I'll act it young, I'll act it sage,
> I'll act it on a public Stage!
> Room, Room, brave gallant boys, come give us room to rhyme!

Whether I rise or stand or fall,
I do my duty to please you all.
But room, brave gallants, room! Room I do require!

And if you don't believe a word of what I say,
Step in St. George, and clear the way!
Folk Play, England, circa 1840

The head of the [Theatre] department was on my panel. Four people were smiling but not him. One of the panel members came running after me in the hall, saying, "Sir, sir, please stop. The chair of the department—he's never worked with someone disabled and he is not going to start now. I just want you to know that you gave one of the best auditions—here is twenty bucks for lunch. Go celebrate because you deserve it."
Brad Rothbart, on his audition at a top-ranked,
undergraduate performing arts conservatory, 1991

Presented here are two poles of theatre access. In the first, a folk play from England, tradition has it that amateur village performers in deep disguise rumble from house to house demanding space to perform their short comic tales of death and resurrection. The cottage inhabitants, the so-called "brave gallants," push aside the kitchen table, roll up their rugs, and hope their lights survive the sword play. St. George enters, followed by the villain, the Slasher or the Turkish Knight, and a battle between good and evil ensues. One or the other is killed and then a doctor arrives to restore the deceased to life. Strong beer and "pocketfuls of money" reward the players' efforts. The masked men depart into the night, moving on to the next house demanding, "Room, room, give us room." At the opposite pole, when a young man seeks entrance into an acting conservatory, the "brave gallants" are not so accommodating. St. George does not appear to sweep the place clean of physical and mental barriers. The wandering player *is* rewarded for his efforts: a twenty-dollar lunch! But not in the room. And the ambiguity is inescapable—a handout or a gift? A beggar or an entertainer?

Like many of my disabled colleagues, I found doors rarely opened on demand. Long before the Americans with Disabilities Act, I made my way to New York's Neighborhood Playhouse in search of actor training. My interview was brief. Neighborhood Playhouse, the interviewer explained, offered *professional* training. The school would not, *could* not, accept me as an acting student. Childhood polio had left me with a pronounced limp and an atrophied leg. I would never work as a professional actor. If I wanted to seek medical advice and somehow eliminate the disability they might reconsider. But I knew there was no "cure" for my condition. St. George would not appear as my champion and no "Noble Doctor" could resurrect my hopes.

Finding traditional training closed, I stumbled upon the thriving, alternative theatre scene of the 1960s and 1970s. For the next six years I received training and work experience as a member of two alternative ensemble companies: Family Circus Theatre in Portland, Oregon, and Lilith, A Woman's Theatre, in San Francisco, both companies part of the surge of "people's theatre" collectives that sprang up on the West Coast in the 1970s, the most prominent and influential of which is the long-lasting San Francisco Mime Troupe. Eventually I made my way to Los Angeles, worked in commercial television and regional theatre, found a creative home for nearly two decades as an artist-in-residence at the Mark Taper Forum, and now teach theatre (including acting) at the university level. So Neighborhood Playhouse was in error when they equated my disability with an inability to work and subsequently regarded me as not eligible for professional training. And as for "curing" my disability in order to participate in their curriculum, ironically, in the alternative ensemble companies that did welcome me, I received a much more physically based training than Neighborhood Playhouse offered at that time. I studied mime, jazz dance,

Alexander, charting my own way through those disciplines given my faulty musculature.[1]

Today, two civil rights laws—the Americans with Disabilities Act (ADA) of 1991 and Section 504 of the Rehabilitation Act of 1977—prohibit discrimination in education and employment on the basis of disability. Schools, public or private, can no longer exclude disabled persons from theatrical training. Theatres and universities must be architecturally accessible, at least those buildings newly constructed or undergoing extensive renovations. We have knocked, demanded, and much has changed.

But, as Brad Rothbart's story documents, the doors to our training institutions are still reluctant to open to aspirants with disabilities. In 1998, a disabled actor with an undergraduate degree in theatre applied to an MFA acting program at a prominent state university. At her final audition the head movement instructor approached the actor, who had a severely scoliosed spine and impaired gait. He stood on his head and then challenged her, "This is what we do in my class. Can you do that?" "No, I cannot," she replied. The instructor did not block her entry to the school but refused to admit her into his classes. These young people in search of professional training in the 1990s heard the same arguments that I had encountered twenty-five years before: because of your disability you will not work and because of your physical impairment you will not be able to fulfill the requirements of our curriculum.

In my experience as a working actress, producer, and theatre educator for the past thirty years, in theatres ranging from grassroots to Equity, and in venues from street fairs to prime-time television, I have found that these two positions—one, that the disabled actor is unemployable and, two, that physically disabled actors will not be able to master significant areas of actor training—are still widely held, if seldom publicly proclaimed. They are maintained by the fearful and the compassionate, in both professional and academic theatre. The decisions or policies that follow from these positions are not seen as discriminatory by the gatekeepers of the training institutions, but rather as pragmatic and based in the realities of American theatre practice. One must, regrettably, sometimes be cruel only to be kind.

But on closer analysis, which I mean to supply here, these practices are based not in reality but on assumptions, myths about both the disabled person as well as the efficacy of theatre training. I begin with two case studies of performers and schools that broke with the field and accepted significantly physically impaired students into their MFA programs. The exploration of three aspects of actor training—movement, voice, and casting—is drawn from the specific experiences of the two young actors as they made their way through their respective MFAs, as well as from additional anecdotal and historical information that establishes a context for such journeys. I argue that serious and rigorous theatrical training is possible for disabled students, provided instructors and degree programs are flexible and at least minimally responsive to cultural changes in the individual and social experience of disability brought about by the disability rights movement that began in the 1970s. [2]

The question of employability touches on critical issues in current discussions concerning the efficacy and responsibilities of theatre-training programs. In the stories presented here we will follow the experiences and reasoning of several leaders in the field of graduate actor training who came to embrace the inclusion of disabled actors in their programs. Here we acknowledge the counter position—that the inclusion of disabled actors, particularly in MFA programs, is a violation of their mandate to provide actors for the industry (regional theatre as well as film and television). From this perspective, any efforts towards inclusive recruiting and expanded casting policies are doomed to irrelevance in the face of an increasingly globalized entertainment marketplace that demands a homogenized, physically perfect product (actor).

In answer, we draw on historical evidence that theatrical policies can contribute to the cultural enfranchisement of minority constituents and, in turn, expand our larger cultural conversations even in latter-day capitalism. Only two generations ago, casting opportunities for African American actors on the legitimate stage were limited and seeking an MFA from an elite conservatory something of a fool's errand. As the civil rights movement reshaped national social expectations, institutions, and laws, gifted African American playwrights created rich and various roles for trained actors of color. Theatre impresarios such as Joseph Papp (Public Theatre) and Bill Bushnell (Los Angeles Theatre Center) mandated nontraditional casting policies for all their productions. I posit that the majority of professional acting programs today do not exclude talented, competitive students of color on the basis of the limited roles available in the industry (even though actors of color still encounter underemployment and discrimination). Nor should they exclude talented, competitive disabled students because casting opportunities are limited. No one can predict what new stories will re-people the American stage. Over the past thirty years, the disability rights movement has effected a similar, if less visible, cultural upheaval, legal and behavioral, and a number of nationally recognized playwrights have created roles best embodied by (trained) disabled actors. For example, Mark Medoff's licensing contract for union productions of *Children of a Lesser God* (1979) required that the roles of Sarah, Orin, and Lydia be played by deaf or hard-of-hearing actors or rights would not be granted. Arguably the legal provision alone might not have been successful without a pool of trained and experienced deaf and hard-of-hearing actors ready to take advantage of this opportunity. But there were. In 1967, the National Theatre of the Deaf (founded just two years before in 1965) established a professional training program which was funded by the United States Congress. Thus, one play and, more importantly, a clear and uncompromised commitment to equal opportunity, *can* revolutionize the artistic development of an entire generation of actors. This chapter is predicated on the belief that artistic leadership and artist advocacy can create policies that will democratize the American stage, and that such efforts are not primarily about good works, but rather good art and good business.

CASE STUDIES

The Gatekeepers

In the late 1990s, both Mel Shapiro, Head of the MFA Acting Program at the UCLA School of Theatre, Film, and Television, and Howard Burman, then Chair of the MFA Theatre Program at California State University Long Beach, accepted significantly disabled actors into their degree programs. Mel Shapiro rejects the claim that an MFA is a guarantee of employment and that therefore the program should only accept students with commercial viability. Shapiro insists: "I can't turn it into a meat market. I never have. I throw away that issue. Most people don't work whether [they're] disabled or not. I just have to deal with—is this someone I want to work with for three years? Is this person gifted enough that we're not fooling each other? And I leave it at that." [3] According to Shapiro, the UCLA MFA in acting is a *professional* training program in the sense that: "You acquire a technique and a way of working that makes you employable in just about any circumstances. You can do film, you can do a play, you can do television. You can act in Ibsen, act in Grotowski. You are there to gain skills. That's about all it is." California State Long Beach's Howard Burman agrees that one of his goals is to take the actor "further down the road of skills training and help them become better performers."[4] But, in addition, Burman emphasizes that an MFA program is in a sense a "licensing agency." The MFA degree is certification of professional competence to teach.

Even so, Shapiro and Burman, both long-time men of the theatre, knew they were pushing the envelope when they opened their doors to Ann Stocking and Diana Jordan. Stocking, 4'9", has a spinal deformity and walks with a limp. Jordan is an African American with cerebral palsy and thus faces a double discrimination in terms of a career. According to Burman, his decision to accept Jordan was pragmatic. "The reason we took Diana into the program was very simple—she was a very good actress. That's it," he insists. "OK, she's handicapped, but that's not the issue here. The issue is—can she benefit from the kind of training we offer and can she perform with our professional program? The answer to both of those questions was yes."[5] Shapiro was not as at ease with Ann Stocking's application for admission to his program. "It was scary," he remembers. "You're looking for people who are going to go through a very physical, rigorously difficult course. I had never dealt with a person who was disabled."[6]

The Petitioners

Ann Stocking was about to give up on graduate training when Edit Villareal, who at the time was the Chair of the MFA in Playwriting at UCLA and had seen Stocking act in the Mark Taper Forum's New Work Festival, convinced her to audition one more time. By the end of her undergraduate education at San Diego State University, Stocking was well-established in the undergraduate theatre program, even playing leads. But the same director/teacher who gave her many of those leads sat her down one day and said, "You know, Annie, this can be an avocation for you, but it cannot be your vocation. The world doesn't work that way. I'm sorry."[7] Undaunted, she auditioned for two prestigious MFA acting programs. "The first was a nightmare. The interviewer sneezed through the entire audition," she recalls. "I was very, very nervous. I couldn't cope with the pressure even though I had the tools." The second audition went better. The interviewer talked with Stocking for a few minutes asking her among other things how she would deal with the dance element. "I felt he was interested but not sold," she observed. Villareal *was* interested and approached Mel Shapiro, recommending that he see Ann. Because of Villareal's enthusiasm, Stocking felt invited to audition. "I think that invitation allowed me to go into the UCLA audition with confidence," she speculates in retrospect. "They knew I was coming. There was an open dialogue about my situation. I felt recruited rather than begging to get in. It helped."

Around the same time, in Chicago, Diana Jordan prepared for the University/Resident Theatre Association (U/RTA) auditions. Jordan had discovered her talent for acting as an undergraduate at the University of Kansas where she majored in occupational therapy in order "to get a real job and please my parents." Once out of school and working as an occupational therapist, she felt "miserable" and decided to try for an MFA. Like any aspiring actor, she was interested in "three years to focus on my craft and not take classes here and there."[8] But Jordan had another goal: eventually to teach theatre to the larger disability community, a community long excluded from the mainstream American cultural scene. At the U/RTA auditions, Howard Burman and his team were struck by Jordan's talent (her audition piece was from the opening monologue of *Richard III*) and her honesty. Burman remembers asking her, "Is stamina going to be an issue for you? This is a very demanding program." And Diana replied, "Am I going to be tired after a long day's work? You bet." Burman laughs, "Now that's a decent answer."[9]

Movement Training

From the very beginning of theatre training, in one way or another, the mind has been telling the body to go to dance class.[10]

Once they were accepted, each woman had to make their own way through a curriculum not designed to serve such wide variations from the norm. The initiations were rocky.

Stocking's very first class at UCLA was hip-hop with Andre Paradis, a former dancing partner of Paula Abdul. Stocking had never taken a dance class in her life. In a phone interview in 2001, Stocking recalls: "I stood in the back with the overweight guy and the guy with gout. We [were] so glad to have each other. But then the first hour was stretching. I could do it." After the class she pursued Paradis through the parking lot, demanding an answer—would it be worthwhile for her to be in his class? And he finally stopped, turned to her and said, "Yeah, I think it's going to be a blast. It's going to be fun. Just . . . yeah . . . show up." Stocking recalls: "That's all I needed, that's all a disabled person needs is an invitation. 'It's going to be a blast. Show up.' And it *was* a blast." But not without a cost. Stocking recalls: "Every day I said a prayer: 'OK, Universe, you want me here. Let's do it.' Every day. Because I was really embarrassed. I was going to look like a fool. In acting classes I knew I could be competitive. Not in that class. But we had so much fun and I got in the best physical condition of my life."

Diana Jordan also experienced challenges in her movement training, most relating to balance. She agreed to drop the second semester of stage combat. "I completed unarmed combat," she recalls in a 2001 conversation, "but next was weaponry and there was a safety issue. I felt a lot of pressure never to make a mistake and I didn't think that was a good learning environment for me." There were successes as well. When Jordan took period dance, she and her partners discovered some of those small kinesthetic adjustments that make life with a disability interesting. "When we did country dance, Virginia reels," she remembers with pleasure, "the guys would give me an extra whip around, an extra push to help me keep up with the others."

Jean-Louis Rodrigue, UCLA's Alexander Technique instructor, was pivotal in Stocking's coming to terms with what she calls a "serious disconnect" between her body and mind. She explains:

> Alexander has completely changed my life, my relationship with my body. Alexander is about learning about the misuse of the body and learning to use it in the correct way. I had been in constant pain before Alexander. I have arthritis in my hip, knee and ankle all on the one side of my body. To learn how to let up on those joints. Part of Alexander is not having to try so hard. I really responded to that.[11]

Stocking also worked with two of the most demanding movement instructors at the school: Jacques Heim, who teaches an acrobatic, risk-taking form of dance, and Amen Santo, who teaches the Brazilian martial art, Capoeira. During the semester that Stocking studied with Heim, one student broke an arm and a kneecap in the class. The technique, which involves catapulting, falling, and tumbling, is risky physical work. How would she complete one of the defining exercises of the class—a dive off a nine-foot wall into the arms of one's classmates? After considering the options, Heim answered: "Well, maybe you won't jump off the nine-foot wall, but the five foot—is ok? You do five feet?" Stocking recalls the exercise, "Being someone who had never been touched in that way—it was very exciting for me. It was important." But the lessons learned through Heim's technique were not so much about dance as about acting. She reflected in 2006:

> What was the essence of the exercise? That you can trust that someone is going to catch you and that you can fly, baby, when you're up on stage ... Go, go, go—trust, trust, trust, trust that the person—your scene partner—is going to catch you.

Ann's next movement class introduced her to an even more formidable technique: Capoeira, a martial arts dance form from Brazil. She volunteered to drop this class but the instructor, Amen Santo, refused. Ann found that:

> There's a spiritual component to Capoeira that is about acceptance and love . . . [Amen] is the model in my experience for how to accommodate a disabled student. He let the class go on and spent just two minutes stretching me while he's watching the others. He is really paying attention to everyone—I'm not a big deal to him and it only takes two minutes—He's not screwing anybody else out of their education—he is just all about acceptance.

Both instructors found ways to incorporate Stocking into their systems without depriving other students of time and attention.

Not every movement professor was so accommodating. One refused to let her in his class. As Stocking recalls, "He insisted, 'I can't teach you, I don't know how to teach you, I can't take time to help you in class. You have to accept the no.'" Arguably, since it was the only such response she encountered in her three years of a rigorous physical program, why couldn't Stocking just be a good sport and "accept the no"? But for Stocking the encounter was not just about her education, but about the precedent her acquiescence would set for other disabled students. "This is the crux of the argument for refusing to let us into these programs,"[12] she reasoned, meaning the disabled student's inability to fulfill the movement curriculum. She chose to move on with her education, but five years later her decision still troubles her.

Disability scholar Carrie Sandahl points out in her insightful essay, "The Tyranny of Neutral," the potentially damaging metaphors that underlie many movement systems used in actor training. Predicated on an ideal body, such methodologies can invalidate the impaired body. But in practice, as Sandahl agrees, some systems are more open than others. For example, she posits that Laban is "more suited to the performance training of disabled people, since it describes in nonjudgmental terms the ways in which bodies actually move."[13] For performance artist and educator Petra Kuppers, Laban is the methodology of choice in working within mental health communities, because:

> It does not matter if one extends an arm, finger, or chin in order to place oneself into a spatial form and experience . . . My creative work . . . explores these potentials by taking the movement to its smallest, invisible, concentrated extreme.[14]

Ann Stocking makes a similar claim for the Alexander technique as a nonjudgmental, infinitely various system, despite Alexander's privileging of a "divine neutral."[15] Stocking insists there is no problem in applying the system to the impaired body, for example, in working with an actor with severe cerebral palsy, because that actor "can do 'forward and up,' 'lengthen and widen' whether his muscles are contracting or not." The goal, for Stocking, is to get to a place where "you can go with your instincts."[16]

If movement systems can be more or less open to variation and modification, the same can be said of instructors. During his undergraduate theatre education, Brad Rothbart (quoted at the beginning of this article), who has cerebral palsy, was unable to follow instructions involving left and right directions. He voluntarily removed himself from a dance class when he was told that he would endanger the other dancers. At Riverside Community College, dance instructor Jo Dierdorff has found another accommodation:

> I have a lot of students with right/left problems. I hardly say "right" [or] "left" anymore. I say, "turn to the office wall, turn to the barre wall, turn to the musicians."[17]

Dierdorff considers that one of her continuing projects as a dance teacher has been, "How to get people to understand, [through] verbal description, or images, or . . . how to understand where movement comes from." An early turning point in her pedagogical development was working with a blind student. She discovered that:

> I was all about demonstrating: it was a "monkey see, monkey do" kind of teaching. Now I had to explain movement. [I] realized it takes so many words to describe one simple movement. I learned a tremendous amount from that. [18]

Over twenty years later she made new discoveries when working with deaf and hard-of-hearing students. Through her interaction with sign language interpreters she became aware of how her instruction depended on "poetic images, French terminology, anatomical terms." The college's dance instructors came together to create a vocabulary sheet for the interpreters, initiating a departmental investigation of the relationship between language, metaphor and technique.[19] Thus we can see an example of how inclusion can benefit the teaching establishment, pushing the discipline forward.

Educational innovator Anne Bogart, who has taught several physically disabled people in her Viewpoint/Suzuki residencies, questions the utility of codified requirements for participation in theatre training:

> I do not look for an idealized body, rather I look for an actor who is willing to put who they are to the test on a daily basis. Watching a person work in the light of tremendous obstacles and seeing them turn their body and spirit into beautiful expression is powerful. For any actor to cross the stage with presence and energy is a tremendous task.[20]

Both Dierdorff and Bogart anticipate a recent development in higher education, Universal Design of Curriculum. Modeled on Universal Design in Architecture, Universal Design of Curriculum calls for teaching practices that provide access to the widest demographic of students in the place of case-by-case special accommodations.[21]

Voice Training

Diana Jordan's greatest concern in the MFA curriculum at California State Long Beach was voice training because she has a speech impediment. If she speaks too quickly or becomes too excited, she is unintelligible. Speech teacher Linda Besisti, while acknowledging Jordan's speech difficulties, also found that "Diana's facility for language and verse is outstanding."[22] How does someone with a speech impediment exhibit a gift for verse? Besisti makes a distinction between physical capability and artistic skill. "If you are correcting an over-sibilancy, poor diction, that is not the same thing as working with an actor who really understands language," she explained. "Diana has a really good sense of the spoken word, so the challenge for her is to be understood."[23]

Jordan found Kristin Linklater voice work more beneficial than years of speech therapy, concentrating as it does on breath support. Jordan explained, "I am learning to feel comfortable with my own vocal patterns which may be slower than other people's. There was a time when I would speed up trying to keep up. We had a guest artist who was jumping my lines . . . He said, 'Well, you should talk faster.' And I said, 'No, you should wait till I'm finished.' . . . I don't need to speed up or catch up. If I am in the moment and connected, the audience will be there."[24]

Carrie Sandahl had a less successful encounter with voice training during her undergraduate theatre years. The voice class was instructed to imagine that their sacrum was the seat of their soul. Sandahl, who was born without a sacrum and the first few of her lumbar vertebrae, asked the instructor how she could fulfill the exercise. The class ground to a halt and the teacher had no answer. Sandahl recalls, "I was really upset—to be told I was missing the seat of my soul!"[25] Sandahl's story decisively illustrates the need for acting instructors to acknowledge the metaphors in their methodologies.

Character/Roles/Casting

> The drama of my life lies in my round back . . . I cannot play roles in which one looks up to heaven.
>
> Charles Dullin

> I was being used and encouraged in my acting class. But I was cast in a particular kind of role—the insane person, the old lady, wacky characters. Fun, fun roles but when you are nineteen or twenty you want to play the ingénue. Just once.
>
> Carrie Sandahl

> One of the main barriers that a disabled actor meets in seeking professional training is that there are no roles.
>
> John Belluso, playwright

Charles Dullin (1885–1949), Copeau's actor of preference and the teacher of Antonin Artaud, Jean Vilar, Jean-Louis Barrault, and Marcel Marceau, was disabled by progressive arthritis and scoliosis. Because of his disability, Dullin was relegated to the marginal characters, the so-called "third roles" in melodramas—madmen, morphine addicts, and bandits.[26] Almost every disabled actor I have known who has performed onstage has been cast in a similar fashion—whatever gender, whatever ethnicity, and whatever physical type, irrespective of the specific physical impairment. Without an awareness of the social and historical redefinition of disability that has occurred over the past twenty to thirty odd years, the theatre educator will be ill-equipped to resist the force of centuries of tradition assigning meaning to the disabled figure in dramatic texts and in performance. Educators are encouraged to become as familiar with the prevailing stereotypes of disabled characters (victims or villains) as they are with those of African American depiction (crooks or clowns) or those of women (madonna or whore).[27]

Turning to "disabled" roles, those that actors with disabilities could "realistically" be cast in, educators should not be surprised that disabled scholars and activists are often critical of those older depictions. Stocking's research into disabled roles led her to the unhappy conclusion that:

> most of those characters were male and they weren't characters I ever wanted to play . . . it was always about overcoming and you [the disabled character] having the problem, not the society. All my research was leading me to the conclusion that it's society that has the problem—stop putting it on us.[28]

Nontraditional casting is very much on the minds of those in the professional theatre, as well as in film and television, thanks to the advocacy of groups within the performing unions as well as organizations like the Non-Traditional Casting Project (recently renamed the Alliance for Inclusion in the Arts). Both Jordan and Stocking played diverse, nonstereotypical roles during their degree programs. Stocking is particularly appreciative of her program's choices:

> I didn't have to fight to not play the maid. But I can imagine that there are a lot of schools where that would still be a problem. Mel [the head of UCLA's Acting program] is a smart guy. He knew he didn't have to use *Glass Menagerie* or *The Miracle Worker* to cast me—he's a smarter guy than that.[29]

Mark Povinelli, the little person whose stunning performance of Torvald in Mabou Mines' adaptation of Henrik Ibsen's *A Doll's House* received much critical acclaim, has taken on some of the stereotypical sorts of roles Stocking refers to since his graduation from Miami University in 1993. He has played everything from the sublime—Nano the dwarf in Ben Jonson's *Volpone* directed by Michael Kahn at the Shakespeare Theatre—to the ridiculous—several years as an elf in a satellite production of the *Radio City Christmas Spectacular*. The latter role paid his yearly financial nut for several years and allowed him to build up his stage resume in Minneapolis. Povinelli is a master manipulator of audience expectations and at this point in his career brings an intelligence and irony to these problematic roles. As he tells the story, this confidence is due in part to the wide range of roles he played in high school and college. He recalls his first role:

> Our [high school] theatre director was a biology teacher. He directed *A Chorus Line* using cafeteria tables as the stage in the gym and cast me as Zach . . . the famed chorographer. There is something beautiful

in that but it was absurd . . . and for the debacle that the program was I got instilled in me that I can play what I want to play.[30]

As a result of this catholic experience of stage personas, which continued in college and was reinforced by strong skill training, Povinelli carries a confidence that he is an actor, "not just a sight gag."

Joe Chaikin reminded us that what "attracts people to the theatre is a kind of discomfort with the limitations of life as it is lived . . . [theatre] present[s] what is possible in society according to what is possible in the imagination."[31] In a sense, nontraditional casting is what we long for when we enter the theatre. At the same time, our life experience is much more diverse than what we see on the stage. Playwright Charles L. Mee has emphasized this disconnect between contemporary public life and conventional casting in his "Note on Casting." As Mee sees it:

> There is not a single role in any one of my plays that must be played by a physically intact white person. And directors should go very far out of their way to avoid creating the bizarre, artificial world of all intact white people, a world that no longer exists where I live, in casting my plays.[32]

How well, we might then ask, is our training establishment fulfilling the mission of the discipline whether conceived of as a catalyst of humanism or as the supplier of talent for the cultural marketplace, if our programs fail to make space for the physically impaired body?

Journey's End

Diana Jordan and Ann Stocking graduated in 2001 with MFAs in Acting from California State University Long Beach and the University of California Los Angeles, respectively. Far from compromising their respective schools they left behind a legacy that will be hard to match. Then Chair Howard Burman evaluated Diana Jordan's three year tenure: "No question that she has made a contribution to our theatre program here. She's greatly admired and respected. To some students she is a great role model and mentor and not just those with disabilities . . . If I had the opportunity to take her again I would do it in a heartbeat. I can't say that about everybody!"[33]

Shapiro's journey was more nuanced. His first fears continued until he had Ann Stocking in his acting class. He recalls, "It was awkward. I didn't know . . . would the disability get in the way of what I could say about it or shouldn't say about it, if I had to be tactful about it. And then I . . . found that her disability was not an obstacle between us. I found that she was very receptive, that she was very emotionally pliable and I sensed working with her that there was a real actress there. So that made me very happy and made the work with her very easy."[34]

In the end, Shapiro concludes: "When I look at it three years later, it was a great learning experience for me. It was a very funny, glorious experience," he recalls. After a thoughtful pause he adds, "We're afraid to deal with things like disabled people, we're afraid to talk about death, we're afraid to talk about the serious things in our lives. The whole thing was very great and very important to me and to the school."[35]

RECOMMENDATIONS

One: Take the Onus off the Student

The university needs to step up, enforce the laws, explore disability as a cultural and historical phenomenon,[36] and actively recruit and welcome disabled theatre students—because without some leadership at the top, whether in the regional theatre or the academic theatre, these initiatives are doomed. This is a loaded proposition, any part of which could initiate a lecture series, a building renovation, a disability studies major or minor, a change in human resources directives, an endowed scholarship or a new faculty hire. But to take one phrase of the recommendation—"actively recruit . . . disabled theatre students." We need more disabled students in the room, because as long as the numbers of disabled students are small, the individual student will suffer from two contradictory dilemmas: one, the student will feel responsible for representing all disabled students; and, two, the student's needs and concerns will be seen as personal, even narcissistic, a playing of the "disability card."

The challenges confronting the pioneering disabled theatre student are already considerable without adding the stress of representing forty-five million other Americans. Stocking explains: "If I didn't do well it would screw it up for other disabled people later. I felt the pressure of being unique in that environment." Seeking accommodations that are covered by anti-discriminatory laws and policies can backfire. In 1981, when Ben Mattlin, who uses an electric wheelchair, entered Harvard University, the *Wall Street Journal* wrote that "In the past three years, Harvard University has spent $680,000 so Ben Mattlin can major in social studies . . . It has widened doorways and installed special ramps, lowered drinking fountains and rebuilt bathrooms . . . Harvard's total bill . . . will run to more than $2 million."[37] Mattlin recalls that he even received hate mail after the article appeared.[38] The disabled student has learned not to draw attention to him or herself, hence Rothbart's dilemma in a movement class when confronted with an instruction he was not able to carry out: "Do I just hide it and soldier on? . . . Or do I say something and make it about me? How to negotiate this? [It's] bad enough in a bachelor's program—worse in a BFA." Although the average age of Stocking's MFA class was twenty-three, Stocking, who was in her early thirties when admitted, insists that she could never have survived the program as a twenty-three-year-old. Without some maturity, spiritual development and a political/cultural understanding of disability, she would have taken all the obstacles as personal failures.[39]

Two: Time

The late playwright John Belluso said of his collaboration with Joe Chaikin (who was aphasiac during the last years of his creative life): "People have to understand: we're not in a race." Time, so essential to the art of theatre, is also one of the qualitative ways in which the lives of many disabled people differ from the nondisabled. How can we accommodate a different cultural valuing of time in an American culture where everyone moves quickly and expects instant results? What do we lose by not adjusting the rhythm?

   People with mobility impairments often experience life at a different pace and with a different choreography. While a graduate student in playwriting at NYU, the late John Belluso was criticized by his professor, a noted American playwright, for having his main character in *Traveling Skin* abandon her wheelchair in favor of crawling, or "slithering" as he put it. Belluso's response to his critic was, "I wanted to make her movement very slow and painful to the audience, something that will take a lot of time and create unease."

   Modern dancer Steve Paxton records a different response to watching a performance of contact improviser Emery Blackwell:

   Emery has said that to get his arm raised above his head requires about 20 seconds of imaging to accomplish. Extension and contraction impulses in his muscles fire frequently and unpredictably and he must somehow select the right impulses consciously, or produce for himself a movement image of the correct quality to get the arm to respond as he wants. We observers can get entranced with what he is doing with his mind. [W]e feel the quandary and see that he is pitched against his nervous system and wins. [40]

Three: Flexible Skill Training.

As Joseph Chaikin said, "Technique is a means to free the artist,"[41] and as Ann Stocking adds, "It's not freedom as in being a rubber band, in being an acrobat who can go wooh-wooh-wooh across the stage."[42] During my years with the people's theatre movement, I became a student of Decroux mime which, as a disabled actor, I found liberating. Here was a technique that allowed me to create a dance from my waist up and to expand and refine my gestural vocabulary. When I began teaching other disabled people, the Decroux technique worked well with a variety of disabilities. But then a woman with cerebral palsy let me know that the rhythms and isolations of the Decroux "keyboard" were the equivalent for her of point exercises in ballet for me with my fused ankle. I made an adjustment. Again, Chaikin: "Exercises can also detour development. [A] dance exercise may be good for the dancer, and an actor can sometimes gain strength and agility through dance, but it shouldn't be confused with body exercises for the actor."[43] Consider offering multiple methodologies—Alexander, Laban (Bartenieff), Mime, Pilates, Feldenkrais—to fulfill movement requirements. You might also consider workshops in contact improvisation and integrated (wheelchair) dance along with more traditional dance forms. Gold standard? Bring in disabled artists skilled in these forms to work with your students.[44]

Four: Active Recruitment

Although many more disabled young people in America are attending university, by the time they leave high school most of them have already gotten the message—the performing arts are not welcoming. There are significant barriers that prevent young people with disabilities from even dreaming about a career in the theatre: low expectations, discouragement from adults, lack of support from vocational counselors, lack of arts programs that accommodate students with disabilities, and the absence of role models to name just a few. If a disabled person does emerge from childhood with a desire to pursue a career in the arts, further obstacles lie ahead, particularly if one is economically disadvantaged and dependent on public support.[45] Consider adding the word "disability" to your audition calls when you stress diversity. Investigate contemporary plays by disabled and deaf and hard-of-hearing playwrights that call for disabled talent.

Five: Apply Critical Standards

Avoid knee-jerk approval for performers solely on the basis of disability. A lack of expectations has been identified as one of the main barriers for disabled students in all fields. Every disabled performer has been in an environment (be it a class, an audition, or a performance) where any work by a disabled performer (whether bad, average, or good) was pronounced fabulous.

As opportunities increase for employment of disabled actors, it is critical that the talent is competitive. Mark Povinelli speaks frankly about the repercussions of failing to apply standards to the training of disabled actors:

> I see a lot of little people who are actors out here [in Los Angeles]. There are so few things where the powers-that-be ask you to do anything of substance. But when that does come along it's invaluable—the experience I've had, the training I've had. Because I just know how to prepare for it. I know what it means. I know how to get there—[how to] come through theatrically cause that's my home I know how to do that whereas there are very few other little people whom I've seen that do.[46]

CODA: A MODEL FOR INCLUSION—MAKING SPACE

In 1999, Teal Sherer enrolled as a communications major at Oglethorpe University, a small liberal arts school in Atlanta, Georgia. Teal's first stop in Atlanta was the Good Shepherd Rehabilitation Center. Teal had been to Shepherd before. After her accident at fourteen her family had brought her to Shepherd because it was known to be one of the country's leading rehabilitation centers for spinal cord injuries with a renowned program for recently injured teens. Now an undergraduate, Teal got a membership at Shepherd's gym, and the arts specialist told her about an integrated (disabled/nondisabled) dance company in town. She began college and simultaneously joined the Full Radius Dance Company, training three days a week for three hours a day and performing throughout the year. She would stay with Full Radius for all four years of college.

In her sophomore year at Oglethorpe, Teal took a beginning acting class as part of the requirements for her communications major. Her instructor integrated her into the class, making adjustments in physical exercises when necessary, but generally just making Teal feel comfortable. Then the teacher, Troy Dwyer, cast her in *The House Of Bernarda Alba*, over the doubts of some of his senior colleagues. Teal went on to take a second major in theatre. Oglethorpe is, not inconsequentially, the site of the Georgia Shakespeare Festival, and the new facilities built to house that event are entirely accessible. During her time at Oglethorpe, Teal not only performed lead roles in mainstage productions, she also stage managed and ran the box office—backstage, front of house, everything was accessible.

Her acting teacher Troy Dwyer was a key contributor to Teal's success. Dwyer had seen disabled performance artist Greg Walloch in New York and was impressed by Walloch's wit and skill. Dwyer, himself a gay man, had experienced the role of the "other" in his own theatrical training. Investigating his initial connection to Teal, he reflects:

> My sense of "otherness" is a big part of how I get through my day. It's my political sensibility, my sense of humor and my POV. So I guess, as an artist and a teacher, I'm always on the lookout for the "others" . . . the fat girls, the sissy boys, the utter weirdos, and yes, the disabled kids. We certainly weren't given opportunities to make space for ourselves when I was doing my acting training, and the only ones of us who went on to work professionally were the ones who (like me) were able to pass for "normal."

Dwyer had experience and a critical vocabulary for recognizing discrimination in the theatre classroom. And Teal met him more than halfway, working harder than any student he has had before.[47]

Dwyer translated the issue of access as a political issue to one of aesthetic possibility, a shift in normal stage geography:

Teal enters a room and challenges the system by virtue of her very presence. Her body says, "OK, the way we think about the role either needs to change so I can inhabit it, or you'd better write another role, dammit." I like that . . . It makes space.

Dwyer is not alone in "making space" for the disabled acting student. There are many "brave gallants" who have taken up the petitioner's request to make room for them, even to anticipate their request, and pull them into their theatres. Mark Povinelli encountered another such educator at Miami University in Ohio, Howard Blanning. Like Teal, Povinelli was playing it safe as a communications major, hoping "to placate my own insecurity and my family's insecurity," about a sensible career choice. But during Povinelli's first week on campus Blanning cast him as Henry Straker in Shaw's *Man and Superman* and continued to use him in major roles for the next four years. Blanning's recruiting of Povinelli into the theatre department "was the greatest experience in my life to that date in time." Legendary actress Linda Hunt's encounter and training with method teacher Robert Lewis played a significant role in her ability to persist through early rejections.[48]

And Teal's story does not hinge on the good intentions of "brave gallants." She was not alone as she knocked at the door. Although Teal did not enter in a troupe of rowdy "guisers," she was the beneficiary of the collective struggle of disabled people since the late 1970s. Teal had a support system in place when she arrived, the Shepherd Center. She had a mixed disabled and nondisabled dance company that she trained and performed with almost daily for the four years of her undergraduate education. She came to university with an expectation of full participation in public life, an expectation made possible by three decades of struggles to secure access to education and employment for all disabled people.[49] The university theatre's physical plant was a model of accessibility. Oglethorpe was a small liberal arts school and not a prestigious conservatory program. The initial gatekeeper, her acting instructor, was flexible and critical about training practices, particularly casting. And, although Teal had little support for theatre in her high school (there was no theatre at the Knoxville school), Teal's mother encouraged her to explore on-camera work as a teen, working as a model in industrials, so Teal was involved with the performing arts before entering higher education. Tangentially, the presence of role models such as Greg Walloch made it possible for Dwyer to imagine a working actor with a disability.[50]

Teal is now in Los Angeles and, like many young actors, nondisabled or disabled, hoping for work in television or film. She lives in a small apartment in West Hollywood, conscientiously attends acting classes, and relies on a tight support system of fellow actors. Some things are different. It took Teal five attempts before she found a cold-reading workshop in an accessible location. But she's part of the game. And if she does carve out that most elusive of all dreams, a working life in the performing arts, no one in her training program will be kicking themselves because they refused to let her in, refused to make room, make a space—in their classes, in their job description, or in their pedagogy—for a talented, driven young artist, looking simply for an education.[51]

> *Whether I rise or stand or fall,*
> *I do my duty to please you all.*
> *But room, brave gallants, room! Room I do require!*

NOTES

1. Some material in this chapter also appeared in my article "O Pioneers!" for *American Theatre* magazine, April 2001, published by Theatre Communication Group.
2. For a good introduction to the disability rights movement, see Joseph Shapiro, *No Pity: People with Disabilities Forging a New Civil Rights Movement* (New York: Random House, 1993). For a more complex historical and political analysis, see James I. Charlton, *Nothing About Us Without Us: Disability, Oppression, and Empowerment* (University of California Press, 1998).
3. Victoria Ann Lewis, "O Pioneers!" *American Theatre*, April 2001, 30.
4. Ibid.
5. Ibid.
6. Ibid.
7. Ann Stocking, interview with author, January 3, 2001.
8. Diana Jordan, phone interview with author, January 14, 2001.
9. Lewis, 30.
10. Nathan Stucky and Jessica Tomell-Presto, "Acting and Movement Training of the Body," in *Teaching Theatre Today: Pedagogical Views of Theatre in Higher Education*, eds. Anne L. Fliotsos and Gail S. Medford (New York: Palgrave Macmillan, 2004), 106.
11. Ann Stocking, phone interview with author, July 23, 2006.
12. Stocking, interview, 2001.
13. Carrie Sandahl, "The Tyranny of the Neutral," in *Bodies in Commotion: Disability and Performance*, eds. Philip Auslander and Carrie Sandahl (Ann Arbor, MI: University of Michigan Press, 2005), 266–267.
14. Petra Kuppers, "Bodies, Hysteria, Pain: Staging the Invisible," in *Bodies in Commotion: Disability and Performance*, eds. Philip Auslander and Carrie Sandahl (Ann Arbor, MI: University of Michigan Press, 2005), 130.
15. As quoted in Sandahl, 260.
16. Stocking, phone interview, 2006.
17. Jo Dierdorff, interview with author, July 25, 2006.
18. Dierdorff, interview.
19. Dierdorff is also a Pilates instructor, a movement system in which "every body is different. Ideally it should be taught one on one. That's how Joe Pilates envisioned it from the start."
20. Anne Bogart, email to author, January 8, 2001.
21. After a two-day workshop on Universal Design of Curriculum at San Francisco State University, Yukihiro Goto, Chair of the Theatre Department, redesigned his beginning movement class so that any student could participate in the class

without special assistance. Rather than finding the universal design directive restrictive, Goto was reenergized in his teaching: "[the] Universal Design for Learning workshop . . . totally blew my mind. Since then my old 'traditional' way of teaching and doing theatre has been seriously challenged." Interview with author, October, 2007.

22. Linda Besisti, phone interview with author, January 9, 2001.
23. Besisti, interview.
24. Jordon, interview.
25. Carrie Sandahl, phone interview with author, January 14, 2001.
26. Frederick Brown *Theatre and Revolution: The Culture of the French Stage* (New York: Viking Press, 1980), 174.
27. See Paul K. Longmore, "Screening Stereotypes: Images of Disabled People in Television and Motion Pictures," in *Why I Burned My Book and Other Essays on Disability* (Philadelphia, PA: Temple University Press, 2003) and Victoria Lewis, "The Dramaturgy of Disability," in *Points of Contact: Disability, Art, and Culture,* eds. Susan Crutchfield and Marcy Epstein (Ann Arbor, MI: University of Michigan Press, 2000).
28. Stocking, interview, 2001.
29. Stocking, interview, 2006.
30. Mark Povinelli, interview with author, March 31, 2007.
31. Joseph Chaikin, *The Presence of the Actor* (New York: Atheneum, 1980), 22–23.
32. Charles L. Mee, "Artist Statement," in *Beyond Victims and Villains: Contemporary Plays by Disabled Playwrights,* ed. Victoria Ann Lewis (New York: TCG, 2006), 231.
33. Lewis, *American Theatre,* 60.
34. Ibid., 31.
35. Lewis, 60.
36. See Lennard J. Davis, "Introduction: Disability, the Missing Term in the Race, Class, Gender Triad," in *Enforcing Normalcy: Disability, Deafness and the Body* (Verso, 1995) and Catherine J. Kudlick "Disability History: Why We Need Another 'Other'" in *The American Historical Review* (Vol. 108, Issue 3).
37. *Wall Street Journal,* February 1, 1981.
38. Ben Mattlin, email to author, August 1, 2006.
39. Stocking, interview, 2006.
40. Steve Paxton as quoted in Ann Cooper Albright's *Choreographing Difference: The body and identity in contemporary dance* (Wesleyan, 2007).
41. Chaikin, 5.
42. Stocking, interview, 2006.
43. Chaikin, 134.
44. I would be remiss if I did not note the pivotal role that contact improvisation has played in the visibility and respect paid the disabled performer in the performing arts. Interested readers are directed to http://nadc.ucla.edu/dance.cfm .
45. The National Endowment for the Arts has sponsored two initiatives to address this problem. One was a National Forum on Careers in the Arts for People with Disabilities, in 1998. Documentation of this event can be found at http://artsedge.kennedy-center.org/forum/. Following that conference, the NEA funded a three-year research project "Experiences of Individuals with Disabilities Pursuing Careers in the Arts: Creating a National Portrait," conducted by the University of Illinois Chicago, Carol Gill, Principal Investigator, Carrie Sandahl, Co-Investigator.
46. Mark Povinelli, interview with author, March 31, 2007.

47. Troy Dwyer, email to author, July 31, 2006.
48. Betty M. Adelson, *The Lives of Dwarfs: Their Journey from Public Curiosity toward Social Liberation* (New Brunswick, NJ: Rutgers University Press, 2005), 262.
49. Playwright John Belluso had this to say about the role of the Disability Civil Rights movement in his successful career: "I think of myself as a writer who is born of the contemporary disability civil rights movement of the mid to late 1970s. I've always felt that it was the creators of that movement who paved the way for the life I live now. Without the civil rights laws they struggled so hard to force into passage, without the history they changed, I doubt I would have been afforded the opportunity to seek out training and create a life for myself in the theatre arts." (from *Beyond Victims and Villains: Contemporary Plays by Disabled Playwrights*. Ed. Victoria Ann Lewis. Theatre Communications Group: 2006.)
50. Walloch and many other disabled performance artists, monologists, and stand-up (sit-down) comics got their training outside traditional training venues, usually on the stage, harkening back to the apprenticeship system which served as training for American actors until the first university programs appeared in the 1880s.
51. In the fall of 2008, actors Teal Sherer and Ann Stocking formed a not-for-profit theatre company, Blue Zone Theatre (the name refers both to the color of handicapped parking spaces and the importance of disabled actors claiming their place in today's theatre). Sherer serves as Producing Director and Stocking as Artistic Director. More information about their company can be found at: http://www.bluezoneproductions.com/.

14 Arrested or Paralyzed?
Reflections on the Erotic Life of an Acting Teacher

Ellen Margolis

You can't work with actors as if they were pawns. You have to be in love with them. And the directors who deny this are lying.[1]

Ariane Mnouchkine

Anne Bogart, whose work as artistic director of the Saratoga International Theatre Institute (SITI) goes hand-in-glove with her longtime commitment to actor training, asserts that erotic openness is paramount in the work of theatre directors, even dedicating one of the seven essays in her 2001 book *A Director Prepares* to eroticism. "The role of attraction and eroticism in the theatre is rarely discussed and yet both are vital ingredients in the creative act and the dynamics between audiences and actors," the chapter begins.[2] According to Bogart, the greater part of theatre is a seduction between actors and audiences:

> [E]rotic tension between the stage and the beholder is part of what makes the theatre experience so attractive. The theatre is a place where it is possible to meet one another in an energetic space unmediated by technology. The sensory stimulation allowed in theatre, authorized by its very form, allows the corporeal imagination to exercise itself.[3]

To witness a theatrical event, to participate as an audience member participates, one must give oneself over to erotic tension in what Bogart describes as a sequence similar to that of sexual seduction: first, you are stopped in your tracks, drawn to the object of attraction; then, sensing the object's energy and power, you become disoriented; next, you make contact; finally, you engage in extended intercourse with the object or partner; and as a result you are changed irrevocably. So an audience meets an actor in the theatre.

Surely Bogart uses the term "erotic" advisedly and with an awareness of its usual implications. Eros, the root of eroticism, is primarily a creative—even a life-preserving—force. Plato's notion of *eros* holds that ideal beauty, reflected in the particular beauty of individuals or objects, draws us to it powerfully. Eroticism is at bottom a creativity that forges powerful connections and gives shape to desires. This most fundamental understanding of "erotic" evokes Bogart's fascination with the creative contribution of audiences to the event of live theatre (a fascination that inspired her creation, with SITI, of *Cabin Pressure* in 1999, a play that probes the electric relationship between performers and their audience).

The director, in his or her function as audience stand-in, has an obligation not to be immune to the sensual and emotional poignancy of the actor. It follows, then, that theatre directors working in the academy—if their production work is to be vital and current and not purely academic—have the same obligations: to be willing and able to be affected and changed by the presence and personal magnetism of actors, to be susceptible to their charms. Even, when casting a show, to recognize which actors are capable of seducing the audience, and each other, and their director.

In other disciplines, students' attractiveness is not part of a professor's concern. Conventional wisdom says it should not even be on his or her radar screen. Nor do other fields share the scenario, not uncommon in our field, where a professor or teaching assistant may be cast opposite an undergraduate in a production and thus (in some cases) be required to behave sexually or romantically with a student. In this fictional dimension, and in other ways, the erotic landscape of student–teacher relations manifests differently for theatre educators than for educators in general.

Such necessary delving into erotic tensions in a studio or rehearsal hall surely carries its own peculiar responsibilities. I would propose that the significance of these tensions is as much pedagogical as personal, insofar as prohibitions against considering students as erotic beings collide with the real value—both artistic and pedagogical—of allowing oneself to be, as Bogart says, "arrested and transformed" by the presence of a student actor laying himself or herself bare.

TRANSFORMATION AND LOSS

In recent years, a number of scholars (often prompted by questions born of feminism) have investigated the eroticism of the classroom. Jane Gallop[4] and others find in the student–teacher relationship a dynamic of mutual desire, irrational emotional response, and thrilling contact analogous to relations between lovers. In her book *Teaching to Transgress*, bell hooks charts the personal challenges and revelations of feminist teaching, including its sometimes erotic nature. While hooks does not address theatre training specifically, readers familiar with Bogart will find much resonance here. A chapter entitled "Eros, Eroticism, and the Pedagogical Process" begins by sounding the same note as the first sentence of Bogart's "Eroticism" chapter. "Professors rarely speak of the place of eros or the erotic in our class rooms," hooks begins. For hooks, the skirting of the erotic begins with the eradication of the body itself[5]:

> Trained in the philosophical context of Western metaphysical dualism, many of us have accepted the notion that there is a split between the body and the mind. Believing this, individuals enter the classroom to teach as though only the mind is present, and not the body. To call attention to the body is to betray the legacy of repression and denial that has been handed down to us by our professorial elders . . . The public world of institutional learning [is] a site where the body [has] to be erased, go unnoticed."

Drawing on Sam Keen's notion of erotic potency as "the moving force that propel[s] every life form from a state of mere potentiality to actuality,"[6] hooks positions eros as intimately connected to other kinds of passions—passion for one's discipline, one's students, one's own potential transformation.

It is the possibility that we ourselves will be transformed that frightens us most, or should. In August 2007, a former student of mine, Kassi Dallmann, died suddenly and unexpectedly after a routine medical procedure. She was twenty-eight, engaged to be married, running a theatre company she'd started with some friends in Chicago. Her death, 2,000 miles away from where I live and years after we'd last spoken, knocked me out for weeks.

In the presence of very courageous people, we are transformed, and so Kassi's courage had transformed me. She lived openly with a panic disorder, and pursued a life in the theatre because she loved performing, despite its many potential triggers for panic. During college, she confided in me shortly after surviving an assault, fiercely resilient even in the near aftermath of the attack. Her honesty gave her a rare radiance, set her apart from the usual self-consciousness of early adulthood, and was for me a kind of touchstone against fear and pretense in the rehearsal hall.

Kassi thanked me a number of times for my faith and support and for helping her to become a better artist. What haunts me, of course, is that I never thanked her. We do thank our students, sometimes, for their good work, even for what we learn from them. But to thank a student for changing us is different, too much. It suggests—as if it were not always quite obvious—that we are in some way using them to complete and educate ourselves. Our erotic yearnings arise from the fact that "we are each incomplete," says Bogart.[7] Is it part of our job as teachers to work only from the parts of us that are whole and unassailable, to insulate our students from those incomplete places within us, always to project wholeness and solvency? Is teaching then somehow the opposite of being human?

Certainly, I never expressed to Kassi how she changed and taught me. And even this statement is an attempt to hold at arm's length the heart-ripping question that ambushed me on my late-night drives home from work for weeks after her death: Did Kassi know I loved her? This was the sort of bloody question I felt I had no right to, being only a former teacher, only someone who had worked with Kassi for a few years while she was in college.

Instinctively, I reached out to share my grief and disorientation with my friend Lissa Tyler Renaud, a dedicated and creative teacher with whom I have shared many conversations about teaching, some of which gave birth to this book. Lissa wrote back with sympathy, and with these singularly comforting words: "A student is so much more than a student." Of course this remarkable teacher would understand the secret love life of another teacher, would provide the recognition of loss I so needed.

A DIRTY JOB

Perhaps because students in acting class reveal so much of themselves, take so many personal risks, and transform right before our eyes, they are so often so much more than students to us. No doubt colleagues in mathematics or history find themselves equally affected by contact with an inspiring student and would be equally devastated by the loss of a promising young professional. But I would propose that the erotic life of the acting teacher in a university setting gets more complicated just about where our teaching and coaching leave theory for practice. Sexual imagery is commonplace in our coaching of scenes, for example. A run-through is "flaccid," a moment is "charged," dialogue "builds to a climax." Moreover, a vast portion of dramatic literature requires that actors embody romance, desire, seduction, consummation. From the ancient mythology of virtually any culture to much of contemporary Western theatre, many plays require that actors— not exempting student actors—engage with sexual impulses in rehearsal and performance. Within four days' time last fall, I had conversations with students about how to negotiate a first homosexual (onstage) kiss, how to thrust one's hips to convincingly sell a stylized rape scene with twenty feet separating the actors, and how to gauge from a brief audition whether a particular first-year acting student would be able to commit to playing a seduction scene in a student-directed project. My fellow acting teachers will recognize that this was not an unusual four-day period, and that such conversations are par for the course.

In both the academic and professional theatre worlds, convention dictates that we treat such matters with a cool detachment befitting our sophistication. We model a respect of persons and privacy; failing to set this example would be failing our responsibility as seasoned theatre people, senior artists, and teachers. Sometimes, working with such material requires us to talk with students about sexual dynamics or acts with which they (or we) are entirely unfamiliar, just as directors are called upon to research, translate, or explain many other kinds of interactions, contexts, or subtexts that may be beyond a particular actor's experience. Such explanations seem comfortably safe when they are only a description of behavior, but what about when they enter the territory of sexual response? Scenes in Wedekind's *Spring Awakening*, for example, make no sense unless the actors involved apprehend and can commit to the sexual volatility of its adolescent characters.

I never ask an acting student about experiences from his or her personal life because, conveniently, such information is extrinsic to my approach to actor training. But, unlike even those colleagues who teach, say, "The Biology of Sexuality" or "The Sociology of Gender," there is an immediacy and utility to how I engage with my students about certain kinds of erotic encounters. Actors cannot afford to regard as merely theoretical or interesting the possibility that somewhere, sometime, people have had such encounters; their job is to fulfill these moments with all possible commitment and conviction.

SEDUCING OUR STUDENTS

About the same time I started teaching, I started writing plays. Among them are a few I've kept at a safe distance from the campuses where I've been employed because they are about various kinds (often the obvious kind) of erotic relationships between teachers and students. I can honestly say I harbor no such designs on my students, but it has always made sense to me that a teacher might choose an imaginary stage to play out the real energies of desire that mark the acts of learning and teaching. Teachers perform, and performance is sexy. Learning is exciting, and excitement is at least partially physical, and at the end of the day, it has to go somewhere. As Jyl Lynn Felman suggests in *Never a Dull Moment: Teaching and the Art of Performance*, "[t]he erotics of the classroom is somewhat like turning the lights on inside the entire corpus, causing a warm current of intellectual erotic energy to burn passionately among all those who are present and engaged."[8]

In order for a student to learn from us, he or she must be excited by us. Generally, theatre students are already nine parts seduced, but still we need to keep up the attraction, keep the romance alive. In some institutions, attracting students—the verb is used routinely[9]—is a matter of personal or departmental survival. For the bulk of my career, I have worked at affordable, crowded state schools where it was taken for granted that a full array of arts offerings was a critical part of the liberal arts mission. Not so at my current campus, a cash-strapped private school where small departments live or die by the number of majors graduating every year, where the theatre department was indefinitely (temporarily, as it happened) eliminated several years ago, and where an associate dean recently told a gathering of department chairs, "Academic integrity is not a good argument around here." (At about the same time, I participated in a common but slightly surreal administrative exercise. As part of a strategic initiative proposal, my Arts Division colleagues and I were called upon to estimate the number of students who would be *attracted* to our university by each item for which new funding was requested. Instructors, courses, and equipment critical for legitimate arts programs had to be not only justified, but wagered on. How many students would pass up School X in our favor if we suddenly had a light board that wasn't obsolete, or a World Theatre course, or working screw guns? It felt a bit like a game of poker. Bid low, and we might not sell the initiative. Bid high, and the administration could call our bluff.)

Day to day, the need to attract students and to keep numbers high plays out in all sorts of pedagogically corrupt, self-abasing behaviors. Prerequisites are waived, attendance policies go by the wayside, students are admitted to classes on the day of the add/drop deadline despite having missed a full two weeks of class. It feels a little slutty. But faculty who maintain their higher standards run the very real risk of losing funding and endangering their own or their colleagues' jobs. Again, one might ask whether such pressures are peculiar to theatre faculty. Perhaps not, but arts enrollments often drop in a recessing economy, and arts programs can be the first to see cuts unless they put out in the only way that counts: high numbers of graduating majors.

Our students are likely innocent of this larger playing field in our professional lives. All they know is that we turn them on or we don't. The attraction emanating from performers (and let us say this extends to teacher–performers) is powerful—as Bogart says, "an invitation to an evanescent journey, to a new way of experiencing life or perceiving reality."[10] We know, or learn, that we can't fake this invitation. When we call students "to the adventure of a relationship," it goes quite a bit deeper than smoke and mirrors. You can only really invite someone into a relationship by revealing yourself. And if that academic excitement or artistic relationship doesn't always know its boundaries, if it sometimes wanders down a chakra or two, well, perhaps it is, as a character in a popular movie has said, that the point of sex isn't recreation or procreation, but concentration, and that it functions (to borrow a useful classroom image) as "biological highlighter."[11]

TO TOUCH OR NOT TO TOUCH

At the 2002 conference of the Voice and Speech Trainers Association (VASTA), an interest group within the Association for Theatre in Higher Education, a roundtable discussion among some sixty teachers of voice and acting found its way to the issue of touch. It was widely—although not unanimously—agreed that touch is a highly effective way for a voice teacher to glean information about what a student is doing with breath, posture, or musculature, and in turn to provide specific and unmediated feedback. Touch, though, especially between people whose relationship is primarily professional, and even more especially when one of those people is perceived to have a great deal of power over the other, can be a very delicate business. Many who took part in this conversation had developed mechanisms for getting a student's consent to touch him or her, and some of these mechanisms, such as permission slips complete with carbon copies and a waiting period, were fairly elaborate. The legalistic savor of these negotiations does not negate these instructors' no doubt very real concern for their students' comfort, but is certainly generated by a system of higher education in which students and faculty stand in formal opposition to each other—and of course a system in which many faculty members have in fact taken advantage of their power to violate their students' trust.

As I listened, I was struck by the realization that I approached my male and female students very differently in terms of touch. And as soon as I observed this imbalance, I recognized the reason for it. In my experience, a great many women have been subject to unbidden and unwanted touch throughout their early lives. My not-entirely-conscious response to this reality was to assume that women in my classes might have troubled, even traumatic, reactions to my touching them, however innocently, in a studio setting. I did not make the same assumption about the men, which I now believe reflects a cultural bias of mine that may or may not bear out in fact.

My reaction to this discovery was to become paralyzed about touching students altogether for about a year, after which time I found myself one day and all at once: placing my hands on a student's shoulders to show her that she was lifting them needlessly when she took a breath, noticing that this was not the *only* way I could have transmitted this information, noticing that this student was female, and noticing that none of this felt earth-shattering. My intentions in that moment were simply to help and instruct.

Is touch inherently erotic? By ordinary glosses, no. By hooks' more inclusive definition, yes, and for exactly that reason, she might argue, we ought neither to proscribe it nor to surround it with supercharged legalities in the studio. My intentions in that moment were simply to help and instruct—and still it is possible that my actions were in error, that I might indeed have made the student uncomfortable. Teachers make mistakes. "The teacher's failings in which the students ripen" reads a line of Lewis Hyde's poem entitled "This Error is the Sign of Love." Hyde, of course, is a teacher as well as a poet.

He is also the author of *The Gift: Imagination and the Erotic Life of Property*. The "erotic" that Hyde's book investigates is that which forms bonds and creates relationships between individuals or groups—very often,

the exchanging of material gifts that serve as fetishes for acts of consummation and consumption and initiation.[12] Most wonderfully, the giving of gifts
encourages the giving of gifts. Is there a more thrilling moment for a teacher
than to have the student show up with a discovery of his or her own? This
erotic exchange not only validates our effective teaching, but convinces us
that our artistic community is fertile, that it will continue to thrive.

THE POLITICS OF PROFESSIONALISM

A few years ago, I wandered into after-show drinks with a young woman
I'll call Peg. In the brief time between completing her first M.A. program
and starting her second, Peg had taken, and almost as quickly left, a teaching job at a community college. Her reason, she said, was not so much
the (truly daunting) workload as the students. "It was ridiculous. It was
supposed to be a theatre program, but I was being asked to work with
a bunch of middle-aged women with families." This casual utterance
reflected assumptions that are, in my experience, shared by a huge number
of American theatre professionals: that no one over thirty has anything of
value to express, that navigating the world for half a century makes one's
artistic voice less interesting, and that the deep investment in the future that
often attends the raising of children is antithetical to the solitary journey of
a real artist. It was wonderful, in a way, that Peg actually articulated this
prejudice. Like most kinds of bigotry, it is far more often held subliminally
and manifest as a passive dismissal.

The profession as a whole does seem to value youth over experience
and to drive away people with personal encumbrances and obligations.
Middle-aged women with families are soft, sloppy. Good theatre is hard,
precise. Middle-aged women with families are overextended. Good artists
are single-minded. Middle-aged women with families are keenly interested
in utility and purpose, are used to compromise, and value reconciliation.
Good art, on the other hand, exists for its own sake, burning in the hot
white flame of individual expression. Middle-aged women's knees don't
bend. Only the buoyancy of youth is worth watching. Middle-aged women
with families should have the good grace to disappear from the world of
theatre. And they should lose some weight while they're at it.

But isn't there a validity to some of these concerns? How can anyone
work in the American theatre (outside the small world of Equity contracts)
if they have to be home at six o'clock to feed a family? How can anyone
do theatre if a sick or uncooperative child might compromise their ability
to be on time to rehearsal? Such complications interfere with the ability to
behave according to professional standards, and certainly "professionalism" is a huge part of what we labor to transmit to our students.

"Professional" of course stands opposed to "amateur," whose root
derives from the Latin word for love. Professionals pursue their trade for

reasons that outrank love in a rational society. Or, conversely, professional standards are necessary when love cannot be counted on to get things accomplished, at least not in a fiscally efficient manner.

What if the theatre our departments made were driven primarily by love? Would middle-aged women find themselves welcomed back to the theatre they left when those families appeared? Would they bring with them an influx of desire? Would they arrive for rehearsal at whatever time they could, work eagerly and with sustained energy, and stay as long as they could without compromising their health or their relationships? Would their ideas for a project be refreshed and inspired by their rich lives outside of the theatre? Or would their "unprofessional" sensibility simply drive their collaborators mad with frustration? Certainly, although I hold the actors in my classes and productions to the strict standards of the profession, I've noticed that every time I've had to make an accommodation for a truly unavoidable major life incident in one of their lives, that yielding has made way for a precious increase in communion and humanity within the project or class.

For those of us working not only in theatre but in the academy, the mutually reinforcing sets of beliefs of both cultures marginalize adults with family or other personal obligations and systematically exclude individuals with full personal lives. Sociologist Martha Beck, probing the origins of the "professional scholar," points us to the historical and social roots of the mind/body separation that bell hooks and others have identified in today's classrooms:

> When the Enlightenment philosophers outlined their ideal society . . . it was a society where every rational individual would do rational work (the kind of work philosophers did), and be equal to every other rational individual. This model of society assumed, as a matter of course, that all rational individuals would have all their traditional work done for them . . . The society of the United States was based on this Enlightenment social model, complete with the assumption that there will always be a large pool of competent adults who are not free-and-equal citizens, but subrational creatures whose only role in life is to provide for the traditional needs of rational men.[13]

For Peg, who has lived out her quarter-century child-free and matriculating through one institution of higher education after another, this model appears to hold water. For many others of us, though, the politics of professionalism in the theatre and the assumptions of the academy require a constant and vigilant patrolling of borders. If, however, actor training and its attendant eroticism are in higher education to stay, perhaps acting professors are, by the nature of their disciplines, positioned to lead the academy to a more humane, less alienating model. If Ariane Mnouchkine is correct about a director's imperative to fall in love with actors, and if that imperative extends legitimately to teachers as well, perhaps we teachers of acting are even now revolutionizing the academy from within.

In trying to model an intellectual life that is neither alienating nor alienated, we will make mistakes, of course. The more informal conversations we engage in every day, the more opportunities we have to look foolish. The more we reveal of ourselves to our students, the more likely it is that those students will see us stumble. The more we are willing to be transformed by them, the less likely that they will revere us. My students and I regularly share halting and awkward exchanges—more of those, frankly, than moments of brilliance and clarity. But then I have come to believe that education, like sex, is messy when it's done right. It is a matter of panic and courage, of love, of hesitation and error and apology. It is a matter, after all, of groping.

NOTES

1. Trans and qtd. in Adrian Kiernander, *Ariane Mnouchkine* (Cambridge, UK: Cambridge University Press, 1993), 27.
2. Anne Bogart, *A Director Prepares: Seven Essays on Art and Theatre* (New York: Routledge, 2001), 61.
3. Ibid., 66.
4. See especially Jane Gallop, *Pedagogy: The Question of Impersonation* (Bloomington, Indiana: Indiana University Press, 1995).
5. bell hooks, *Teaching to Transgress* (New York: Routledge, 1994), 191.
6. Sam Keen, *The Passionate Life* (New York: HarperOne, 1992), 5.
7. Bogart, 64.
8. Jyl Lynn Felman, *Never a Dull Moment: Teaching and the Art of Performance* (New York: Routledge, 2001), 114.
9. As is—increasingly and incorrectly, but perhaps tellingly—"servicing."
10. Bogart, 62.
11. *The Opposite of Sex*, DVD, directed by Don Roos (1998; Culver City, CA: Sony Pictures Classics, 1998).
12. Lewis Hyde, *The Gift: Imagination and the Erotic Life of Property* (New York: Random House, 1979).
13. Martha Beck, *Breaking Point: Why Women Fall Apart and How They Can Re-Create Their Lives* (New York: Random House, 1992), 34.

Contributors

Donna B. Aronson (BFA, Acting, Virginia Commonwealth University; MFA, PhD, Florida State University) is Vice President for Academic Affairs, Millikin University, Illinois. After teaching graduate acting (Brandeis), she was longtime Professor, Director of Theatre, and Dean, University of the Incarnate Word, Texas. She has been on numerous state and national committees; for the Association for Theatre in Higher Education, she has served the Board and Governing Council as Forum Chair, Vice President for Conference, Secretary, and President.

Sharon Marie Carnicke (MA in Russian/Theatre Arts, New York University; PhD in Russian Literature, Columbia University) is Professor of Theatre and Slavic Studies and Associate Dean of Theatre at the University of Southern California. She has worked professionally as an actor, director, dancer, and teacher. Author of *Stanislavsky in Focus,* she is known as one of the foremost scholars of Stanislavsky. Her wide-ranging publications include her latest co-authored book (with Cynthia Baron), *Reframing Screen Performance,* 2008.

Jonathan Chambers (MFA, Acting, Virginia Commonwealth University; PhD, Theatre History and Criticism, Southern Illinois University at Carbondale) is Associate Professor in the Department of Theatre and Film, Bowling Green State University. His work onstage and behind-the-scenes is extensive. He is former Editor of "Theatre Topics." He writes broadly; his book, *Messiah of the New Technique: John Howard Lawson, Communism, and American Theatre, 1923–1937,* was published by Southern Illinois University Press, 2006.

Chandradasan (MS, Chemistry; PhD, ABD, Theatre, Kerala Kalamandalam University for Art and Culture) is a major force in Indian theatre. He is Artistic Director of Lokadharmi Theatre Centre, a widely published theatre scholar, and a multilingual director and translator. His work has been seen throughout the Indian subcontinent and in Europe. He is recipient of India's most coveted national theatre awards: Best Director, Best Actor, Best Play, and Outstanding Contribution to Indian Theatre.

Mary Cutler (PhD, Theatre, Bowling Green State University, Ohio) is currently Full Professor, University of North Dakota, teaching dramatic literature and voice. She was the Director of Graduate Studies from 1998 to 2005, and has taught all levels of acting. She writes on lesbian/gay performance, musicals, the classics, and new works. She has studied Alexander Technique (LA), with Patsy Rodenburg (NY), and acted many same- and cross-gender roles. Recipient of UND's Outstanding Teacher Award, she is President of the Officers, Mid-America Theatre Conference.

Micha Espinosa (BFA, Stephens College; MFA, Acting, University of California San Diego) is Assistant Professor of Voice and Acting, Arizona State University. She is also an actor (member AFTRA, SAG), teaching workshops nationally and abroad. Espinosa is certified to teach Fitzmaurice Voicework and yoga, with extensive Feldenkrais training. For the Voice and Speech Trainers Association, she is Associate Conference Planner and writes for their journal, among others. She is Associate Editor, International Dialects of English Archive (IDEA).

Victoria Ann Lewis (BA, Dunbarton College; MA, Columbia University; PhD in Theatre, University of California Los Angeles) is Associate Professor of Theatre Arts, University of Redlands. She works primarily in documentary theatre, collective and solo. She is known for her writings on disability and performance; she was Editor of *Beyond Victims and Villains: Contemporary Plays by Disabled Playwrights*. Ms. Lewis received the Director's Award for Outstanding Contribution to the Arts from the California Arts Council, 2005.

Ellen Margolis (MFA, Acting, University of California, Davis; PhD, Theatre History, University of California, Santa Barbara), co-editor of this volume, is Associate Professor and Chair of Theatre, Pacific University, Oregon. She is an award-winning director and actor, with writings published in *Radical Acts* anthology, in theatre journals and short play collections. As playwright, she has done productions and workshops with Vital Theatre, Theatre Limina, Portland Center Stage/PlayGroup, and received commissions from the Susan G. Komen Foundation and Mile Square Theatre. She served as Literary Director, International Centre for Women Playwrights, 2002–2004.

Derek Mudd (BA, Theatre, BA, English, Morehead State University; MFA, Acting, Louisiana State University; PhD (in progress), Performance Studies, Louisiana State University) teaches acting, voice, and public speaking. He has appeared professionally in dozens of regional theatre productions, in films, commercials and solo performances, in Louisville and Austin. He has served as Assistant for the Drama Major at the Kentucky Governor's Scholars Program, and as Administrator of Contracts and Evaluations for the Texas Commission on the Arts.

Antonio Ocampo-Guzman (BFA, Teatro Libre School in Colombia; Voice Diploma and MFA in Directing, York University, Toronto) is Assistant Professor at Northeastern University, where he teaches acting, voice, movement and Shakespeare. A professional actor and director, he has both worked and taught workshops in Europe and South America, specializing in bi-lingual actor training. He is a Designated Linklater instructor, as well as Chair of the Diversity Committee for the Voice and Speech Trainers Association.

Venus Opal Reese (BFA, Theatre, Adelphi University; MFA, Acting, Ohio State University; MA/PhD in Directing/Critical Theory, Stanford University) is Associate Professor of Aesthetic Studies, University of Texas at Dallas. She is an award-winning solo performer, playwright, director, choreographer, and poet, seen nationally and in Europe. Her scholarly writing is featured in the March 2006 issue of *Women and Performance*, and in *Recharting the Black Atlantic: Modern Cultures, Local Communities, Global Connections*, 2008.

Lissa Tyler Renaud (BA Acting, MA, Directing, PhD, Theatre History/Criticism, University of California, Berkeley), co-editor of this volume, has been Director of California-based Actors' Training Project since 1985. Recipient of National Science Foundation and Ford Foundation grants among others, she spent six years overseas as Visiting Professor/Master Teacher of Directing, Theory, Acting, Voice and Ideokinesis. She is a recitalist and award-winning actress, and lectures and publishes widely on the avant-garde and contemporary actor training, in the U.S. and Asia. She serves as co-editor for the International Association of Theatre Critics.

David Eulus Wiles (BA, History, University of Cincinnati; MFA, Acting, Yale University) is Associate Professor at Carleton College, where he teaches acting, voice, theatre history, dramatic literature, and also directs. As a professional actor, appearances include Yale Rep, Aquila Theatre Company, Shakespeare and Company, and the Guthrie Theatre. He trains with Shakespeare & Company and is a student of Patsy Rodenburg. His article, "Burdens of Representation: The Method and the Audience," appears in *Method Acting Reconsidered*.

Leigh Woods (MFA, Acting, Columbia University; PhD, University of California Berkeley) is Professor and Head of Theatre Studies, University of Michigan, Ann Arbor. He has played over one hundred roles at professional and academic theatres nationally, including premieres by Heiner Müller, George W. D. Trow, and Wendy Wasserstein. He is a widely published scholar of performance and history of acting; his latest book, *Transatlantic Stage Stars in Vaudeville and Variety: Celebrity Turns*, was published by Palgrave Macmillan, 2006.

Index

Lightning Source UK Ltd.
Milton Keynes UK
173591UK00010B/40/P